Social Development in Asia

Social Development in Asia

Diversity and Implications

Murli Desai

RAWAT PUBLICATIONS

Jaipur • New Delhi • Bangalore • Hyderabad • Guwahati • Kolkata

ISBN 978-81-316-0700-8

Published by
Prem Rawat for **Rawat Publications**
Satyam Apts, Sector 3, Jawahar Nagar, Jaipur 302 004 (India)
Phone: 0141 265 1748 / 7006 Fax: 0141 265 1748
E-mail: info@rawatbooks.com
Website: www.rawatbooks.com

New Delhi Office
4858/24, Ansari Road, Daryaganj, New Delhi 110 002
Phone: 011 2326 3290

Also at *Bangalore, Hyderabad, Guwahati* and *Kolkata*

Typeset by Rawat Computers, Jaipur

Printed at Chaman Enterprises, New Delhi

Contents

Part 2
Diversity in Social Development Progress in Asia and Implications

List of Tables

Preface

Importance of Asia's Social Development

Asia is the most populated continent of the world, known for its ancient civilizations, origin of religions as well as its recent history of colonization. Asia is also known for the phenomenal economic progress that it has made in four waves, the first three considered the 'Asian Miracle' by the World Bank (1993):

1. Japan recovered quickly from the Second World War and has been prominent since the late 1960s. It was the first country in East Asia to develop economically and, thus, served as a model for East and South East Asia.
2. The four Asian Tigers – Hong Kong, South Korea, Taiwan and Singapore – excelled economically from the 1970s onwards.
3. Following closely were countries like Thailand, Malaysia and Indonesia.
4. Since the early 1990s, China and India have embarked on similarly rapid economic development (Tang, 2000).

Industrialization in the West was supported by the modern ideologies that led to liberal capitalism, emergence of the nation-states, individualism and resources from the colonized world such as Asia. However, industrialization in Asia took place in the absence of liberal capitalism, mostly by authoritarian states, in collectivistic societies, through development aid by these countries, as their own resources were in control of and exploited by them.

Development in Asia has, thus, thrown up questions about the necessity of modern ideologies, liberal capitalism and individualism considered essential for development. When the Reagan-Thatcher era of the 1980s promoted the neo-liberal Washington Consensus that emphasized minimum government interference and considered market as the sole social regulator, Stiglitz (1998) noted that the East Asian countries had achieved the 'Asian Miracle' due to a prominent role of the state, without following the requirements of the Washington Consensus. According to him, the Washington Consensus fails to provide the right framework for understanding either the success of the East Asian economies or the Asian Financial Crisis. He argued that IMF policies contributed to bringing about the Asian Financial Crisis and the failure of Russia's conversion to a market economy. Based on his critique of the Washington Consensus, he promoted what is called the post-Washington Consensus, promoting participatory approaches, incorporation of environmental concerns, and attention to governance, institutional reform, and so on (Haynes, 2008). Thus, lessons learnt from development in this region have contributed to changes in the international strategies for development.

Ghosh (2005) notes that Asia is now the most 'globally integrated' region in the world, with the highest average ratios of trade to GDP, the largest absolute inflows of foreign direct investment, substantial financial capital flows and even significant movements of labour. Asia is also seen as the part of the world that has benefitted the most from the process of globalization. According to research carried out at the Goldman Sachs by Wilson and Purushothaman in 2003, over the next 50 years, Brazil, Russia, India and China – the BRICs economies – could become a much larger force in the world economy. It is Asia that is seen as increasingly central is the rebalancing of world economic growth away from the USA (and UK) (Kilmister, 2008). Harris, Moore and Schmitz (2009) note that the fast economic growth in Asia has eroded the apparent 'superiority' of the First World. The 2013 Human Development Report on 'The Rise of the South: Human Progress in a Diverse World' examines the profound shift in global dynamics driven by the fast-rising new powers of the developing world and its long-term implications for human development. The rise of the South is radically reshaping the world of the 21st century, with developing nations driving economic growth, lifting hundreds of millions of people from poverty, and propelling billions more into a new global middle class, says the Report. China has already overtaken Japan as the world's second biggest economy while lifting hundreds of millions of its people out of poverty. India is reshaping its future with new entrepreneurial creativity and social policy innovation.

While Asia is known for its fast economic development and explanations for it are sought in an 'Asian development model' and 'Asian values', this region is also known for the largest number of poor people in the world. The UNESCAP Fact Sheets on Millennium Development Goals (MDGs) in Asia (2006 and 2007a, b) note that although Asia as a whole is expected to halve, between 1990 and 2015, the proportion of people whose income is less than one US dollar a day by 2015, the region continues to have the largest number of poor people. In fact the fast economic growth has to a large extent been responsible for the widespread poverty through social exclusion and inequalities, environmental degradation and neglect of social policy. Today, social development is more important in Asia than anywhere in the world due to the prices it has paid for the economic development. However, one cannot generalize about development in Asia as its economic development as well as social development range from very high level to the very low level. The diversity in development in Asia is probably due to it being one of the most diverse continents with reference to geographical, religious-cultural and political background. A need was, therefore, felt for a comprehensive analysis of social development in Asia in the international context.

Gap in Literature

A perusal of the literature showed that few edited books have been published on social development in Asia which comprise articles on different countries by different authors, without a common framework for comparison. The few books found on comparative studies on social development across select countries or sub-regions of Asia either focus on select issues or select countries/sub-regions. The Human Development Reports published annually by the United Nations Development Programme (UNDP) and the reports on the Millennium Development Goals (MDGs) published by United Nations

Economic and Social Commission for Asia and the Pacific, Asian Development Bank and the UNDP have generated a lot of comparable cross-country data of Asia. However, their purpose is not to comprehensively seek explanation for the similarities and differences. The need was felt for a comparative study of social development in Asian sub-regions.

Objectives

The aim of the book is to carry out a comparative study of social development in Asian sub-regions to explore the following questions:

- What is the status of social development in Asia with reference to progress, gaps and contradictions, if any?
- Is social development in Asian sub-regions homogenous or diverse?
- Why is Asia rising? Is it a miracle? What factors explain the diversity in social development progress across Asian sub-regions?
- Are there Asian values or development approaches that cut across Asian sub-regions? What are they and what determine them?
- What does Asia and the Asian sub-regions need to do for better progress in social development?
- What are the implications for international social development if Asia is rising?

To examine the diversity in Asia, the book focuses on comparison across sub-regions; however, the sub-regions themselves are not homogenous within themselves. There is diversity within sub-regions and within the countries also, but the book does not go into details of diversity within the countries.

Conceptual Framework and Sources

The conceptual framework for analysis of social development progress comprises the following dependent, intermediate and independent constructs.

Dependent Construct

The dependent construct is the progress of social development that comprises economic development, poverty eradication and food security, investment in people's basic needs, environmental sustainability and social justice. Since the international measures of social development progress developed and promoted by the UN are the human development measures reported in the HDRs and progress on the MDGs in Asia published by the United Nations Economic and Social Commission for Asia and the Pacific (UNESCAP), the Asian Development Bank (ADB) and the UNDP, these are used as the main measures of social development progress in this book. Based on these measures, the following indicators are being examined in this book:

1. Overall progress of social development.
2. Progress of economic development, poverty eradication and food security.
3. Progress of investments in basic needs with reference to health and education.
4. Progress of social justice with reference to gender equality.
5. Progress of environmental sustainability.

Following are the limitations of the above constructs:

- Progress of investments in basic needs could be ascertained only with reference to health and education as the human development measures and MDGs do not go beyond these two basic needs.
- Progress of social justice could be ascertained only with reference to gender equality as the MDGs do not focus on other inequalities.

The data also has limitations. The 2013 HDR notes that because national and international data agencies continually improve their data series, the data – including the HDI values and ranks – presented in this Report is not comparable to those published in earlier editions. The HDR also mentions that national and international data estimates can vary because international agencies harmonize national data for comparability across countries, produce an estimate of missing data or do not incorporate the most recent national data (United Nations Development Programme, 2013). Similarly, countries that report on the MDG progress use different data sources and may not be comparable. Moreover, as noted above, some highly developed and some least developed countries do not report on all the indicators. Due to these limitations of the data, the book uses this data to examine the trends but does not use quantitative methods of analysis.

Intermediate Constructs

This book has researched diverse multidisciplinary sources for an analysis of the intermediate and independent constructs. The intermediate constructs used to explain the progress of social development at the sub-regional level are:

- Role of development systems: Development systems are systems that influence, formulate and implement development policies. The main developmental systems are state, civil society and regional/sub-regional institutions.
- Social development policy approaches: According to Midgley and Sherraden (2000), social development seeks to end the bifurcation of economic and social policy and to ensure that social policy is not subsidiary to the economy. Thus, social development policy approaches comprises economic and social policy approaches.

Independent Constructs

The geographical and historical background of social development is used as an independent construct to explain the strength of development systems and social development policy approaches. Background of development comprises:

- Geographical background.
- Historical background: religious-cultural background, pre-colonial civilizations and political background.

Directions

Based on the above analysis, the book draws directions for ideologies, roles of development systems and social development policy approaches to promote the progress of social development in Asia, and lessons for the rest of the world.

Table 1
Conceptual Framework for Analysis of Diversity of Social Development

Independent Constructs				
Geographical Background	**Historical Background**			
	Religious Background	**Cultural Background**	**Pre-Colonial Civilizations**	**Political Back-ground**
Intermediate Construct				
Role of Development Systems: State Civil Society Sub-Regional Institutions	Social Development Policy Approaches: Economic Policy Approaches Social Policy Approaches			
Dependent Construct: Progress of Social Development				
Overall Social Development	Economic Development, Poverty Eradication and Food Security	Investments in Basic Needs: Health and Education	Social Justice: Gender Equality	Environmental Sustainability

Chapter Plan

The book is divided into two parts and 13 chapters as follows:

Part 1: Overall Diversity in Social Development in Asia

1. Emergence of the Social Development Paradigm
2. Introduction to Diversity in Social Development Progress in Asia
3. Geographical and Historical Background of Social Development in Asia
4. Political Background of Social Development in Asia
5. Role of State and Civil Society in Social Development in Asia
6. Economic Policy Approaches and Role of Regional Institutions in Social Development in Asia
7. Social Policy Approaches and Social Development in Asia

Part 2: Diversity in Social Development Progress in Asia and Implications

8. Diversity in Progress in Poverty Eradication and Food Security in Asia

9. Diversity in Progress in Investment in Health in Asia
10. Diversity in Progress in Investment in Education in Asia
11. Diversity in Progress in Gender Equality in Asia
12. Diversity in Progress in Environmental Sustainability in Asia
13. Discussion of Diversity in Social Development Progress in Asia and Implications

The first chapter on Emergence of the Social Development Paradigm aims to review the following:

1. The paradigm of economic development comprising the western modern ideologies, industrial capitalism, modernization theory and policy approaches of development aid-giving international systems.
2. Critique of the economic development paradigm and recognition of the need for an alternative development paradigm.
3. Emergence of the paradigm of social development based on alternate ideologies emerging from the civil society, leading to alternate development approaches and policy approaches of the United Nations.

Chapter 2 on Introduction to Diversity in Social Development Progress in Asia aims to introduce the following:

1. Asian sub-regions of East Asia, South East Asia, South Asia and North and Central Asia.
2. Overall progress of economic development in Asia and diversity in Asian sub-regions.
3. Overall progress of social development in Asia and diversity in Asian sub-regions.

Chapter 3 on Geographical and Historical Background of Social Development in Asia aims to review the following:

1. Geographical background of Asian sub-regions with reference to diversity in geographical adjacency and geopolitics, the temperate/tropical zones, the landlocked developing countries and Small Island Developing States and their implications for social development.
2. Religious background of Asia with reference to diversity in religious ideologies and their implications for social development.
3. Collectivistic culture in Asia and its implications for social development.

4. Pre-colonial civilizations in Asia with specific reference to China and India.

Chapter 4 on Political Background of Social Development in Asia reviews the following:

1. The political background of Asia with reference to colonization, decolonization, neocolonialism and the Cold War and their implications.
2. Diversity in political background and implications for social development in Asian sub-regions.

Chapter 5 on Role of State and Civil Society in Social Development in Asia aims to review the following:

1. Role of state in Asia with reference to type of state and corruption.
2. Diversity in state role in Asian sub-regions and implications for social development.
3. Role of civil society in Asia with reference to the specific role of non-government organizations in relation to the role of the state.
4. Diversity in role of civil society in Asian sub-regions and implications for social development.

Chapter 6 on Economic Policy Approaches and Role of Regional Institutions in Social Development in Asia aims to review the following:

1. The economic policy approaches in Asia with reference to state economic planning, process of industrialization, and causes and effects of the Asian Financial Crisis and the American Financial Crisis.
2. Diversity in economic policy approaches in Asian sub-regions with reference to development state approach, centrally planned economy approach and mixed economy approach.
3. Role of regional and sub-regional institutions for social development in Asia.
4. Diversity in role of sub-regional institutions in social development in Asian sub-regions.

Chapter 7 on Social Policy Approaches and Social Development in Asia reviews the following:

1. The overall social policy approaches in Asia with reference to history of social policy, policy approach for social protection and policy approach to human rights.
2. Diversity of social policy approaches and social development in Asian sub-regions.

Chapter 8 on Diversity in Progress in Poverty Eradication and Food Security in Asia aims to review the following:

1. Concepts and causes of poverty in Asia with reference to the social exclusion profile, fast economic development, environmental degradation and weak social policy.
2. Progress in reduction of poverty in Asia with reference to Human Poverty Index and reduction of poverty as an MDG and diversity in Asian sub-regions and implications for policy for poverty eradication.
3. Concepts and causes of food insecurity with reference to poverty, barriers in agriculture, market-based food insecurity, speculation and price rise and problems with quality of food in Asia.
4. Progress in reduction of food insecurity as an MDG in Asia with reference to underweight children under-five, malnourishment and Global Hunger Index and diversity in Asian sub-regions and implications for policy for food security.

Chapter 9 on Diversity in Progress in Investment in Health in Asia aims to review the following:

1. Concepts of investment in and importance of health, barriers to health and right to health.
2. Progress in investment in health in Asia with reference to public spending on health, life expectancy, reduction of child mortality and maternal mortality and combating HIV/AIDS, Malaria and other diseases.
3. Diversity in progress in investment in health in Asian sub-regions.
4. Implications for health policy in Asia.

Chapter 10 on Diversity in Progress in Investment in Education in Asia aims to review the following:

1. Concepts of investment in and importance of education, barriers to education and right to education.
2. Progress in investment in education in Asia with reference to public spending on education, EFA Development Index, progress in school education and progress in youth and adult literacy.
3. Diversity in progress in investment in education in Asian sub-regions.
4. Implications for education policy in Asia.

Chapter 11 on Diversity in Progress in Gender Equality in Asia aims to review the following:

1. Concepts of gender and gender equality, causes of gender inequality, feminism and women's movement.
2. Progress in gender measures in Asian sub-regions with reference to Gender-related Development Index, Gender Empowerment Measure, Gender Inequality Index and sex ratio and diversity in Asian sub-regions.
3. Diversity in progress in MDG targets of gender equality in Asian sub-regions with reference to education, youth literacy, wage employment and political participation and diversity in Asian sub-regions.

Chapter 12 on Diversity in Progress in Environmental Sustainability in Asia aims to review the following:

1. Concepts, causes and effects of environmental degradation, ecologism and environmental movement.
2. Progress in reversal of the loss of environmental resources in Asia with reference to forest cover, protected area, and CO_2 emissions and ODP CFC consumption and diversity in Asian sub-regions.
3. Progress in access to sustainable water sources and sanitation facilities in urban and rural Asia and diversity in Asian sub-regions.
4. Progress in the lives of slum dwellers in Asia and diversity in Asian sub-regions.

The last chapter on Discussion of Diversity in Social Development Progress in Asia and Implications aims to discuss the above through a summarization of the following:

1. Overall social development progress, gaps and contradictions in Asia.
2. Diversity in social development progress in Asia.
3. Factors affecting diversity in social development progress in Asia.
4. Policy implications for social development in Asia and for international social development.

Readership

The book is prepared for a comprehensive understanding of social development in Asia so that it can feed into policy planning of development systems and teaching social development in Asian countries as well as in other countries interested in Asian social development. Some of the systems that can make good use of this book are listed below:

1. United Nations Systems:
   - United Nations Commission for Social Development
   - United Nations Development Programme
   - United Nations Educational, Scientific and Cultural Organization
   - United Nations Environment Programme
   - United Nations Millennium Project
   - United Nations Office of the High Commissioner for Human Rights
   - United Nations Research Institute for Social Development
   - World Bank
2. Regional and Sub-regional Institutions:
   - United Nations Economic and Social Commission for the Asia and Pacific
   - Asian Development Bank
   - ASEAN
   - SAARC
3. Academic Departments/Schools in the following Disciplines:
   - Political Economy
   - Social Policy and Social Work
   - Development Studies
   - Asian Studies
   - International Relations
4. Training Institutions of Development Systems:
   - United Nations University and Training Systems
   - Government Training Institutions
   - Training Programmes by Civil Society Organizations
5. Social Work Professional Associations:
   - International Association of Schools of Social Work and Asia-Pacific Association for Social Work Education
   - International Consortium of Social Development and the Asia-Pacific Branch of the International Consortium of Social Development

Acknowledgements

When I taught the courses on 'Comparative Social Service Systems in South East Asia' at the National University of Singapore and 'Social Development of the World' at the Seoul National University (SNU), I undertook an extensive theoretical and research review of the multidisciplinary field of development studies. Based on this review, I wrote *The Paradigm of International Social Development: Ideologies, Development Systems and Policy Approaches* published by Routledge in 2013. While working at the SNU, I carried out 'A Comparative Study on Social Development across Asian Sub-Regions'. I used my experience of research and teaching on social development and social work in India (South Asia), then Singapore (South East Asia) and lastly South Korea (East Asia). I added the Asian sub-region of Central Asia to complete the comparison of Asian sub-regions, although I have never worked there. West Asia was not included as historically and popularly it is better known as the Middle East than West Asia. This book on *Diversity and Contradictions in the Rise of Asia: Economic versus Social Development* is based on my forthcoming book on *The Paradigm of International Social Development: Role of Ideologies, Development Systems and Policy Approaches* and this study.

I would like to place on record my appreciation for my seniors, colleagues, students and the libraries of the academic institutions that provided me with the opportunities to experience and study social development in Asia: Tata Institute of Social Sciences, National University of Singapore and Seoul National University.

June 8, 2014

Murli Desai

murlidesai@gmail.com

Part 1

Overall Diversity in Social Development in Asia

Chapter 1

Emergence of the Social Development Paradigm

Introduction

Concept of Social Development

Midgley (1995) defined social development as a process of planned social change designed to promote the well-being of the population as a whole and in conjunction with a dynamic process of economic development. According to him, the development perspective in social welfare is universal, comprehensive and macro-focused, drawing on the insights of political economy. According to Midgley and Sherraden (2000), social development seeks to end the bifurcation of economic and social policy and to ensure that social policy is not subsidiary to the economy. The social development perspective does not rely on transfer of resources from the productive economy to those in need. It transcends these debates by encouraging the adoption of social programmes that are primarily concerned not with providing social services but with enhancing the capacities of needy people to participate in the productive economy. Social development proponents believe that such participation is the primary means by which most people meet their social needs. It is, therefore, also known as the social investment or the productivist approach to social policy. Unlike the traditional social service approach, the social development perspective seeks to shift the emphasis from consumption-based and maintenance-oriented services to social programmes that contribute directly to economic development. Social development is also concerned with ensuring that economic development brings tangible benefits to ordinary people. It focuses not only on the recipients of the social services but also on economic policies that enhance the welfare of the whole population (Midgley and Sherraden, 2000).

Chapter Objectives

The chapter on emergence of the social development paradigm aims to review the following:

1. The paradigm of economic development comprising the western modern ideologies, industrial capitalism, modernization theory and policy approaches of development aid-giving international systems.
2. Critique of the economic development paradigm and recognition of the need for an alternative development paradigm.
3. Emergence of the paradigm of social development based on alternate ideologies emerging from the civil society, leading to alternate development approaches and policy approaches of the United Nations.

The Paradigm of Economic Development

Western Modern Ideologies and Historical Background of Development

Concept of Ideology

According to Heywood (2007: 11–12), 'An ideology is a more or less coherent set of ideas that provides the basis for organized political action, whether this is intended to preserve, modify or overthrow the existing system of power.' All ideologies, therefore, have the following features:

1. They offer an account of the existing order, usually in the form of a world view.
2. They advance a model of a desired future, a vision of the good society.
3. They explain how political change can and should be brought about – how to get from (1) to (2).

Heywood stated that because ideology is deeply embedded within a set of normative or prescriptive beliefs, it has a powerful emotional or affective character. According to Hunt (1978), the most important element in ideology is the inevitability of choice and its urgency. People, who accept an ideology, usually reject all other systems concerned with the same content. It is the ideological perspective that leads to development of paradigms, on which scientific activity is built, and scientific revolution brings about a paradigmatic change (Kuhn 1970, cited by Payne, 2005).

Western Modern Ideologies and Industrial Capitalism

In Europe, the ideology of secular humanism formed the intellectual core of the Renaissance which revived the importance of human beings in the religion-dominated feudal society of the medieval Western world. It led to the modern period that was launched off by the ideology of rationalism, a philosophic outlook that ushered in an Age of Reason or Enlightenment for humankind. When the ideologies of secular humanism, rationalism and scientism replaced religion with science, democracy, liberalism and utilitarianism emerged with the ideas of individual initiative and individual control. Economic liberalism influenced the political economy of capitalism or free enterprise which, together with science and technology, led to industrialization in Europe.

Capitalism and industrialization led to class stratification, labour exploitation and an individualistic culture. As an economic system, industrialism is characterized by large-scale production, the accumulation of capital and relentless growth. As a philosophy, it is dedicated to materialism, utilitarian values, and absolute faith in science and technology (Heywood, 2007). As a result of capitalism, classes developed as groups of people, one of which can appropriate the labour of another, owing to the different places they occupy in the economic system. It also resulted in understanding physical labour as participating in production and mental labour as enjoying its fruits (Rao, 1997). The determinant of status in class stratification is supposed to be individual merit, which has to be proved by competition. However, this does not happen in practice, because the majority has already been deprived of the means of production and, therefore, also of the fruits of production (Kappen, 1994). Western modern ideologies and industrialization led to individualistic culture in Europe, since the 19th century as individualism became essential for economic growth. Individualism is a political and social ideology that places high value on the self-directed, self-contained, and comparatively unrestrained individual or ego. The unlimited pursuit of pleasure is considered the ultimate right of every person, thus transmuting selfishness into a universal virtue. In this context, social values are considered secondary to the creation and satisfaction of wants (Pereira, 1997).

Social Darwinism

Social Darwinism was a modern ideology that attempted to apply Darwin's theory of natural selection and the struggle for existence to the evolution of human society (Macarov, 1995). According to Rist (2008: 40), the doctrine of social evolutionism was firmly rooted in the popular imagination of the supposed superiority of the West over other societies with agreement on three essential points:

- Progress has the same substance (or nature) as history.
- All nations travel the same road.
- All do not advance at the same speed as the Western society, which therefore has the undisputable lead because of the greater size of its production, the dominant role that reason plays within it and the scale of its scientific and technological discoveries.

Social Darwinism became a rationalization for racism and/or prejudice against ethnic groups of various kinds (Macarov, 1995). Social Darwinism divided people into hierarchical dichotomies of 'worthy and not worthy' and 'deserving and non-deserving', which led to dichotomies of 'haves and have-nots'. The Protestant ethics made the negatively defined seem immoral and the liberalists made them appear deviant as they are presumably uninterested in competing with others in the open market. They were justifiably refused the fundamental life support resources and were even deemed expendable (Ramsay, 1999). The dichotomies of 'primitive and civilized', 'backward and advanced', and 'superstitious and scientific' were used to justify colonization (Gardner and Lewis, 1996).

Colonization

During the Age of Discovery, a period starting in the early 15th century and continuing till the 17th century, voyagers from Western

Europe, led by Spain and Portugal, set out across the world in search of alternative trade routes to 'the East Indies' (now South and South East Asia), in search of gold, silver and spices. In the 18th century, the Industrial Revolution made European nationalism aggressive and expansionist, promoting international trade and colonization of Asian and African countries. The European nation-states, in vantage positions to increase the productive capacities of their own economies, acquired command over the resources as also the people of the colonies, and thus reinforced their home economies (Sharma, 1998). They began to establish extensive trading networks in Latin America and Asia. By the 19th century, the European Empires and/or European-derived powers controlled nine-tenth of the entire globe (Young, 2003). Tan (2000) noted that by the beginning of the 20th century, most of the countries in East, South East and South Asia had been colonized by western imperial powers, namely the British, Spanish, French and the Dutch. The exceptions were China, Japan, Nepal, Bhutan and Thailand but they were also subjugated by these powers. Colonization led to disturbance in their industrial and agricultural systems, Eurocentrism, imposition of the state and individualism, cultural homogenization, and global polarization.

Socialism

The modern ideology of socialism, with core values of social cooperation, social justice and equality, emerged as the counter ideology of liberalism. Marx and Engels proposed a revolutionary socialism in which the working class seizes political power, expropriates private capital, and democratically controls a planned economy designed to utilize the productive forces developed by capitalism to the benefit of all members of society (Hudelson, 1993). Marxist ideas influenced development of labour movements that led to communist rule in Russia, followed by other adjacent countries, which together formed the Soviet Union. The paradigm of development adopted by the socialist countries was largely industrial, the same as that of the capitalistic world. The difference was that decision regarding production, use and distribution, however, was not in the arena of market forces but under the command of the political system (Sharma, 1998).

Decolonization

During the 20th century, the doctrine of nationalism spread throughout the globe as the peoples in the colonies rose in opposition to the colonial rule. They came to resist the established domination of the European colonists, also because they had the vitality and capacity for self-renewal which Europeans had far too easily dismissed as uncivilized. The European powers responded initially with a variety of strategies to delay the inevitable; the overall process saw repression, accommodation, war and, finally, withdrawal after the Second World War (Preston, 1996). The Second World War (1939–1945) brought unparalleled levels of death, devastation, privation, and disorder. It left not only much of Europe and Asia in ruins but the old international order as well (McMahon, 2003). It was these greater upheavals of the Second World War which made decolonization inevitable (Young, 2003).

Social Construction of Development

Social Construction of 'Underdevelopment'

The US and the Soviet Union emerged as the most powerful nations after the Second World War. Their competition for world supremacy to promote their respective contrasting ideologies of capitalism and communism in the world, led to what was later known as the Cold War between the First World comprising the capitalist countries and the Second World comprising the communist countries. The former colonies that remained unaligned either to the First or the Second World were labelled as the Third World. These countries were the focal point of the Cold War. 'Development' of the 'underdeveloped' or 'developing' countries was socially constructed as a tool of the Cold War.

In 1949, the US President Harry Truman stated the fourth objective of his foreign policy as 'making the benefits of their scientific advances and industrial progress available for the improvement and growth of 'underdeveloped' areas', implying mainly the decolonized former colonies. Since then, Esteva (2010: 2) notes, billions of people ceased being what they were, in all their diversity, and were transmogrified into an inverted mirror of others' reality, in the terms of a homogenizing and narrow minority. Rist (2008) argues that by defining 'underdevelopment' as a lack rather than the result of historical circumstances, the 'underdeveloped' were simply treated as poor without seeking the reasons for their destitution. He further observes that this new identity was accepted by those who headed the independent states, because it was a way of asserting their claim to benefit from the aid that was supposed to lead to 'development'. In gaining political independence, they forfeited their identity and their economic autonomy, and were now forced to travel the development path mapped out for them by others. Around the 1960s, with nationalist sentiments becoming vocal, the term 'less developed' was added, as it was considered less pejorative than 'underdeveloped'. The development economists coined the following triad of stages that societies have to pass through to become 'developed': Underdeveloped → Developing → Developed (Girvan, 2005).

In one of its first reports in 1948, the World Bank closely correlated the problem of global poverty with countries' GNP. It postulated that countries with an average per capita income of US$ 100 are, by definition, poor and underdeveloped. Thus, for the first time in history, entire nations came to be considered as poor, on the grounds that their overall income is insignificant in comparison with those now dominating the world economy (Rahnema, 2010).

The World Bank's main criterion for classifying economies is GNI per capita, replacing the earlier used term GNP. Based on its GNI per capita, every economy is classified as low income, middle income (subdivided into lower middle and upper middle), or high income. In 2009:

- High income economies are those with an income of $12,196 or more.
- Lower middle income economies are those with an income of $996–$3,945 and upper middle income economies are those with an income of $3,946–$12,195.
- Low-income economies are those with an income of $995 or less. The low- and middle-income economies are commonly referred to as developing economies (http://data.worldbank.org/news/dev-economies-increase-share-of-global-output).

Social Construction of 'Development'

The term development is generally linked to growth, evolution and maturation, implying a favourable change, a step from the simple to the complex, from the inferior to the superior, from worse to better (Esteva, 2010). As far as countries were concerned, the term 'civilization' was used until the end of the First World War (Rist, 2008: 25).

According to Wolfgang Sachs (2010: xvii), it was the rising influence of the Soviet Union that forced Truman to come up with a vision of 'development' that would engage the loyalty of the decolonizing countries in order to sustain his struggle against communism. Since 1949, the usage of the word 'development' for human societies was, thus, popularized to describe the process through which the former colonies, which had achieved independence, were to be transformed into modern, developing nations from what their colonizers saw as backward, primitive and 'underdeveloped' societies (Reddock, 2000). In operational terms, development comprises an array of interventions for promoting economic growth (Sachs, 2010). According to Ivan Illich (1980), in both theory and practice, development means the transformation of subsistence-oriented cultures and their integration into an economic system. It entails the expansion of a formally economic sphere at the cost of subsistence-oriented activities; and this expansion proceeds at the cost of all other traditional forms of exchange.

Theories of Development

Modernization Theory of Development

In the 1950s, a new sub-discipline of development economics provided a set of analytical and policy tools that responded to the political need for the 'development' of the 'underdeveloped' countries (Girvan, 2005). In the 1950s and early 1960s, the work in development economics was complemented by (mainly American) political scientists and public administration theorists who addressed the difficulties involved in building democratic states and modern bureaucracies, and by anthropologists and sociologists concerned with tensions generated by the interaction between traditional and modern value and knowledge systems. The social scientists who comprised the modernization theorists assumed that these transitions would be relatively rapid and painless, by importing Western capital, technology and organizational systems (Brett, 2009). They, too, developed a triad: Traditional → Transitional → Modern (Girvan, 2005). These theories also implied a covertly Western-centered evolutionism insofar as they assumed that poor countries had stagnated on a relatively low level of development and could and should develop, or modernize, in the direction of a

Western-type society. This development discourse was eurocentric in the sense that it was not the economies but also the indigenous people who had to be modernized, by adopting the values of the White race (Kennett, 2001).

Wallerstein (2004) noted that for the post-1945 social scientists, the social construction of development allowed to distinguish between various kinds of development, economic, political and social, and thereby maintain intact the classical distinction that undergirded the three great disciplines of the social sciences. But on the other hand, it allowed the social scientists to overcome the Western world versus *others* distinction now out of favor by adding the codicil that different countries were at different *stages* of development. This had the advantage of being universalist. The operations of all states worldwide were explained by the same concept of development and, therefore, were said to be pursuing the same trajectory or model of development. On the other hand, the states were also different (or particular) at the present time, because they were at different 'stages' of the same developmental process. In addition, 'development' had a third virtue. One could derive from its study useful parables for political advice: if 'underdeveloped' countries copied the wisdom of 'developed' ones, they would advance more rapidly along the universal path of societal development. As a result, the gap between the 'developed' and the 'underdeveloped' would inevitably close. In this way, modernization theory put forth a very optimistic view of the future of those states that were still poor and struggling (Wallerstein, 2004).

Dependency Theory of Development

In the late 1960s and early 1970s, a related strand of development thinking drew on the Marxist critique of Western capitalism for its explanations of Third World poverty. These theorists critiqued the modernization theory's assumptions about development and how to achieve it. They argued that modernization was the cause of Third World underdevelopment, rather than its solution. Called dependency theorists, they argued that the capitalist system benefitted from a dependent, peripheral Third World and that the capitalist system was designed to perpetuate this dependency (Connelly et al., 2000). According to them, over time, the world economy divided into *core* (that is industrially developed) states and *peripheral* (that is less industrialized) countries that relied for export earnings on production and sale of primary products abroad. Between the blocs of core and peripheral countries there was situated the category of *semi-peripheral* countries which occupied a kind of half-way house position. Economic surplus was said to flow from periphery to core maintaining the division between the wealthy and non-wealthy states (Haynes, 2008).

The dependency theory questioned the dualistic model of the 'traditional' and 'modern' of the modernization theory. It argued that the obstacles to development are not the internal socio-cultural characteristics of the 'traditional' societies but are external to the underdeveloped countries, based in the legacy of colonialism. It was critical of the structures of the Western imperial capitalism within and through which Third World economies had become enmeshed in such a way as to create and maintain 'underdevelopment' and exploitation. The one-way transfer of resources from the Third World to the Western world was maintained and reinforced through the agents of capitalism such as multinational corporations (MNCs), international banks, inter-governmental agencies such as the International Monetary Fund (IMF) and the World Bank, and the local elites (Midgley, 1997, cited in Kennett, 2001).

The dependency theorists argued that the perpetuation of these unequal relations is managed by a clientele class in the South that collaborates with the dominant capitalist class in the North. To overcome this, the dependency theorists called for a critical attitude toward Western technology, the overthrow of this clientele class, an end to links with the North, and a focus on self-reliant development. This perspective and its prescriptions attracted many intellectuals (and some policymakers) in the South, who saw in it both an explanation for their legacy of underdevelopment and a means to overcome that legacy (Connelly et al., 2000). However, the dependency theory is criticized as it explained the origin of underdevelopment but did not challenge the basic presupposition of modernization theory that growth and modernization are necessary for these countries (Rist, 2008). Moreover, the dependency theory lost ground when significant economic development occurred in some developing countries which are called the newly industrialized countries (NICs) such as South Korea, Hong Kong and Taiwan, and the Middle Eastern oil-producing states (Haynes, 2008).

Aid-Giving International Development Systems and their Policy Approaches

Decolonization was a relatively minor move from direct to indirect rule. Development aid by the developed countries worked as neocolonialism (Young, 2003) through the establishment of the International Financial Institutions (IFIs) such as the International Monetary Fund (IMF) and the World Bank. During the Cold War, the US provided military aid to the newly independent countries to fight civil wars with their own people to combat communism. As its anti-communist allies, the US also provided them with economic aid which was tied; it was to be spent only on purchasing US goods (Chan, 1993). The IMF pressed the aid-receiving countries to liberalize their trade and payments. Its philosophy called for the widest possible freedom of play for market forces and frowned on many kinds of government interventions such as price subsidies, rationing, or protection of domestic industries as 'distortions' of free market relations. The IMF strategy resulted in the takeover of the domestically owned businesses by their foreign competitors and devaluation raised the cost of living. Developing countries found that the IMF ordered them like debt slaves as their debt kept them tied to their creditors. If they remain within the system, the debtor countries were doomed to perpetual underdevelopment, or rather to development of their exports at the service of multinational enterprises, at the expense of development for the needs of their own citizens (Payer, 1974).

A well-functioning market system is often absent in developing nations and, therefore, state economic planning was used in the newly independent countries as a deliberate governmental attempt to coordinate economic decision-making (Todaro and Smith, 2009). At the same time, for many countries, external debt exceeded their total GNP (United Nations Development Programme, 1991). The Third World debt crisis of the late 1970s was followed by the Reagan-Thatcher era of the 1980s that promoted the ideology of neo-liberalism. Neo-liberalism emphasizes minimum government interference and considers market as the sole social regulator. In this era of neo-liberal backlash, the World Bank and the IMF argued that the debt crisis had been a result of the inward-oriented, statist development strategies of the 1950s and 1960s. They promoted the Structural Adjustment Programme (SAP), through which the developing countries were made, as a condition to loans, to cut what was regarded as excessive public spending to balance their books and enable the development of their private economies, often through a strategy of export-led growth (Deacon, 2007). Neoliberalism, together with the dissolution of the Soviet Union, led to collapse of the economic development project.

Conclusion on the Economic Development Paradigm

Thus, development in the economic development paradigm is:

- Based in the ideologies of liberalism, utilitarianism, capitalism, nationalism, Social Darwinism and neo-colonialism.
- Aims at economic growth and accumulation of capital.
- Controlled by state-based development systems of developed countries, IFIs, development aid systems, the state, global corporations and regional institutions.
- Through policy approaches namely, industrialization, export-led growth, modernization, consumption, structural adjustment, regulation by market and residual, social policy/welfare capitalism/pluralism.
- Where the outcome is measured by the Gross National Income (GNI).

Critique of the Economic Development Paradigm and Need for an Alternative Development Paradigm

Critique of Industrialization

Mahatma Gandhi had forecasted that industrialization on a mass scale will necessarily lead to passive or active exploitation of the villagers as the problems of competition and market come in and that is what happened. Rahnema (2010: 179) notes that the industrial era accelerated the breakdown of vernacular societies, disembedding them from their socio-cultural roots and subjecting them to economic ones.

Critique of Modernization

Frank (1963, cited in Preston, 2002) criticized that the modernization approach attributed a history to the developed countries but denied all history to the underdeveloped ones. According to him, it is precisely the histories they do have that explain their present circumstances. People commonly described as 'primitive', 'traditional', 'backward', or 'underdeveloped' are not frozen in a static past but represent particular local, creative adaptations to economic and cultural conditions (Connelly et al., 2000). On the other hand, as Rahnema (2010) notes, the modern economy reduced everyone to becoming the agent of an invisible national or world economy, geared only to producing things for whoever can pay for them. In most developing countries, neither the production of economic resources and commodities nor the extension of social services has ultimately served the poor. More often than not, they have resulted in further diminishing their capacity to meet their real needs, which they used to do in the context of their vernacular livelihood. Such approach to poverty alleviation only forces the poor to work for others rather than for themselves.

Brett (2009: xiv) notes that the processes of modernization rarely went according to plan. Democratic rule gave way to authoritarianism, planned economies were destabilized by balance of payments and fiscal crisis, and social cohesion was undermined by the inability to protect people from rapid and disruptive transfers of assets and increases in exclusion and insecurity. According to Sachs (2010: xviii), 'The campaign to turn traditional man into modern man has failed. The old ways have been smashed; the new ways are not viable.... Shunned by the advanced sector and cut off from the old ways, they are expatriates in their own country'.

Critique of Development

According to Illich (1980), development signifies a violent exclusion of those who want to survive without dependence on consumption from the environment's utilization values. Rist (2008) argues that it is in the nature of 'development' to produce inequality and exclusion as sacrifices are demanded of many to guarantee the prosperity of few. Such a development became an instrument of the privileged class. In spite of all the critique, Rist observes that the belief in 'development' as economic growth remains unchallenged as it assures the good life for all through technological progress and ever-rising production of goods and services, from which everyone will eventually benefit.

According to Amartya Sen (1999), winner of the Nobel Prize for Economics, it is narrow to identify development with the growth of the Gross National Product (GNP, measure of the accrual of income or the value of the output, produced by the nationals), or with the rise in personal incomes, or with industrialization, or with technological advance, or with social modernization. Sen argued that we use income and commodities as the material basis of our well-being, but following are five sources of variation between our real incomes and the advantages of well-being and freedom we get out of them:

- Personal Heterogeneities: People have disparate physical characteristics connected with disability, illness, age or gender, and these make their needs diverse.
- Environmental Diversities: Variations in environmental conditions, such as climatic circumstances can influence what a person gets out of a given level of income.
- Variations in Social Climate: Social conditions including public educational arrangements, and the prevalence or absence of crime and violence in the particular location influence the conversion of personal incomes and resources.
- Differences in Relational Perspectives: The commodity requirements of established patterns of behaviour may vary between communities, depending on conventions and customs.
- Distribution within the Family: Distributional rules followed within the family can make a major difference to the attainments and predicaments of individual members (Sen, 1999: 70–71).

Alkire and Deneulin (2009) have critically examined and rejected the following assumptions for the dominance of economic development by giving evidence to the contrary:

1. A high Gross Domestic Product (GDP, market value of all the output produced in a nation) per capita is necessary for human quality of life.
2. Families with a good income will not be deprived in other dimensions.
3. Economic growth will automatically reduce other kinds of poverty such as malnutrition.

4. Data for income and expenditure are better than other poverty data.
5. It is easier to promote economic growth than human flourishing.
6. Economic growth can be sustained without considerations for human flourishing.

Need for an Alternative Development Model

Haq, the Pakistani economist who played a key role in formulating the human development paradigm, came to recognize the need for an alternative development model due to many factors, including the following:

- Growing evidence that did not support the then prevailing belief in the 'trickle down' power of market forces to spread economic benefits and end poverty.
- The human costs of Structural Adjustment Programmes became more apparent.
- Social ills (crime, weakening of social fabric, HIV/AIDS, pollution, etc.) were still spreading even in cases of strong and consistent economic growth.
- A wave of democratization in the early 1990s raised hopes for people- centered models (http://hdr.undp.org/en/humandev/origins/).

The Paradigm of Social Development

Civil Society and Alternate Ideologies

In the context of the criticism of the economic growth-based development paradigm as narrow, the alternative to this paradigm emerged from the global exchange and alliances of civil society actors at the UN level. Besides Karl Marx, Mahatma Gandhi and Paulo Freire are some of the most well-known critical thinkers who have significantly influenced alternate ideologies and alternate development approaches. The new social movements such as women's movement, indigenous people's movement and environmental movement have challenged the dominant ideas as to how society should be organized, and drawn attention to needs not currently attended to under existing social arrangements. The main alternate ideologies that emerged are postmodernism, post-colonialism, multiculturalism, feminism, ecologism and human rights.

Postmodernism

Postmodernism suggested that the grand narratives of modernization and dependency theories cannot explain or predict complex and diverse patterns of historical change. It drew attention to social and cultural diversity, the primacy of localized experiences, the roles played by resistance movements of various types and the colonial roots of development discourses. In the early 1990s, these grand narratives of development were replaced by post-development perspectives which suggested that development in any form was not a solution to problems of global poverty and inequality, but a highly restrictive and controlling discourse that simply served to extend the power of richer countries over the poorer ones (Lewis and Kanji, 2009). Post-development focuses on the underlying premises and motives of development, and what sets it apart from other critical approaches is its rejection of development (Pieterse, 2010).

Post-Colonialism

Post-structuralism and postmodernism have provided the impetus to the post-colonial studies through a clear critique of the Western civilization (Gandhi, 1998). The postcolonial theory has emerged as a conceptual reorientation towards the perspectives of knowledge, as well as needs, developed in the former colonies. It combines and draws on elements from radical socialism, feminism, and environmentalism. It seeks to intervene and force its alternative knowledge into power structures of the West as well as the non-West (Young, 2003).

Multiculturalism

Multiculturalism is one of the offshoots of post-colonialism as it sought to challenge and overturn the cultural dimensions of imperial rule by establishing the legitimacy of non-Western and sometimes anti-Western political ideas and traditions. As a descriptive term, it has been taken to refer to cultural diversity that arises from the existence within a society of two or more groups whose beliefs and practices generate a distinctive sense of collective identity. Multiculturalism, in this sense, is invariably reserved for communal diversity that arises from racial, ethnic and language differences. As a normative term, multiculturalism implies a positive endorsement, even a celebration of communal diversity. By challenging the predominantly Eurocentric world view, multiculturalism allowed non-Western religions, ideas and philosophies to be taken more seriously (Heywood, 2007: 313–314).

Feminism

Feminism and postmodernism, both, call for the development of new paradigms of social criticism that do not rely on traditional philosophical underpinnings. Postcolonial feminism involves any challenge to the dominant patriarchal ideologies by women of the former colonies. The anti-colonial campaigns were directed against the colonial regime towards the political goal of sovereignty, and the postcolonial struggles are directed against the postcolonial state as well as against the Western interests that enforce the neo-colonial status. Such activism consists of contesting local power structures, as well as challenging racist or Eurocentric views of men and women in the First World (Young, 2003). According to the postcolonial third-world feminism, development is not possible without greater equity and participation for women. In their vision, feminism has at its very core a process of economic and social development geared to human needs through wider access to economic and political power. Equality, peace and development by and for the poor and oppressed are inextricably interlinked with equality, peace and development by and for women (Sen and Grown, 1987). Eco-feminists see the patriarchal domination of women by men as the prototype of all domination and exploitation. They point out that the exploitation of nature has gone hand in hand with that of women, who have been identified with nature throughout the ages. They see female experiential knowledge as a major source for an ecological vision of reality (Capra, 1996).

Ecologism

Ecologism is an ideology based on the belief that nature is an interconnected whole, embracing humans and non-humans, as well as the inanimate world. Deep ecology is strong ecologism, based on the more challenging idea that the purpose of human life is to help sustain nature, and not the other way round (Heywood, 2007). According to Capra (1996), a deep ecologist, the world is not a collection of isolated objects, but a network of phenomena that are fundamentally interconnected and interdependent. In nature, there is no 'above' or 'below', and there are no hierarchies. There are only networks nesting within other networks. According to him, the principles of the planet's ecosystems organize themselves through interdependence, recycling, partnership, flexibility, and diversity. One of the most significant assumptions of deep ecology is biocentric equality, which views natural entities as morally independent of their perceived usefulness for human purposes. This underscores the intrinsic worth of all natural things. From this assumption flows deep ecology's ideas of non-anthropocentrism, tolerance of different views, open relational communication with nature, the inclusion of animals and plants in the community and creating the need for heightened preservation and conservation efforts (Naess, 1995, cited by Besthorn, 2003).

Human Rights

According to the UN (1992), human rights could be generally defined as those rights that are inherent in our nature and without which we cannot live as human beings. After the colonies achieved independence, development and human rights followed parallel tracks in the context of the Cold War. The entry of the newly independent Southern countries into the UN in the 1960s and 1970s spurred the beginnings of attempts to bridge the two domains of human rights and development with the CESCR as an important starting point. The Declaration on the Right to Development of 1986 placed an emphasis on the global inequalities and the achievement of international cooperation in solving international problems of an economic, social, cultural or humanitarian nature (UN, 2006). Triggered by the World Conference on Human Rights in 1993, the rights-based approach to development rose in the 21st century in the context of neoliberal globalization, on the one hand, and democratization in many authoritarian countries, on the other (Mitlin and Hickey, 2009). The importance of rights-based development lies in its emphasis that development is not a charity but legally enforceable (Munro, 2009). In this approach, human rights is seen as an intrinsic part of development, and development as a means to realizing human rights. It also brought a holistic as against the atomistic approach used so far for development planning (United Nations Development Programme, 2000).

Alternate Development Approaches

Participatory Approach

These alternate ideologies led to the alternate development approaches that attempt to push back the predominance of the economic world-view and put people back at centre stage. Participation was the slogan which gave the development discourse a new lease of life, in the hope that it would finally enable development to meet everyone's basic needs. Participatory development emphasizes:

- Bottom-up approaches where people have direct or indirect access to decision-making and power in the economic, social, cultural and political processes that affect their lives.
- Development as empowerment for marginal strata with the emphasis on grassroots work and collective action.
- Local people's knowledge over bureaucratic expertise (Przeworski, 2006).

However, there is a danger in the bottom-up struggles of the poor and marginalized people, as it can lead to an exaggeration of their capacity to cope and progress under structural constraints (Cleaver, 2009).

Human Development Approach

The alternate ideologies converged into the human development approach. As a result of the growing criticism of the economic development approach and the loss in development progress in the 1980s, the human development approach arose in the 1990s, aiming to put people back at centre stage. Based on Amartya Sen's concept of development as freedom, human development is defined as 'the expansion of people's freedoms to live long, healthy and creative lives; to advance other goals they have reason to value; and to engage actively in shaping development equitably and sustainably on a shared planet. People are, both, the beneficiaries and drivers of human development, as individuals and in groups. Thus stated, human development has three components:

- *Well-being:* expanding people's real freedoms – so that people can flourish.
- *Empowerment and agency:* enabling people and groups to act – to drive valuable outcomes.
- *Justice:* expanding equity, sustaining outcomes over time and respecting human rights and other goals of society' (United Nations Development Programme, 2010).

According to Haq (1999: 20–21), the human development paradigm is holistic, it covers all aspects of development, whether economic growth or international trade, budget deficits or fiscal policy, saving or investment or technology, basic social services or safety nets for the poor. Following are the essential aspects of the human development paradigm according to him:

- Development must put people at the centre of its concerns.
- The purpose of development is to enlarge all human choices, not just income.
- The human development paradigm is concerned with building up human capabilities (through investment in people) and with using those human capabilities fully (through an enabling framework for growth and employment).
- Human development has four essential pillars: equality, sustainability, productivity and empowerment.

Dissatisfaction with the GNP as the measure of human welfare, because it leaves out all the activities that are not monetized, and fails to capture the cultural, social, political and many other choices that people make, the human development approach developed a new composite index of socioeconomic progress, the human development measures (Haq, 1999).

Policy Approaches of the United Nations

The policy approaches of the UN as the key development system shifted from economic to social development through the four UN Decades of Development. In the First UN Decade of Development, the starting focus was on economic development and the shift to social development took place in the middle of the Decade. The highlights of the Second UN Decade of Development are the proposal for a NIEO by the Southern countries, proposal for a basic needs strategy, and the beginning of the focus on women's issues. The highlights of the Third UN Decade of Development are the neoliberal Washington Consensus, conferences on the LDCs, Declaration on the Right to Development, proposal for adjustment/development with a human face, publication of *Our Common Future* that defined the concept and objectives of sustainable development, and launching of the human development approach. The highlights of the Fourth UN Decade of Development are the post-Washington Consensus, World Conference on Human Rights, the World Summit for Social Development, and the HIPC.

The economic and social initiatives of the 1990s had highlighted that neither growth nor development necessarily eliminates poverty. The UN concluded that sustainable development, of both urban and rural human settlements, was directly linked to the alleviation of poverty. The first UN Decade for the Eradication of Poverty was launched in 1997 and extended through 2006. In 2000, the UN General Assembly adopted the Millennium Declaration based in the fundamental values of freedom, equality, solidarity, tolerance, respect for nature and shared responsibility. The key objectives of the Declaration are peace, security and disarmament; development and poverty eradication; protecting our common environment; human rights, democracy and good governance; protecting the vulnerable; meeting the special needs of Africa; and strengthening the UN.

The UN functions as a multilateral development aid agency. The bilateral development aid agencies function on a country-to-country basis. These systems are found to have problems with their effects on the NGOs, development, power structure and governance in the recipient countries. The UN policy initiatives for development aid systems comprise the 20: 20 initiative, HIPC, global partnership as a Millennium Development Goal (MDG), and the UN conferences on financing for development. The core strategies that have merged through these initiatives are aid allocation for human priority areas; peace dividend; development cooperation in which economic partnership would be based on mutual interests, not charity, cooperation, not confrontation, equitable sharing of market opportunities, not protectionism, and far-sighted internationalism, not stubborn nationalism, country ownership, aid harmonization and so on. In 2005, donor coordination in providing aid is improving, there is less use of tied aid, and more emphasis is being placed on country ownership. Many donors have been reducing tied aid, but the practice remains widely prevalent and underreported.

Conclusion on the Social Development Paradigm

Thus, the social development paradigm that is emerging comprises development that:

- Is based in ideologies of post-colonialism, postmodernism, multiculturalism, feminism, ecologism and human rights.
- Aims at economic development, investment in people's basic needs, poverty eradication, environmental sustainability and social justice.
- To be achieved through participatory, inclusive and empowering, sustainable and rights-based economic and social policy approaches by national and international state and civil society systems and democratic and good governance and partnership among themselves.
- Assesses the outcome by human development measures.

The social development paradigm is compared with the economic development paradigm in Table 1.1.

Table 1.1
Comparison between the Economic Development and the Social Development Paradigms

	Economic Development Paradigm	Social Development Paradigm
Ideologies	Liberalism	Post-Colonialism
	Utilitarianism	Postmodernism
	Capitalism	Multiculturalism
	Nationalism	Feminism
	Social Darwinism	Ecologism
	Neo-Liberalism	Human Rights
Development Systems	State-based Development Systems:	State-based Development Systems:
	Developed Countries	United Nations
	International Financial Institutions	Development Aid Agencies as Partners

Cont'd...

...Cont'd

	Tied Aid by Development Aid Systems	State
	State	Regional Institutions
	Global Corporations	Non-State-based Development Systems:
	Regional Institutions	Civil Society
		Non-Government Organizations
		Development Studies
		Think-Tanks
Systems Approach	Control	Democratic and Good Governance
		Partnership
Aims	Economic Growth	Economic Development
	Accumulation of Capital	Investment in People's Basic Needs
		Poverty Eradication
		Environmental Sustainability
		Social Justice
Policy Approaches	Industrialization	Economic and Social Policy Approaches to be:
	Export-led Growth	Participatory
	Modernization	Inclusive and Empowering
	Consumption	Sustainable
	Structural Adjustment	Rights-Based
	Regulation by Market	
	Residual, Social Policy/Welfare Capitalism/Pluralism	
Outcome Measures	Gross National Income	Human Development Measures
		Income Gini Coefficient
		Millennium Development Goals

Source: Desai, 2013.

References

Alkire, S. and Deneulin, S. (2009). A normative framework for development. In S. Deneulin and L. Shahani (eds), *An Introduction to the Human Development and Capability Approach: Freedom and Agency* (pp. 3–21). London: Earthscan.

Besthorn, F.H. (2003). Radical ecologisms: Insights for educating social workers in ecological activism and social justice. *Critical Social Work*, 4(1). Retrieved 30 July 2011 from http://www.uwindsor.ca/critical socialwork/radical-ecologisms-insights-for-educating-social-worker s-in-ecological-activism-and-social-justice

Brett, E.A. (2009). *Reconstructing Development Theory: International Inequality, Institutional Reform and Social Emancipation.* London: Palgrave Macmillan.

Capra, F. (1996). *The Web of Life.* New York: Anchor Books.

Chan, S. (1993). *East Asian Dynamism: Growth, Order, and Security in the Pacific Region.* Oxford: Westview Press.

Cleaver, F. (2009). Rethinking agency, rights and natural resource management. In D. Mitlin and S. Hickey (eds), *Rights-based Approach to Development: Exploring the Potential and Pitfalls* (pp. 127–144). Sterling, VA: Kumarian Press.

Connelly, P., Li, T.M., MacDonald, M. and Parpart, J.L. (2000). Feminism and development: Theoretical perspectives. In J.L. Parpart, M.P. Connelly and V.E. Barriteau (eds), *Theoretical Perspectives on Gender and Development.* Ottawa: International Development Research Center. Retrieved 8 December 2009 from http://www.idrc.ca/es/ev-27444-201-1-DO_TOPIC.html

Deacon, B. (2007). *Global Social Policy and Governance.* Los Angeles: Sage Publications.

Desai, M. (2013). *The Paradigm of International Social Development: Ideologies, Development Systems and Policy Approaches.* New York: Routledge.

Esteva, G. (2010). Development. In W. Sachs (ed.), *The Development Dictionary: A Guide to Knowledge as Power* (2nd ed.). (pp. 1–23). New York: Zed Books.

Gandhi, L. (1998). *Postcolonial Theory: A Critical Introduction.* New Delhi: Oxford India Paperbacks.

Gardner, K., and Lewis, D. (1996). *Anthropology, Development and the Post-modern Challenge.* London: Pluto Press.

Girvan, N. (2005). *The Search for Policy Autonomy in the South.* Geneva: United Nations Research Institute for Social Development.

Haq, M.U. (1999). *Reflections on Human Development.* Delhi: Oxford University Press.

Haynes, J. (2008). *Development Studies.* Cambridge: Polity Press.

Heywood, A. (2007). *Political Ideologies: An Introduction* (4th ed.). New York: Palgrave Macmillan.

Hudelson, R.H. (1993). *The Rise and Fall of Communism.* Oxford: Westview Press.

Hunt, I. (1978). Social work and ideology. In N. Timms and D. Watson (eds), *Philosophy in Social Work* (pp. 7–25). London: Routledge and Kegan Paul.

Illich, I. (1980). The de-linking of peace and development, Opening address on the occasion of the first meeting of the Asian Peace Research Association, Yokohama. Retrieved 27 June 2010 from http://www.pudel.uni- bremen.de/pdf/DELINK.pdf

Kappen, S. (1994). *Tradition Modernity Counterculture: An Asian Perspective.* Bangalore: Visthar.

Kennett, P. (2001). *Comparative Social Policy: Theory and Research.* Philadelphia: Open University Press.

Lewis, D. and Kanji, N. (2009). *Non-governmental Organisations and Development.* London: Routledge.

Macarov, D. (1995). *Social Welfare: Structure and Practice.* London: Sage Publications.

McMahon, R.J. (2003). *The Cold War: A Very Short Introduction.* New York: Oxford University Press.

Midgley, J. (1995). *Social Development: The Developmental Perspective in Social Welfare.* London: Sage Publications.

Midgley, J. and Sherraden, M. (2000). The social development perspective. In J. Midgley, M.B. Tracy and M. Livermore (eds), *The Handbook of Social Policy* (pp. 435–446). London: Sage Publications.

Mitlin, D. and Hickey, S. (2009). Introduction. In D. Mitlin and S. Hickey (eds), *Rights-based Approach to Development: Exploring the Potential and Pitfalls* (pp. 3–20). Sterling, VA: Kumarian Press.

Munro, L.T. (2009). The 'human rights-based approach to programming': A contradiction in terms? In D. Mitlin and S. Hickey (eds), *Rights-based Approach to Development: Exploring the Potential and Pitfalls* (pp. 187–208). Sterling, VA: Kumarian Press.

Payer, C. (1974). *The Debt Trap: The International Monetary Fund and the Third World.* New York: Monthly Review Press.

Payne, M. (2005). *Social Work Theory.* Houndmills, Basingstoke: Macmillan.

Pereira, W. (1997). *Inhuman Rights: The Western System and Global Human Rights Abuse.* Mapusa, Goa: The Other India Press.

Pieterse, J.N. (2010). *Development Theory* (2nd ed.). Los Angeles: Sage Publications.

Preston, P.W. (1996). *Development Theory: An Introduction.* Oxford: Blackwell Publishing.

Przeworski, A. (2006). Democracy, social inclusion, and development. In *Participatory Governance and the Millennium Development Goals (MDGs).* New York: United Nations. Retrieved 12 November 2009 from http://unpan1.un.org/intradoc/groups/public/documents/un/unpan028359.pdf

Rahnema, M. (2010). Poverty. In W. Sachs (ed.), *The Development Dictionary: A Guide to Knowledge as Power* (2nd ed.). (pp. 174–194). New York: Zed Books.

Ramsay, R.F. (1999). Toward a common paradigmatic home: Social work in the 21st century. *The Indian Journal of Social Work, 60*(1), 69-86.

Rao, V.V. (1997). People's movements: The role of a writer. *Lokayan Bulletin*, 13(6), 1–18.

Reddock, R. (2000). Why gender? Why development? In J.L. Parpart, M.P. Connelly and V.E. Barriteau (eds), *Theoretical Perspectives on Gender and Development.* Ottawa: International Development Research Center. Retrieved 8 December 2009 from http://www.idrc.ca/es/ev-27443- 201-1-DO_TOPIC.html

Rist, G. (2008). *The History of Development: From Western Origins to Global Faith* (3rd ed.). New York: Zed Books.

Sachs, W. (2010). Introduction. In W. Sachs (ed.), *The Development Dictionary: A Guide to Knowledge as Power* (2nd ed.). (pp. xv–xx). New York: Zed Books.

Sen, A. (1999). *Development as Freedom*. New York: Random House.

Sen, G. and Grown, C. (1987). *Development crises and alternative visions.* London: Earthscan Publications.

Sharma, B.D. (1998). The people versus the system. In M. Desai, A. Monteiro and L. Narayan (eds), *Towards People-centred Development* (pp. 44–61). Mumbai: Tata Institute of Social Sciences.

Tan, G. (2000). *Asian Development: An Introduction to Economic, Social and Political Change in Asia.* Singapore: Times Academic Press.

Todaro, M.P. and Smith, S.C. (2009). *Economic Development* (10th ed.). Essex: Pearson Education Ltd.

United Nations. (1992). *Human Rights: Teaching and Learning about Human Rights.* New York.

——. (2006). Social justice in an open world: The role of the United Nations. DESA, New York. Retrieved 22 February 2011 from http://www.un.org/esa/socdev/documents/ifsd/SocialJustice.pdf

United Nations Development Program. (1991). *Human Development Report: Financing Human Development.* New York: Oxford University Press.

——. (2000). *Human Development Report: Human Rights and Human Development.* New York: Oxford University Press.

——. (2010). *Human Development Report: The Real Wealth of Nations: Pathways to Human Development.* New York: Oxford University Press.

Wallerstein, I. (2004). World-systems analysis. In G. Modelski and R.A. Denemark (eds), *World System History*. Oxford: EOLSS Publishers.

Young, R.J.C. (2003). *Postcolonialism: A Very Short Introduction*. New York: Oxford University Press.

CHAPTER 2

Introduction to Diversity in Social Development Progress in Asia

Introduction

Introduction to Rise in Asia

Asia, located in the Eastern part of the Northern Hemisphere, is the most populated continent of the world, with 4.1 billion, that is 60 per cent of the world's seven billion people. It is known for its ancient civilizations, origin of major religions, diversity of ethnic groups, recent history of colonization and now the newly industrialized countries. The temptation to see Asia as one unit reveals a distinctly Eurocentric perspective (Sen, 1997). On the contrary, because of its diversity of cultures, limited experience with cooperation and low levels of interdependence, there is absence of a clear concept of Asia as a region (Karns and Mingst, 2010). As far as development is concerned, it is economically the fastest developing region in the world. The 2013 Human Development Report (HDR) on 'The Rise of the South: Human Progress in a Diverse World' examines the profound shift in global dynamics driven by the fast-rising new powers of the developing world and its long-term implications for human development. The rise of the South is radically reshaping the world of the 21st century, with developing nations driving economic growth, lifting hundreds of millions of people from poverty, and propelling billions more into a new global middle class, says the Report. Several high achievers have not only boosted national income, but also had better than average performance on social indicators in areas such as health and education. In Asia, these high achievers include the larger countries such as China and India, as well as smaller countries such as Bangladesh, Indonesia, South Korea, Malaysia, Thailand and Vietnam (United Nations Development Programme, 2013).

Some of the questions raised by this development is why is Asia rising? Is it rising only economically or also socially? Are there contradictions between economic and social development in Asia? Is it rising homogenously? If Asian sub-regions differ, what are the factors that explain the diversity in Asian sub-regions? Are there Asian values or development approaches that cut across Asian sub-regions? What are they and what determines them? What are the implications for international social development if Asia is rising?

Chapter Objectives

This chapter on introduction to diversity in social development progress in Asia aims to introduce the following:

1. Asian sub-regions of East Asia, South East Asia, South Asia and North and Central Asia.
2. Overall progress of economic development in Asia and diversity in Asian sub-regions.
3. Overall progress of social development in Asia and diversity in Asian sub-regions.

Introduction to Asian Sub-Regions

The United Nations Economic and Social Commission for Asia and the Pacific (UNESCAP) has divided Asia into the following sub-regions:

- East and Northeast Asia that includes the People's Republic of China (China), Democratic People's Republic of Korea (North Korea), Japan, Mongolia, the Republic of Korea (South Korea) and the Russian Federation (Russia);
- North and Central Asia that includes the Commonwealth of Independent States (former Soviet Union) in Asia (CIS Asia), namely, Armenia, Azerbaijan, Georgia, Kazakhstan, Kyrgyzstan, Russia, Tajikistan, Turkmenistan and Uzbekistan;
- South and Southwest Asia that includes Afghanistan (Afghanistan would participate in activities relating to Central Asia as a member of the UN Special Programme for the Economies of

Central Asia), Bangladesh, Bhutan, India, the Islamic Republic of Iran (Iran), Maldives, Nepal, Pakistan, Sri Lanka and Turkey; and

- South East Asia that includes Brunei Darussalam (Brunei), Cambodia, Indonesia, Lao People's Democratic Republic (Laos), Malaysia, Myanmar, the Philippines, Singapore, Thailand, Timor-Leste and Vietnam.

This book has retained the sub-region of South East Asia as above and made changes in the others for meaningful groupings by sub-regions, as follows:

- South Asia is separated from Southwest Asia and Afghanistan is not included in South Asia as it overlaps with Southwest Asia, South Asia and Central Asia.
- Southwest Asia is excluded from the study as though UNESCAP includes only Iran and Turkey into this sub-region; it is sometimes used as coterminous with the Middle East and not considered part of Asia.
- East Asia is separated from the grouping with North Asia.
- Northeast Asia is renamed as North Asia because Russia is located in the North and not Northeast of Asia.
- Mongolia is included in North Asia due to its political commonalities with Russia rather than China.
- Armenia, Azerbaijan and Georgia are excluded from North and Central Asia as these comprise the South Caucasus, historically and culturally different from the rest of the five countries generally considered as Central Asia.

Thus, this book covers the four Asian sub-regions of East Asia, North and Central Asia, South East Asia and South Asia with 29 countries listed in the table below with its population:

Table 2.1
Asian Sub-Regions by Countries and Population

Asian Sub-Region	Countries	Population Mid-2012 (in millions)*
North Asia	Russia	143.2
	Mongolia	2.9
Central Asia	Kazakhstan	16.8
	Kyrgyzstan	5.7

Cont'd...

...Cont'd

	Tajikistan	7.1
	Turkmenistan	5.2
	Uzbekistan	29.8
South Asia	Bangladesh	152.9
	Bhutan	0.7
	India	1259.7
	Maldives	0.3
	Nepal	30.9
	Pakistan	180.4
	Sri Lanka	21.2
South East Asia	Brunei	0.4
	Cambodia	15
	Indonesia	241
	Laos	6.5
	Malaysia	29
	Myanmar	54.6
	Philippines	96.2
	Singapore	5.3
	Thailand	69.9
	Timor-Leste	1.1
	Vietnam	89
East Asia	China	1350.4
	Japan	127.6
	North Korea	24.6
	South Korea	48.9
Total		

**Source:* Population Reference Bureau, 2012

The world's most populated countries China and India are located in Asia, totalling to 8610 million people. The third highly populated country in Asia is Indonesia with 241 million people. On the other hand, Asia's least populated countries are Maldives with 0.3 million people, Brunei with 0.4 million people and Bhutan with 0.7 million people.

Introduction to Economic Development Progress in Asia

Overall Economic Development Progress

Asian Miracle

Asia has made phenomenal economic progress that has occurred in four waves, the first three considered the 'Asian Miracle' by the World Bank (1993):

1. Japan recovered quickly from the Second World War and has been prominent since the late 1960s. It was the first country in East Asia to develop economically and, thus, served as a model for East and South East Asia.
2. The four Asian Tigers Hong Kong, South Korea, Taiwan and Singapore excelled economically from the 1970s onwards.
3. Following closely were countries like Thailand, Malaysia and Indonesia.
4. Since the early 1990s China and India have embarked on similarly rapid economic development (Tang, 2000).

Implications of the Rise of Asia

Ghosh (2005) notes that the past two decades have been momentous for Asia. This is now the most 'globally integrated' region in the world, with the highest average ratios of trade to GDP, the largest absolute inflows of foreign direct investment, substantial financial capital flows and even significant movements of labour. Asia is also seen as the part of the world that has benefitted the most from the process of globalization. In terms of growth rates of aggregate GDP, Asia, and especially East Asia and India, far outperformed the rest of the world. High rates of growth in East Asia are of course dominated by the performance of China.

According to research carried out at the Goldman Sachs by Wilson and Purushothaman in 2003, over the next 50 years, Brazil, Russia, India and China – the BRIC economies – could become a much larger force in the world economy. When they mapped out GDP growth, income per capita and currency movements in these economies until 2050, the results were startling. If things go right, in less than 40 years, these economies together could be larger than the G6 (group of six powerful European countries) in US dollar terms. By 2025, they could account for over half the size of the G6. Of the current G6, only the US and Japan may be among the six largest economies in US dollar terms in 2050. The 2013 HDR (United Nations Development Programme, 2013) notes that the combined outputs of Brazil, China and India is about equal to the combined GDP of the long-standing industrial powers of Canada, France, Germany, Italy, UK and US. Brazil, China, India, Russia and South Africa have proposed a BRICS Development Bank that would draw upon their considerable reserves to finance projects in developing countries. This flow of resources would also assist with global financial rebalancing.

Kilmister (2008) observes that one issue in particular seen as increasingly central is the rebalancing of world economic growth away from the US (and UK) towards the surplus economies of Asia and elsewhere, especially China. Harris, Moore and Schmitz (2009) note that the tripartite (First, Second, Third World) and dichotomous (developed–developing countries; donor–recipient countries) classifications of the world countries need a rethinking. The apparent 'superiority' of the First World has been eroded by the fast economic growth in Asia. Some of the fast growing large economies, notably China and India, now exercise considerable geopolitical and economic power at the global level.

According to Zoellick (2010), President of the World Bank Group, 'Asia's share of the global economy in purchasing power parity terms has risen steadily from 7 per cent in 1980 to 21 per cent in 2008. Asia's stock markets now account for 32 per cent of global market capitalization, ahead of the United States at 30 per cent and Europe at 25 per cent. ...the developing world is becoming a driver of the global economy. Much of the recovery in world trade has been due to strong demand for imports among developing countries.' According to him, '... 2009 saw the end of what was known as the 'Third World': We are now in a new, fast-evolving multi-polar world economy – in which some developing countries are emerging as economic powers; others are moving towards becoming additional poles of growth; and some are struggling to attain their potential within this new system – where North and South, East and West, are now points on a compass, not economic destinies ...'.

The HDR of 2013 notes that with the rise of the South, the current institutions and principles for international governance require rethinking as they were designed in the post-Second World War context, that does not match the contemporary reality. The UN

Security Council is a significant body that has the ultimate responsibility for meeting threats to international peace and security. However, the five permanent veto-wielding seats are reserved for the victors of the Second World War, namely the US, Soviet Union (now Russia), the UK, France and China (earlier Taiwan). In the two most powerful international financial institutions, the IMF and the World Bank, the current voting system allows the west to dominate. Moreover, no Asian has been the head of either of these organizations. India's Prime Minister Manmohan Singh said in his speech in 2006, '...we need global institutions and new global 'rules of the game' that can facilitate the peaceful rise of new nations in Asia. It also means that existing global institutions and frameworks of cooperation must evolve and change to accommodate this new reality. This is as true for the reform and revitalization of the United Nations and the restructuring of the United Nations Security Council, as it is true for the management of multilateral trading system, or for the protection of global environment or for the security of world energy supplies.' According to Mahubani (2008), with the rise of Asia, rethinking of these structures has become an imperative as only monarchies and dictators enjoy perpetual rule, without seeking re-election and without being held accountable.

Diversity in Economic Development Progress in Asian Sub-Regions

Table 2.2 on Asian countries by economic development provides information on the per capita GNI of each country, its classification by its economic development progress by the World Bank, and the Income Gini Coefficient.

Table 2.2
Diversity in Economic Development Progress in Asian Sub-Regions

Countries	Per Capita GNI in USD 2012	World Bank Classification (based on GNI per Capita in 2011)	Income Gini Coefficient 2000–2010
East Asia			
Japan	32,545	High Income	NA
South Korea	28,231	High Income	NA
Hong Kong	45,598	High Income	NA
China	07,945	Upper Middle Income	42.5

Cont'd...

...Cont'd

North Korea	NA	Low Income	NA
South East Asia			
Singapore	52,613	High Income	NA
Brunei	45,690	High Income	NA
Malaysia	13,676	Upper Middle Income	46.2
Thailand	07,722	Upper Middle Income	40.0
Philippines	03,752	Lower Middle Income	43.0
Indonesia	04,154	Lower Middle Income	34.0
Vietnam	02,970	Lower Middle Income	35.6
Timor-Leste	05,446	Lower Middle Income	31.9
Laos	02,435	Lower Middle Income	36.7
Cambodia	02,095	Low Income	37.9
Myanmar	01,817	Low Income	NA
North and Central Asia			
Russia	14,461	Upper Middle Income	40.1
Kazakhstan	10,451	Upper Middle Income	29.0
Turkmenistan	07,782	Upper Middle Income	NA
Mongolia	04,245	Lower Middle Income	36.5
Uzbekistan	03,201	Lower Middle Income	36.7
Kyrgyzstan	02,009	NA	36.2
Tajikistan	02,119	Low Income	30.8
South Asia			
Maldives	07,478	Upper Middle Income	37.4
Sri Lanka	05,170	Lower Middle Income	40.3
India	03.285	Lower Middle Income	33.4
Bhutan	05,246	Lower Middle Income	38.1
Pakistan	02,566	Lower Middle Income	30.0
Bangladesh	01,785	Low Income	32.1
Nepal	01,137	Low Income	32.8

Sources: Columns 1 and 3: United Nations Development Programme, 2013; Column 2: World Bank classification of Asian countries by economic development as of 2011 (http://databank.worldbank.org/ddp/viewClassifications?HIERARCHY=Classification&DIMENSION=WDI_Ctry)

Gross National Income and Development

Table 2.2 shows that the per capita GNI is the highest in Singapore, Brunei, Japan and South Korea and lowest in Nepal, Bangladesh and Myanmar. Sub-regionwise, it is highest in East Asia and the lowest in South Asia. The World Bank classification of Asian economies shows that most of the countries in Asia are categorized as lower middle income countries.

Income Gini Coefficient

The Income Gini Coefficient is a measure of the deviation of the distribution of income (or consumption) among individuals or households within a country from a perfectly equal distribution. A value of zero represents absolute equality and a value of 100 represent absolute inequality. Data on the Income Gini Coefficient of Asian countries at very high level of human development and some at low level of human development are not available. Of the countries for which it is available, Table 2.2 shows that inequality in income is prevalent throughout Asia, and cuts across the levels of economic development. Minimum income inequality is in Kazakhstan (29.0) and Pakistan (30), and maximum income inequality is in Malaysia (46.2), Philippines (43.0) and China (42.5). Sub-regionwise:

- In South East Asia, Timor-Leste has minimum and Malaysia and the Philippines have maximum inequality.
- In North and Central Asia, Kazakhstan has minimum and Russia has maximum inequality.
- In South Asia, Pakistan has minimum and Sri Lanka has maximum inequality.

Least Developed Countries

Mainly based on economic measures, since 2003, the Economic and Social Council of the UN use the following three criteria for the identification of the least developed countries (LDCs):

- A low-income criterion, based on a three-year average estimate of the gross national income (GNI) per capita (under $750 for inclusion, above $900 for graduation);
- A human resource weakness criterion, involving a composite Human Assets Index (HAI) based on indicators of: (a) nutrition; (b) health; (c) education; and (d) adult literacy; and
- The composite Economic Vulnerability Index (EVI).

To be added to the LDC list, a country must satisfy all three criteria. To qualify for graduation, a country must meet the thresholds for two of the three criteria in two consecutive triennial reviews. In addition, since fundamentally the LDC category recognizes structural handicaps, it excludes large economies; so the population must not exceed 75 million (Source: http://www.un.org/special-rep/ohrlls/ldc/ldc%20criteria.htm).

In two Asian sub-regions, the following eight countries are identified as LDCs:

- South East Asia: Cambodia, Laos, Myanmar and Timor-Leste
- South Asia: Bangladesh, Bhutan, Maldives and Nepal

Absence of North Korea in the LDC list is also surprising as it is a low income country.

Discussion

Thus, though Asia is considered 'rising':

- It is diverse as the World Bank classification for economic development in the sub-regions ranges from mainly high income in East Asia, to mainly upper middle income in North and Central Asia, to mainly lower middle income in South East and South Asia to low income in some countries.
- The contradiction lies in the fact that inequality in income is prevalent throughout Asia, and cuts across the levels of economic development.

Introduction to Social Development Progress in Asia

Measures of Social Development Progress

The international measures of social development progress developed and promoted by the UN are the human development measures and progress on the MDGs and, therefore, used as the main measures of social development progress in this book.

Human Development Measures

Human Development Index

The Human Development Index (HDI) was developed in 1990 as a new measure of social progress to reinforce the paradigm shift from economic development to social development. At the onset, the HDI followed six basic principles as guidelines (Haq, 1995, cited by Kovacevic, 2010):

1. Measure the basic purpose of human development - to enlarge people's choices.
2. Include a limited number of variables to keep it simple and manageable.
3. Be composite rather than a plethora of separate indices.
4. Cover both social and economic choices.
5. Be sufficiently flexible in both coverage and methodology to allow gradual refinements, once better alternatives became available.
6. Not be inhibited by lack of reliable and up-to-date data series.

The HDI has three key components:

1. Longevity measured by life expectancy at birth
2. Knowledge measured by adult literacy (two-third weightage) and mean years of schooling (one-third weightage)
3. Real GDP per capita income in purchasing power parity (PPP) dollars (Haq, 1999).

These three dimensions are standardized to values between zero and one, and the simple average is taken to arrive at the overall HDI value, also in the range of zero to one. Countries are then ranked on the basis of this value with a rank of one representing the highest HDI value. HDI classifications into four levels of human development: very high, high, medium and low, is relative – based on quartiles of HDI distribution across the 187 countries. The 2010 HDR introduces the Inequality-adjusted HDI (IHDI), a measure of the level of human development of people in a society that accounts for inequality. Under perfect equality the HDI and the IHDI are equal. When there is inequality in the distribution of health, education and income, the HDI of an average person in a society is less than the aggregate HDI; the lower the IHDI (and the greater the difference between it and the HDI), the greater the inequality (United Nations Development Programme, 2010).

Human Development Reports

Since 1990, the United Nations Development Programme (UNDP) annually publishes an HDR, which monitors the progress of humanity through the country rankings by the HDI. Each HDR annually addresses, as its main issue, the question of how economic growth translates, or fails to translate, into human development. The reports are intended to assess the quality of life of a population and be an advocacy tool for its improvement. In assessing the state of a population from a people-centred perspective, these reports have the political purpose of raising awareness and generating debate on public issues and concerns which would otherwise not be on the political agenda (Alkire and Deneulin, 2009). The global HDR's analytical framework and inclusive approach carry over into regional, national and local HDRs, also supported by the UNDP.

Critique

Ever since the HDI was first published, it has drawn critiques from many sides. Kovacevic (2010) summarizes that these critiques have centred on two general areas, first, how to define human development and how to observe and measure its components and determinants, and second, how to aggregate the different indicators to obtain a commonly acceptable single index of human development in order to measure its improvement. The 2013 HDR notes that because national and international data agencies continually improve their data series, the data-including the HDI values and ranks-presented in this Report are not comparable to those published in earlier editions. The HDR also mentions that national and international data estimates can vary because international agencies harmonize national data for comparability across countries, produce an estimate of missing data or do not incorporate the most recent national data (United Nations Development Programme, 2013).

Millennium Development Goals

Millennium Development Goals

In 2000, the UN General Assembly adopted the Millennium Declaration based in the fundamental values of freedom, equality, solidarity, tolerance, respect for nature and shared responsibility.

Under the objective of Development and Poverty Eradication of the Millennium Declaration, the following eight MDGs were identified to be met by the year 2015:

1. Eradicate extreme poverty and hunger

- Reduce by half the proportion of people living on less than one US dollar a day.
- Reduce by half the proportion of people who suffer from hunger.
- Increase the amount of food for those who suffer from hunger.

2. Achieve universal primary education

- Ensure that all boys and girls complete a full course of primary schooling.
- Increased enrollment must be accompanied by efforts to ensure that all children remain in school and receive a high-quality education.

3. Promote gender equality and empower women

- Eliminate gender disparity in primary and secondary education preferably by 2005, and at all levels by 2015.

4. Reduce child mortality

- Reduce the mortality rate among children under five by two-thirds.

5. Improve maternal health

- Reduce the maternal mortality ratio by three quarters.

6. Combat HIV/AIDS, malaria, and other diseases

- Halt and begin to reverse the spread of HIV/AIDS.
- Halt and begin to reverse the incidence of malaria and other major diseases.

7. Ensure environmental sustainability

- Integrate the principles of sustainable development into country policies and programmes reverse loss of environmental resources.

- Reduce by half the proportion of people without sustainable access to safe drinking water.
- Achieve significant improvement in lives of at least 100 million slum dwellers, by 2020.

8. Develop a global partnership for development

- Develop further an open trading and financial system that is rule-based, predictable and non-discriminatory. Includes a commitment to good governance, development and poverty reduction – nationally and internationally.
- Address the least developed countries' special needs. This includes tariff- and quota-free access for their exports; enhanced debt relief for heavily indebted poor countries; cancellation of official bilateral debt; and more generous official development assistance for countries committed to poverty reduction.
- Address the special needs of landlocked and Small Island Developing States.
- Deal comprehensively with developing countries' debt problems through national and international measures to make debt sustainable in the long term.
- In cooperation with the developing countries, develop decent and productive work for youth.
- In cooperation with pharmaceutical companies, provide access to affordable essential drugs in developing countries.
- In cooperation with the private sector, make available the benefits of new technologies - especially information and communications technologies.

The variation in progress of the MDGs ranges as follows:

- Early achiever (has already met the target),
- On track (expected to hit the target by 2015),
- Off track – slow (expected to hit the target, but after 2015) and
- Off track – regressing (slipping backwards, or stagnating).

Critique

Rist (2008: 234–235) observes that development which was previously regarded as a coherent phenomenon has been broken up into a set of objectives whose links with one another are scarcely explained. This division, he says, actually paralyses thought and stands in the way of their systemic linkage. The example he gives is about Asia where the proportion of people living on less than one US dollar per day has fallen considerably but inequalities have widened and the consumption share of the poorest 20 per cent has declined. Although the numbers of the poor have declined, this has been at the price of increased pollution and growing inequalities.

According to the UN Office of the High Commissioner for Human Rights (UNOHCHR, 2008) there are some similarities between the MDGs and human rights. The content of the MDGs partly resembles some economic and social rights, and both provide tools to hold governments accountable. They can also reinforce each other, because MDGs potentially provide benchmarks for economic and social rights, and human rights strategies can offer enhanced legitimacy, equity and sustainability to the types of policies needed to achieve the MDGs. However, it is concerned that:

- Human rights have not yet played a significant role in supporting and influencing MDG-based development planning.
- The MDG agenda departs too much from the Millennium Declaration, from which they were drawn and which contained significant references to human rights.
- The MDG targets are not sufficiently focused on the poorest of the poor or on inequality within a country; several require only the halving of a certain indicator.
- A number of MDG targets are not consistent with human rights and potentially diminish gains enshrined in international human rights treaties. For example, MDG 2 ignores the crucial requirement of free primary education, which is an immediate obligation in international human rights treaties.
- There is lack of participation of Southern countries and civil society organizations in drafting the MDGs and targets.
- There is lack of effective accountability mechanisms for the MDGs, particularly for donor countries.

Overall Social Development Progress

According to the 2010–11 Report, the MDGs in Asia Pacific (United Nations Economic and Social Commission for Asia and the Pacific, Asian Development Bank and United Nations Development Programme, 2010–11), one of the greatest MDG successes in this region, has been that of poverty reduction. Between 1990 and 2008, the countries of the region reduced the number of people living on less than $1.25 a day from 1.5 billion to 947 million; thus, the region is on track for the poverty goal. However, due to its size, the region continues to have the largest number of poor people.

For the following indicators, the Asia-Pacific region as a whole has already achieved the targets:

- Reducing gender disparities in primary, secondary and tertiary education enrolment.
- Preventing a rise in HIV prevalence.
- Stopping the spread of TB.
- Reducing consumption of ozone-depleting substances.
- Halving the proportion of people without access to safe drinking water.

On the other hand, the region is lagging in the following major areas:

- Reducing the extent of hunger.
- Reducing child mortality.
- Improving maternal health provision.
- Ensuring that girls and boys reach the last grade of primary education.
- Providing basic sanitation.

Diversity in Social Development Progress in Asian Sub-Regions

Diversity in Human Development Measures

The latest HDR (United Nations Development Programme, 2013) provides the progress in HDI Rank, HDI Value and Inequality-adjusted HDI Value by level of development of 29 countries in Asia (Hong Kong is listed separately from China and data is not available for North Korea) as presented in Table 2.3.

...Cont'd

		4 Countries with Low Human Development			
26	Pakistan	146	0.515	0.356	30.9
27	Bangladesh	146	0.515	0.374	27.4
28	Myanmar	149	0.498	—	—
29	Nepal	157	0.463	0.304	34.2

*Data for China do not include Hong Kong, Macao and Taiwan.

Table 2.3 shows the diversity of the countries in Asia ranging from very high human development to low human development. The majority of the Asian countries (55.2%) fall in the medium human development category. Although the economic and the social paradigms are so different, there seems to be a high correlation between the economic and social aspects of development:

- All the four countries with very high level of human development are also the countries classified as high income countries by the World Bank.
- Except Sri Lanka, all the countries with high level of human development belong to the upper middle income category as Sri Lanka has higher level of human development than its economic development.
- Although most of the countries in the category of medium level of human development are same as those classified as lower middle income countries, the exceptions are China, Thailand, Turkmenistan and Maldives which are considered upper middle income countries. Thus, their economic development is higher than their human development. On the other hand, Cambodia and Tajikistan which are at medium level of human development are categorized as low income countries; probably their human development is better than their economic development.

The Inequality-adjusted HDI Value is not calculated for most of the countries with very high human development. For all the countries for which it is calculated, it is lower than the HDI Value, indicating inequality in human development in all the countries of Asia. However, the level of inequality varies:

- The maximum percentage loss in HDI indicating inequality in Asia is in Nepal (34.2%), Timor-Leste (33.0%), Pakistan

(30.9%), India (29.3%), Bangladesh (27.4%), Cambodia (25.9%), Maldives (25.2%) and Laos (24.7%), most of which are countries of South Asia.

- The minimum percentage loss in HDI because of inequality is observed in Kazakhstan (13.6%), Vietnam (14.0%), Sri Lanka (15.1%), Uzbekistan (15.8%), Mongolia (15.9%), South Korea (16.5%), Kyrgyzstan (17.1%), and Tajikistan (18.4%), most of which are the former Soviet Union countries.

The diversity in Asian sub-regions is discussed in the following sections.

East Asian Countries by Human Development

Following is the distribution of countries in East Asia by level of human development:

- Very High Level of Human Development: Japan, Hong Kong and South Korea
- Medium Level of Human Development: China
- North Korea (Data not available)

Thus, East Asia has the highest level of human development in Asia.

The HDR of 2013 notes that China's performance over 1990–2010 was dominated by growth in income in part because when reforms began in the late 1970s, China's achievements in health and education were already high. South Korea, despite lower economic growth than China, had the biggest gains in HDI value (United Nations Development Programme, 2013).

South East Asian Countries by Human Development

Following is the distribution of countries in South East Asia by level of human development:

- Very High Level of Human Development: Singapore and Brunei
- High Level of Human Development: Malaysia
- Medium Level of Human Development: Thailand, Philippines, Indonesia, Vietnam, Laos, Cambodia and Timor-Leste
- Low Level of Human Development: Myanmar

Thus, South East Asian countries are most diverse in Asia with reference to the range from very high to low level of human development.

The HDR of 2013 notes that Vietnam fared well, ranking third in income growth and among the top 20 in HDI improvement in the world (United Nations Development Programme, 2013).

North and Central Asian Countries by Human Development

Following is the distribution of North and Central Asian countries by level of human development:

- High Level of Human Development: Russia and Kazakhstan
- Medium Level of Human Development: Turkmenistan, Mongolia, Uzbekistan, Kyrgyzstan and Tajikistan

The Inequality-adjusted HDI Value shows low level of inequality in Russia, Kazakhstan, Mongolia, Kyrgyzstan and Uzbekistan. Thus in Asia, inequality in human development is minimum in the former Soviet Union countries of North and Central Asia.

South Asian Countries by Human Development

Following is the distribution of countries in South Asia by level of human development:

- High Level of Human Development: Sri Lanka
- Medium Level of Human Development: Maldives, India and Bhutan
- Low Level of Human Development: Pakistan, Bangladesh and Nepal

Three out of four countries with low level of human development are in South Asia. The Inequality-adjusted HDI Value shows high level of inequality in South Asian countries such as Nepal, Pakistan, India, Bangladesh and Bhutan. Thus in Asia, South Asia has the lowest level of human development and highest level of inequality.

The HDR of 2013 notes that Sri Lanka has had high income growth as well a notable reduction in HDI shortfall despite years of internal conflict. India's economic performance has been impressive but its per capita income is still low (United Nations Development Programme, 2013).

Diversity in Progress of Millennium Development Goals

Following is the comparative progress of the MDGs in the Asian sub-regions. Asia includes the world's two most populous countries, China and India, so the region's overall achievement on the MDGs are swayed by their performance. Excluding these two countries, Asia's performance is worse.

East Asia

According to the United Nations Economic and Social Commission for Asia and the Pacific (UNESCAP), Asian Development Bank (ADB) and United Nations Development Programme (UNDP) (2009–10):

- South Korea: South Korea started in 1990 with its indicators at high levels, leaving less scope for further advances. However, this country has made slow progress in gender equality in tertiary education.
- China: Macao has low indicators coverage, less than 40 per cent, and is off track on half of them. Data availability is also weak for Hong Kong, with coverage of a little over 40 per cent, and it had regressed in primary education between 2001 and 2005. China has demonstrated some of the sub-region's greatest advances, especially in poverty. Between 1990 and 2005, the poverty rate fell from 60 to 16 per cent. On the other hand, it has made slow progress in reducing child mortality and in providing basic sanitation.
- North Korea: It is difficult to assess the progress of North Korea since, although it reports on more than 60 per cent of the indicators, these do not include those on poverty, education, or gender equality. For its reported indicators, the country has not made progress on reducing child and maternal mortality and on providing basic sanitation.

South East Asia

According to the UNESCAP, ADB and UNDP (2009–10), most countries in South East Asia have reported data on more than 80 per cent of the indicators. The exceptions are two wealthy countries, Brunei and Singapore, and two LDCs, Timor-Leste and Myanmar. According to the subsequent report of the UNESCAP, ADB and UNDP (2012–13), South East Asia has made the greatest progress, being on track for two, and an early achiever for 12, of the 21 indicators. It is slow on just six, mainly those related to child and maternal health, and for only one, forest cover, it is classified as regressing or without progress.

North and Central Asia

According to the UNESCAP, ADB and UNDP (2009–10), Russia reports on 85 per cent of the indicators. However, on most of these indicators Russia already had good starting levels in 1990. Most countries in Central Asia have reported data on more than 90 per cent of the indicators. According to the UNESCAP, ADB and UNDP (2012–13), North and Central Asia is an early achiever on 12 indicators but slow in other six – child, infant and maternal mortality, skilled birth attendance and access to water and sanitation. Russia is the largest influence in this sub-region; nevertheless the outcomes for the sub-region without it are similar to those for the sub-region as a whole. North and Central Asia excluding Russia is an early achiever in 13 indicators, slow in other five and regressing or making no progress in two – primary enrollment and HIV prevalence. The reduced sub-region is an early achiever in access to basic sanitation, whereas the whole sub-region is slow.

South Asia

According to the UNESCAP, ADB and UNDP et al. (2009–10), All the South Asian countries except Maldives have reported on more than 80 per cent of the 21 indicators assessed in this report. Starting from a low base on many MDG indicators, South Asia is an early achiever for seven, on track for three and slow for the rest of the indicators. Significant advances are visible in Goals 6 and 7, except for basic sanitation, where the sub-region has been making slow progress. Another area where the sub-region has performed very well is in achieving gender parity in primary education. The sub-region is behind on reducing malnutrition and improving child and maternal health. In this case, India has the largest influence. For poverty, the outcomes for the sub-region excluding India are more positive than those for the sub-region as a whole. However, in many other cases, the reduced sub-region does worse – as with primary enrollment, forest cover and tuberculosis incidence. The reduced sub-region is on track for two, and an early achiever for only five indicators, while it is slow for 12 and regressing for two (UNESCAP, ADB and UNDP, 2012–13).

Least Developed Countries

As might be expected, the countries off track on the highest proportion of indicators are the LDCs. Some LDCs are emerging from conflicts and others are highly fragile. The group as a whole has been making no or slow progress on 11 indicators. On the other hand, the group is an early achiever in seven indicators and on track in another three. For example, many LDCs for which data is available have done well in poverty reduction and several other MDGs. Nepal and Cambodia are early achievers and Laos is on track. Similarly, Bangladesh, Cambodia, Laos and Timor-Leste are all on track in reducing maternal mortality. The case of Nepal is interesting: despite a period of internal conflict, the country has managed to reduce the incidence of poverty from 53 per cent in 2003 to 25 per cent in 2010. This impressive achievement seems to be a combination of several factors including a decrease in household size, increased access to services, an increase in remittances, improvements in real wages and rapid urbanization (UNESCAP, ADB and UNDP, 2012–13).

Limitations

Limitation of the MDG progress data is that some highly developed and some least developed countries do not report on all the indicators. Moreover, countries that report on the MDG progress often use different data sources and may not be comparable.

References

Alkire, S. and Deneulin, S. (2009). A normative framework for development. In S. Deneulin and L. Shahani (eds), *An Introduction to the Human Development and Capability Approach: Freedom and Agency* (pp. 3–21). London: Earthscan.

Ghosh, J. (2005). Globalisation and economic empowerment of women: Emerging issues in Asia. In *UNESCAP, Asia and the Pacific Beijing+10: Selected Issues.* New York. Retrieved 13 May 2010 from http://www.unescap.org/esid/gad/ PDF/AsiaandPacificBeijing+10.pdf

Haq, M.U. (1999). *Reflections on Human Development.* Delhi: Oxford University Press.

Harris, D., Moore, M. and Schmitz, H. (2009). Country classifications for a changing world. Institute of Development Studies, Working Paper No.

326. Retrieved 18 December 2010 from http://www.kef-online.at/en/r4d-news/ids-working-paper-country-classifications-for-a-changing-world.html

Karns, M.P. and Mingst, K.A. (2010). *International Organizations: The Politics and Processes of Global Governance.* London: Lynne Rienner Publishers.

Kilmister, A. (2008). The economic crisis and its effects. Retrieved 3 April 2010 from http://www.internationalviewpoint.org/spip.php?article 1581

Kovacevic, M. (2010). Review of HDI critiques and potential improvements. Human Development Research Paper, United Nations Development Program. Retrieved 28 April 2013 from http://hdr.undp.org/en/reports/global/hdr2010/papers/HDRP_2010_33.pdf

Mahubani, K. (2008). *The New Asian Hemisphere: The Irresistible Shift of Global Power to the East.* New York: Public Affairs.

Population Reference Bureau. (2012). *2012 World Population Data Sheet.* Retrieved 17 June 2013 from http://www.prb.org/pdf12/2012-population-data-sheet_eng.pdf

Rist, G. (2008). *The History of Development: From Western Origins to Global Faith* (3rd ed.). New York: Zed Books.

Sen, A. (1997). *Human Rights and Asian Values, Sixteenth Morgenthau Memorial Lecture on Ethics and Foreign Policy.* New York: Carnegie Council on Ethics and International Affairs.

Singh, M. (2006). Speech by Dr Manmohan Singh, Prime Minister of India, to the LSE Asia Forum, New Delhi. Retrieved 27 April 2013 from http://www2.lse.ac.uk/lseasiaforum/pdf/manmohansingh_openingaddress.pdf

Tang, K.L. (ed.) (2000). *Social Development in Asia.* The Netherlands: Kluwer Academic Publishers.

United Nations Development Programme. (2010). *Human Development Report: The Real Wealth of Nations: Pathways to Human Development.* New York: Oxford University Press.

——. (2013). *Human Development Report: The Rise of the South: Human Progress in a Diverse World.* New York.

United Nations Economic and Social Commission for Asia and the Pacific, Asian Development Bank and United Nations Development Program. (2009–10). *Achieving the Millennium Development Goals in an Era of Global Uncertainty: Asia-Pacific Regional Report.* Retrieved 9 January 2010 from http://www.mdgasiapacific.org/regional-report-2009–10

——. (2010–11). *Paths to 2015: MDG Priorities in Asia and the Pacific.* Retrieved 2 December 2010 from http://www.adb.org/Documents/Reports/ Asia-Pacific-MDG-2010/default.asp

——. (2012–13). *Perspectives for a Post-2015 Development Agenda: Asia-Pacific Regional MDGs Report 2012/13.*

United Nations Office of the High Commissioner for Human Rights. (2008). *Claiming the Millennium Development Goals: A Human Rights Approach.* New York.

Wilson, D. and Purushothaman, R. (2003). Dreaming with BRICs: The path to 2050. Goldman Sachs, Global Paper No. 99. Retrieved 31 March 2010 from http://www.goldmansachs.com/our-thinking/brics/brics-repo rts-pdfs/brics-dream.pdf

World Bank. (1993). *The East Asian Miracle: Economic Growth and Public Policy.* Washington, DC.

Zoellick, R.B. (2010). The end of the Third World? Modernizing multilateralism for a multipolar world. Retrieved 21 April 2010 from http:// web.worldbank.org/WBSITE/EXTERNAL/NEWS/0,,content MDK:22541126~ pagePK: 34370~piPK: 42770~theSitePK: 4607,00.html

CHAPTER 3

Geographical and Historical Background of Social Development in Asia

Introduction

This chapter on geographical and historical background of social development in Asia reviews the following:

1. Geographical background of Asian sub-regions with reference to diversity in geographical adjacency and geopolitics, the temperate/tropical zones, the landlocked developing countries and Small Island Developing States and their implications for social development.
2. Religious background of Asia with reference to diversity in religious ideologies and their implications for social development.
3. Collectivistic culture in Asia and its implications for social development.
4. Pre-colonial civilizations in Asia with specific reference to China and India.

Geographical Background of Social Development in Asia

Table 3.1 provides the geographical background of the Asian sub-regions with reference to the zonal location, geographical adjacency, countries and level of human development in these regions:

Table 3.1
Diversity in Geographical Background of Asian Sub-Regions

Asian Sub-Region	Geographical Adjacency	Countries	Level of Human Development
	Temperate Zone		
Central Asia	Landlocked between:	Kazakhstan	High
	South of Russia	Kyrgyzstan	Medium
	East of the Caspian Sea	Turkmenistan	Medium
	West of China	Uzbekistan	Medium
	North of Southwest Asia	Tajikistan	Medium
North Asia	South of Arctic Ocean	Russia (largest)	High
	East of Europe		
	North of Central Asia and China	Mongolia	Medium
East Asia	South of Mongolia and Russia	Japan	Very High
	East of Central Asia	South Korea	Very High
	West of North Pacific Ocean	China (largest)	Medium
	North of South East Asia	North Korea	Low
	Tropical Zone		
South East Asia	Indo-China:	Thailand	Medium
	South of China	Vietnam	Medium
	East of India	Cambodia	Medium
		Laos	Medium
		Myanmar	Low
	Maritime South East Asia: Island States North of Indian Ocean	Singapore	Very High
		Brunei	Very High
		Malaysia	High
		Indonesia (largest)	Medium
		Philippines	Medium
		Timor-Leste	Medium
South Asia	North/Mainland Countries:	India (largest)	Medium
	South of China	Bhutan	Medium

Cont'd...

...Cont'd

Between Southwest Asia and South East Asia	Pakistan	Low
North of Indian Ocean	Bangladesh	Low
	Nepal	Low
South/Island Countries:	Sri Lanka	High
Islands in Indian Ocean	Maldives	Medium

Geographical Adjacency and Geopolitics

The adjacency between sub-regions and between countries has played an important geopolitical role in the ideological-cultural and political development of the respective sub-regions as discussed later:

North and Central Asia

Russia has had geopolitical power in these sub-regions due to its adjacency to East Europe and Central Asia both of which had joined it to form the former Soviet Union. Southwest Asia has influenced Central Asia with the spread of Islam.

East Asia

China being the largest country in East Asia has had geopolitical power over other countries in East Asia as well as in the adjacent South East Asia. Through the Silk Route across North India and Central Asia it traded in silk with the Western world.

South East Asia

South East Asia has been significantly influenced by the geopolitical power of China and India. The mainland countries of South East Asia namely, Myanmar, Thailand, Cambodia, Laos and Vietnam are together also known as Indo-China. Malaysia and the southern island countries of South East Asia namely, Brunei, Indonesia, the Philippines, Singapore and Timor-Leste are called Maritime South East Asia. Compared to Indo-China, the South East Asian countries in the Maritime South East Asia are at a higher level of human development.

South Asia

With the Himalayas in the North and the sea in the South, India has had a unified but diverse civilization in the wide area in between

(Nehru, 1945). India, being the largest country, has had significant geopolitical power over other South Asian countries as well as on South East Asia. First through trade and then through spread of Buddhism India influenced South East Asia. Southwest Asia has influenced the northern countries of Bangladesh, Bhutan, North India, Nepal and Pakistan. Compared to the South Asian countries in the mainland, the island countries in South Asia are better developed, similar to the Maritime South East Asian countries.

Temperate/Tropical Zones

Landes (1999) identified geography as one of the reasons for the rich countries being rich and the poor countries being poor. He noted that the rich countries lie in the temperate zones, particularly in the northern hemisphere; poor countries in the tropics and semi-tropics. According to him, the discomfort of heat exceeds that of cold. The easiest way to reduce heat is to not work and have siesta at mid-day. Heat also encourages the proliferation of life forms hostile to human beings. The result is faster transmission of disease and development of immunities to counter measures.

In Asia, most of the countries at very high level of human development in Asia, namely Japan, Hong Kong and South Korea and most of the countries at high level, namely Russia and Kazakhstan do lie in the temperate zone in the northern hemisphere. Only North Korea is at the low level of human development in this region. However, most of the countries in this geographical region, namely, China, Mongolia, and other Central Asian countries are not at very high or high levels of human development. Although four of the five countries at low level of human development lie in the tropical zone, Singapore and Brunei are at very high level of human development and Malaysia is at high level of human development but located in the tropical zone. Thus, the background of temperate/tropical zones only partly explains the level of a country's development. Thus, the temperate/tropical zone does not totally explain the level of development.

Landlocked Developing Countries

According to the United Nations Office of the High Representative for the Least Developed Countries, Landlocked Developing Countries and Small Island Developing States (UNOHRLLS at http://www.unohrlls.org/en/lldc/31/), lack of territorial access to the sea, remoteness and isolation from world markets and high transit costs continue to impose serious constraints on the overall socio-economic development of landlocked developing countries. Their sea-borne trade unavoidably depends on transit through other countries. The economic performance of landlocked developing countries reflects the direct and indirect impact of geographical situation on key-economic variables. Landlocked developing countries are generally among the poorest of the developing countries, with the weakest growth rates, and are typically heavily dependent on a very limited number of commodities for their export earnings. In most cases their transit neighbours are themselves developing countries, often of broadly similar economic structure and beset by similar scarcities of resources. The recorded trade between landlocked and transit developing countries tends to be relatively insignificant. In most cases, the transit developing countries are in no position to offer transport systems of high technical and administrative standards to which their landlocked neighbours might link themselves effectively by the development of their own internal transport systems.

Table 3.2 on the list of countries in Asia that are landlocked shows that their level of human development varies from high to low, the most common being the medium level of development. Thus, landlocking of a country does not totally explain inadequacy of development.

Table 3.2
Diversity in Landlocked Developing Countries and Social Development in Asia

Asian Sub-Region	Landlocked Country	Level of Human Development
South East Asia	Laos	Medium
North and Central Asia	Mongolia	Medium
	Kazakhstan	High
	Kyrgyzstan	Medium
	Tajikistan	Medium
	Turkmenistan	Medium
	Uzbekistan	Medium
South Asia	Bhutan	Medium
	Nepal	Low

Small-Island Developing States

Small Island Developing States (SIDS) were recognized as a distinct group of developing countries facing specific social, economic and environmental vulnerabilities at the UN Conference on Environment and Development, also known as the Earth Summit, held in Rio de Janeiro, in 1992. SIDS also tend to confront constraints in their sustainable development efforts, such as a narrow resource base depriving them of the benefits of economies of scale; small domestic markets and heavy dependence on a few external and remote markets; high costs for energy, infrastructure, transportation, communication and servicing; long distances from export markets and import resources; low and irregular international traffic volumes; little resilience to natural disasters; growing populations; high volatility of economic growth; limited opportunities for the private sector and a proportionately large reliance of their economies on their public sector; and fragile natural environments (http://www.unohrlls.org/en/sids/43/).

Table 3.3 shows that both the SIDS countries in Asia have medium level of human development. Thus, being a small-island developing state does not explain inadequacy of development.

Table 3.3
Diversity in Small-Island Developing States and Social Development in Asia

Asian Sub-Region	Small-Island Developing State	Level of Human Development
South East Asia	Timor-Leste	Medium
South Asia	Maldives	Medium

Diversity in Religious Ideologies and Social Development in Asia

Religion has had a strong influence on ideologies and culture in Asia. India is the origin of Hinduism and Buddhism which have had strong influence in South Asia. China is the origin of Confucianism which has had strong influence in East Asia and South East Asia. Hindusim and Confucianism both translate into ethical structure governing behaviour (United Nations, 2010). The following briefs on these religions show that their ideologies are quite different from each other. However, as Jawaharlal Nehru (1945) noted, what is common among the Asian religious ideologies is that they affected all aspects of life with the intention of producing equilibrium and a sense of harmony as against the modern capitalist ideology of just how to be comfortable.

Asia has also been influenced by Judeo-Christian religions such as Islam as well as Christianity. Whole of Central Asia is predominantly Islamic, being adjacent to the Middle East, the origin of Islam. Pakistan and Bangladesh in South Asia and the Malay world of Malaysia, Brunei and Indonesia are also predominantly Islamic. Most Muslims live in Asia as Indonesia, India, Pakistan and Bangladesh have the world's largest Muslim populations. Russia, Philippines and Timor-Leste are predominantly under the influence of Christianity. So Asia is not homogenous with reference to religious ideologies. However, religions that have originated in the sub-regions seem to have had a strong impact on all aspects of life, including development, in the sub-regions of origin and adjacent sub-regions.

Hindu Ideologies and Implications

Origin and Spread

The main source of what we call today the Hindu religion lies in the *Vedas*, written during 4000 to 1000 BC, by the priestly group of Aryans who invaded India around 1500 BC. The Rig Veda, the first of the Vedas, is probably the earliest book that humanity possesses. It comprises hymns used by the Aryan priests, the Brahmins, in their rituals directed towards nature gods such as *Agni*, the god of fire, and *Indra*, the god of sky (Black, 1999). This religion has the largest number of scriptures, written over a long period of time. Besides India being the origin of Hinduism, Nepal is a Hindu country. Besides Hindusim, countries in South Asia are also influenced by Buddhism and Islam and Hinduism has also influenced the South East Asian societies.

Philosophy

Following are key philosophical concepts according to the Vedic scriptures:

- *Brahman* is the ultimate reality, which means that everything in the world is but the manifestation of a part of *Brahman*. If *Brahman* is the ultimate reality and if we are not different from it, birth cannot be our beginning or death our end.

- *Samsara* means transmigration or the flow of *atman* (soul) from beyond birth to beyond death. Thus, *atman* is eternal and birth and death relate to the integration and disintegration of the elements that compose the body.
- The kind of birth the *atman* takes and the type of enjoyment that falls to its lot are determined by its own past, or *karma*. The term *karma* means work and its result. The law of *karma* states that the sphere of morality is an ordered realm, and is the moral equivalent of the physical law of causality. The sufferings of people are usually understood to be the result of their bad *karma*.
- Freedom from the cycle of *karma* is called *moksha*, which is not only possible, but is one's ultimate goal and destiny. What prevents the soul from realizing it is its own ignorance, which when dispelled through wisdom of the nature of the self, one attains release. *Moksha* is attainable in this life, by achieving an exalted mode of existence, freed from the shackles of egoity and ignorance (Mahadevan, 1982).

Caste System

According to the Aryan theory of race, when the Aryans first came to India they were divided into three occupational groups: *Brahmins*, the priests; *Kshatriyas*, the warriors; and *Vaishyas*, the traders. The heredity of occupations was not a recognized principle in the early Vedic age. The darker coloured native inhabitants of India, whom they conquered, were considered *Shudras or Ati-Shudras* (considered untouchables). This interface seems to have been the cause of the development of the system of *Varna* (color). As the *Varna* of a person had been assigned to him/her by virtue of his/her birth into it, it was also called the *jati* system, which the west translates as caste. Endogamy prevailed as marriages were permitted only within the caste. The hereditary caste system is supposed to have burgeoned in the later Vedic age (Singhal, 1983). Casteism justified hierarchy of castes based on natural and social inferiority of a large number of communities. Suffering of the lower castes is usually explained by their *karmas*, in this life or the previous lives (Gore, 1966).

Implications for Development

Weber (1958) notes that the other-worldly philosophy of Hinduism gives less importance to improving the conditions in this world. He also observed that the belief in *karma* makes Hindus fatalistic about the caste system which hinders development in South Asia. However, as Black (1999) noted, since the 1950s, the Westerners who reject the Western materialism and work ethics turn to Hinduism and Buddhism, which are found to be more positive and less repressive orders. Indian practices such as meditation and yoga have become very popular in the West due to its spiritual benefits.

Buddhist Ideologies and Implications

Origin and Spread

Around 6th to 5th century BC, when the Vedic ideology had lost its original purity, giving rise to ritualism and caste system, Buddhism challenged the authority of the *Vedas*. Buddhism is an egalitarian religion, admitting into its fold, all peoples, irrespective of their castes. Buddhism crossed over its frontiers into Asia and then became an Asian religion. In Central Asia, it developed along the Silk Route. In China, Buddhism was influenced by Taoism. This combination was called Zen when it reached Korea and Japan. Zen has no dogmas and no rituals as it is mystical. Today, Bhutan and Sri Lanka in South Asia, Myanmar, Thailand, Laos and Cambodia in the South East Asian peninsula, and Mongolia are predominantly Buddhist countries and China, Korea, Japan, Singapore and Vietnam have a strong Buddhist influence.

Four Noble Truths

According to Buddha, there are Four Noble Truths:

- *Dukha* or suffering or pain that seeps at some level into all finite existence on occasions such as birth, sickness, old age, the phobia of death, to be tied to what one abhors and separation from loved ones.
- The cause of the suffering is *tanha* or desire, is our captivity, in the form of selfish craving.
- Therefore, the cure of suffering lies in being released from the narrow limits of such self-interest into the vast expanse of universal life.
- The overcoming of *tanha* is through the Eightfold Path. The Eightfold Path consists of right knowledge, right aspiration, right speech, right behavior, right livelihood, right effort, right mindfulness and right absorption (Smith, 1958).

Implications for Development

According to Schumacher's classic book titled *Small is Beautiful*, (1973), 'right livelihood' as one of the requirements of Buddha's Noble Eightfold Path takes the function of work to be at least threefold:

- To give human beings a chance to utilize and develop their faculties.
- To enable them to overcome their ego-centredness by joining with other people in a common task.
- To bring forth the goods and services needed for a becoming existence.

Schumacher (1973) noted the following endless consequences that flow from this view. To organise work in such a manner that it becomes meaningless, boring, stultifying, or nerve-racking for the worker would be little short of criminal; it would indicate a greater concern with goods than with people, an evil lack of compassion and a soul-destroying degree of attachment to the most primitive side of this worldly existence. Equally, to strive for leisure as an alternative to work would be considered a complete misunderstanding of one of the basic truths of human existence, namely that work and leisure are complementary parts of the same living process and cannot be separated without destroying the joy of work and the bliss of leisure. While the materialist is mainly interested in goods, the Buddhist is mainly interested in liberation. But Buddhism is 'The Middle Way' and, therefore, in no way antagonistic to physical well-being. It is not wealth that stands in the way of liberation but the attachment to wealth; not the enjoyment of pleasurable things but the craving for them. The keynote of Buddhist economics, therefore, is simplicity and non-violence. From an economist's point of view, the marvel of the Buddhist way of life is the utter rationality of its pattern, amazingly small means leading to extraordinarily satisfactory results.

According to Schumacher (1973), it is therefore clear that there must be such a thing as Buddhist economics. All the same, Buddhist countries invariably assume that they can model their economic development plans in accordance with modern economics, and they call upon modern economists from so-called advanced countries to advise them, to formulate the policies to be pursued, and to construct the grand design for development. No one seems to think that a Buddhist way of life would call for Buddhist economics.

As befitting a Buddhist country, Bhutan has introduced Gross National Happiness (GNH), a concept that implies that sustainable development should take a holistic approach towards notions of progress and give equal importance to non-economic aspects of well-being. The concept of GNH has often been explained by its four pillars: good governance, sustainable socio-economic development, cultural preservation, and environmental conservation. Lately, the four pillars have been further classified into nine domains in order to create widespread understanding of GNH and to reflect the holistic range of GNH values. The nine domains are: psychological well-being, health, education, time use, cultural diversity and resilience, good governance, community vitality, ecological diversity and resilience, and living standards. The domains represents each of the components of well-being of the Bhutanese people, and the term 'well-being' here refers to fulfilling conditions of a 'good life' as per the values and principles laid down by the concept of Gross National Happiness (http://www.grossnationalhappiness.com/articles/).

Confucius Ideologies and Implications

Origin and Spread

Confucianism is not a religion, but the traditional view of life and code of manners of the Chinese gentry for 2000 years. It was not founded but edited by Confucius who was born around 551 BC. In 130 BC, it was made the basic discipline for the training of government officials, a pattern which continued until the establishment of the Republic of China in 1912 (Graham, 1959; Smith, 1958). After the communist rule, Confucian teachings were condemned and the faith was abolished. However, besides China, Korea, Japan, Singapore and Vietnam are predominantly under Confucian (besides Buddhist) influence.

Goals of Character and Social Life

According to Confucius, the goals of character and social life comprise the following:

- *Jen:* Jen refers to goodness. It involves simultaneously a feeling of humanity toward others and respect for oneself.
- *Chun-tzu:* The focus is not on what one can get, but on what one can do to accommodate.
- *Li:* Li refers to propriety. Five relationships that make up the warp and woof of social life are between father and son, elder brother and junior brother, husband and wife, elder friend and junior friend and ruler and subject. Three of the five relationships prescribe that the bulk of respect flows from the young to the old. Confucius continued the Chinese belief that the family is the basic unit of society. The strongest of Confucian duties is filial piety. A son must obey his father absolutely, not only in childhood, but until his father's death.
- *Te:* Te refers to government by virtue. The three essentials of government are economic sufficiency, military sufficiency and the confidence of the people.
- *Wen:* Wen refers to the arts of peace as relevant for international relations (Smith, 1958).

Influences on Confucianism

Around 4th century BC, Chuang Tzu wrote the *Tao te Ching,* which is the central text for Taoism in China. Tao means the Way, that is the order of nature. According to this philosophy, the world is continually changing and so spontaneity and intuition are our only guides to a sane life. It advocates spontaneity, humility, and the mystical communion with nature. The philosophy abandons Confucian artificiality, ritual formalism, the pursuit of wealth and power and attempts to coerce either people or nature. From around the middle of the 1st century AD, there was a marked decline in philosophical and contemplative Taoism and a new form of Taoism emerged that used magic potions, alchemy, astrology and forms of sexual yoga (Black, 1999). The coexistence of Confucianism with Taoism gave rise to a civil imperial bureaucracy. The early Confucianism primarily concerned itself with the needs of society. Neo-Confucianism emerged from merging of Buddhist and Taoist thoughts into Confucius traditions, including ideas such as the nature of the soul and the relation of the individual to the cosmos, ideas not fully explored by Confucianism. In Japan, Confucianism got fused with Shintoism. It was based upon a loyalty understood as submission to the orders of superiors, facilitated the development of a feudal military bureaucracy (Amin, 2008).

Implications for Development

The real testament to Confucius' influence is the character of the civilization he largely molded. A cross-section of Chinese life through the centuries reveals his imprint at almost every point. Nowhere has family solidarity been greater. Age has uniformly been accorded respect, even veneration (Smith, 1958). Confucian social ethics provides the foundations for a model of the family-based 'Confucian Welfare State'. The notion of Confucian familism, involving a strong reliance on the family as the site of social welfare and service delivery, is often considered a core feature of such a welfare state (Goodman and Peng, 1996, cited by Cook and Kwon, 2007).

Fulcher (2004) noted that Confucianist beliefs in orderliness of both the natural and social worlds encouraged social stability rather than the dynamism characteristic of capitalism. Therefore, for long, Asian culture was seen as an obstacle to the region's modernization. However, in the current context of fast economic development in East and South East Asia, Asian models of economic and political organization are championed by zealous advocates to challenge the western political vision (Inoguchi and Newman, 1997; Khong, 1997). According to Schech and Haggis (2000), the following Confucian cultural features are the most prominent in explanations of East Asian economic development:

- Human relations and social harmony based on the idea of filial piety.
- Respect for authority and a strong identity with the organization.
- Subjugation of individual rights in favour of community obligations.
- Diligence.

When the western world refers to 'Asian values', they generally refer to these Confucius East Asian values and claim that the rest of Asia is rather similar (Sen, 1997).

However, the Asian Human Rights Charter of 1998 notes that 'Authoritarianism has in many states been raised to the level of national ideology, with the deprivation of the rights and freedoms of their citizens, which are denounced as foreign ideas inappropriate to the religious and cultural traditions of Asia. Instead there is the exhortation of spurious theories of 'Asian Values' which are a thin disguise for their authoritarianism.'

Collectivistic Culture and Social Development

Culture is related to ideology as it is a set of values, beliefs, and norms for socially acceptable language patterns, behaviours and standards for ideal role types that represent the social structure of a given society. Cultural values affect the way people construe and evaluate problems, situations and the actions taken in pursuit of important goals (Timberlake, Zajicek-Farber and Sabatino, 2008). Culture is derived from ethnicity, race, religion and nation (Fenton, 2010). Asia is one region where culture and tradition play an important role, affecting almost every part of life. Religious ideologies under lie these dominant cultures (United Nations, 2010).

Besides importance of religion, what seems to be common across Asian countries is the cultural value of collectivism. Besides Confucius promoting this value, collectivism is found in most agricultural and traditional societies. For the developing Asian countries, the jump from an agricultural to an industrial society was too abrupt, they have therefore remained more collectivistic and less industrialized (Triandis, 1988). The communist countries in Asia are also more collectivistic based on the ideals of socialism.

According to Heywood (2007), collectivism is the belief that collective human endeavour is of greater practical and moral value than individual self-striving. Inoguchi and Newman (1997) observed that the Asian societies are more group conscious than are those in the liberal, atomized West; Asian people work for the good of society, are less selfish and accept that the cohesion and stability of society are more important, and logically prior to, the rights of individuals. Behaviour is said to be motivated primarily not by concerns of individual rights but equally by duties and responsibilities. Hamilton (2007) notes that collectivist cultures tend to have less wealth. When resources are scarce:

- People are more likely to work together to survive and thrive.
- Interdependence is valued and finances and other resources are therefore shared.
- People maintain close ties with family members and relatives and family rituals are attended by everyone.
- An individual's identity is closely connected to the group identity (Hamilton, 2007).

According to Heywood (2007), some Asian states have been resistant to the attractions of liberal capitalism because their political cultures have emphasized community rather than the individual. Haynes (2008) cited the Asian political leaders such as Muhammad Mahathir of Malaysia and Lee Kuan Yew of Singapore who claim that liberal democracy is actually alien to their countries. Culturally several Asian countries are more collectivistic than individualistic, so the western-style liberal democracy, with its individualistic premises, is seen as misplaced. Where capitalism has been successfully established, as in Japan, it has tended to assume a corporate rather than an individualistic character (Heywood, 2007). Hamilton (1996, cited by Flynn, 1999) also noted that even business in Asia is based on networks of relationships based on obligations other than those arising from short-term economic transactions.

Pre-Colonial Civilizations in Asia

At least 2000 years ago, the global system was organized around three major centres of India, China and the Middle East, while Africa, Japan and South East Asia were peripheries of those centres. There were intensive relations not only of goods but also of technologies, knowledge, philosophies, religions, and so on. Additionally, the distribution of income between those parts of the old system was not very unequal (Amin, 1999). The rise of China and India in the present times is, thus, not a miracle. They have strong foundations of pre-modern civilizations that have contributed significantly to the civilizations in the world.

Pre-Colonial Chinese Civilization

The long list of major technological innovations achieved in China during the pre-modern period include redesigned ploughshares, hydraulic engineering, gunpowder, the tapping of natural gas, the compass, mechanical clocks, paper, printing, lavishly embroidered silk fabrics, and sophisticated metalworking techniques (Steger, 2009). According to Peter Watson, who has written a classic book on world history of ideas (2005), by the Middle Ages, the most sophisticated country and the most technologically advanced country in the world was China. The Chinese silk travelled West along the Silk Routes format at least 1200 BC; until 200 AD, only the Chinese knew how to process silk worms. In addition to innovation in paper and printing technology, Chinese advances in iron and steel manufacture were several hundred years ahead of Europe. Coal was being mined from the 8th century onwards and used in furnaces that produced high quality iron and steel.

Pre-Colonial Indian Civilization

In ancient India, ship-building was a well-developed and flourishing industry and overseas trade flourished with well-established ports. Among the exports from India were silks, muslins, cutlery and armour, brocades, embroideries and rugs, perfumes and drugs, ivory and ivory work, jewellery and gold. Indians had developed the sciences of mathematics, astronomy, economics, political science and medicine. The foundations of the modern arithmetic and algebra were laid in India. It had two internationally well-known universities called Nalanda and Takshila, where students came to study from different parts of the world. Throughout the first millennium of the Christian era, India was highly developed in manufacturing industries: textile industry and dyeing, tempering of steel, ship-building and others. India's trade was widespread and Indian merchants controlled many foreign markets. Pepper and other spices went from India or from Southeast Asia via India to the West. Its banking system was efficient and well organized throughout the country (Nehru, 1945).

Peter Watson (2005) notes that in the year 499, India calculated pi as 3.1416 and the length of the solar year as 365.358 days and discovered that the earth was a sphere spinning on its own axis and revolving around the sun, discovered by the West a 1000 years later. Indian thought in the Middle Ages was in several areas far ahead of European ideas. The importance of grammar in the history of Sanskrit is unequalled anywhere else in the world. India was the destination for all the travelling that took place during the Age of Discovery. China, the Islamic world and Europe were all drawn towards its commercial centres, with Arab traders, Chinese merchants and spice dealers from the Malay archipelago, all conducting transactions in Indian markets (Black, 1999).

Pre-Colonial Civilization of South East Asia

The culture of South East Asia has been significantly influenced by the cultures of China and India. Instead of conflict between the two, this dual influence resulted in a mixed Indo-Chinese civilization emerged in these countries. The mainland countries of South East Asia, Myanmar, Thailand, the Cambodia, Laos and Vietnam are together known as Indo-China, though the majority of people in the region are neither Chinese nor Indian. Cambodia, Laos, Myanmar and Thailand are influenced mainly by India with a smaller influence from China. Thailand is called *swarnabhoomi* which is Sanskrit for the golden land. There were centres of Sanskrit learning in some of these countries. The names of the rulers of the various states and empires that arose are purely Indian/Sanskrit. State ceremonies were Indian and conducted in Sanskrit. Cambodian alphabet is derived from the Indian *devnagri*. Vietnam is more heavily influenced by Chinese culture with only minor cultural influences from India. The Maritime South East Asian sub-region is sometimes referred to as Greater India. The languages are derived from Sanskrit. The old literature in Indonesia is full of Indian mythological stories (Nehru, 1945).

References

Amin, S. (1999). Globalisation yesterday and today. In W. Fernandes and A. Dutta (eds), *Colonialism to Globalisation: Five Centuries after Vasco da Gama. Volume 1: Main Issues around Colonialism and Globalisation* (pp. 22–26). New Delhi: Indian Social Institute.

Amin, S. (2008). *Eurocentrism.* Delhi: Aakar Books.

Black, J. (ed.) (1999). *Encyclopedia of World History.* Bath, UK: Parragon.

Cook, S. and Kwon, H. (2007). Economic reform and social protection in East Asia, paper presented at the RC19 Annual Conference at Florence University. Retrieved 15 May 2009 from https://docs.google.com/viewer?url=http://www.unifi.it/confsp/papers/pdf/Kwon_Cook.doc&pli=1

Fenton, S. (2010). *Ethnicity.* Malden, MA: Polity Press.

Flynn, N. (1999). *Miracle to Meltdown in Asia: Business, Government, and Society.* New York: Oxford University Press.

Fulcher, J. (2004). *Capitalism: A Very Short Introduction.* New York: Oxford University Press.

Gore, M.S. (1966). The cultural perspective in social work in India. *International Social Work*, 9(3), 6–16.

Graham, A.C. (1959). Confucianism. In R.C. Zaehner (ed.), *The Concise Encyclopaedia of Living Faiths.* Boston: Beacon Press.

Hamilton, V.M. (2007). *Human Relations: The Art and Science of Building Effective Relationships.* Upper Saddle River, NJ: Pearson Prentice Hall.

Haynes, J. (2008). *Development Studies.* Cambridge: Polity Press.

Heywood, A. (2007). *Political Ideologies: An Introduction* (4th ed.). New York: Palgrave Macmillan.

Inoguchi, T. and Newman, E. (1997). Introduction: 'Asian values' and democracy in Asia. In *'Asian Values' and Democracy in Asia.* Proceedings of a Conference organized by the Shizuoka Prefectural Government and the Oganising Committee of the Asia-Pacific Forum in Japan.

Khong, C.O. (1997). Asian values: The debate revisited. In *'Asian Values' and Democracy in Asia.* Proceedings of a Conference organized by the Shizuoka Prefectural Government and the Oganising Committee of the Asia-Pacific Forum in Japan.

Landes, D.S. (1999). *The Wealth and Poverty of Nations: Why Some are So Rich and Some So Poor.* New York: Norton.

Mahadevan, T.M.P. (1982). The Religio-Philosophic culture of India. In *The Cultural Heritage of India*, Volume I (pp. 163–181). Calcutta: The Ramakrishna Mission Institute of Culture.

Nehru, J. (1945). *The Discovery of India.* Calcutta: Oxford University Press.

Schech, S. and Haggis, J. (2000). *Culture and Development: A Critical Introduction.* Oxford: Blackwell Publishers.

Schumacher, E.F. (1973). *Small is Beautiful: Economics as if People Mattered.* New York: Harper & Row Publishers.

Sen, A. (1997). *Human Rights and Asian Values, Sixteenth Morgenthau Memorial Lecture on Ethics and Foreign Policy.* New York: Carnegie Council on Ethics and International Affairs.

Singhal, D.P. (1983). *A History of the Indian People.* London: Methuen.

Smith, H. (1958). *The Religions of Man.* New York: Harper & Row.

Steger, M.B. (2009). *Globalization: A Very Short Introduction.* Oxford: Oxford University Press.

Timberlake, E.M., Zajicek-Farber, M.L. and Sabatino, C.A. (2008). *Generalist Social Work Practice: A Strengths-based Problem Solving Approach.* Boston, MA: Allyn & Bacon.

Triandis, H.C. (1988). Collectivism and development. In D. Sinha and H.S.R. Kao (eds), *Social Values and Development: Asian Perspectives* (pp. 285–303). New Delhi: Sage Publications.

United Nations. (2010). *Strengthening National Mechanisms for Gender Equality and the Empowerment of Women: Regional Study – Asia and the Pacific*. Bangkok.

Watson, P. (2005). *Ideas: A History from Fire to Freud*. London: Weidenfeld & Nicolson.

Weber, M. (1958). *The Protestant Ethic and the Spirit of Capitalism*. New York: Charles Scribner's Sons.

CHAPTER 4

Political Background of Social Development in Asia

Introduction

Concept of Political Background

Political background of a country is the background of governance or organized control over people. It influences the social and institutional processes through which certain groups of economic and political elites influence the allocation of scarce productive resources, either for their own benefit exclusively or for that of the larger population as well (Todaro and Smith, 2009). It affects development significantly as economic processes do not take place in isolation from social and political processes.

Chapter Objectives

This chapter on political background of social development in Asia reviews the following:

1. Political background of Asia with reference to colonization, decolonization, neocolonialism and the Cold War and their implications.
2. Diversity in political background and implications for social development in Asian sub-regions.

Political Background of Social Development in Asia and Implications

Political Background of Social Development in Asia

Colonization

Process of Colonization

During the Age of Discovery, a period starting in the early 15th century and continuing to the 17th century, voyagers from Western Europe, led by Spain and Portugal, set out across the world in search of alternative trade routes to 'the East Indies' (now South and South East Asia), in search of gold, silver and spices. In this process, two events in the 1490s are considered as marking the beginning of colonization, Christopher Columbus reached the Americas, and Vasco da Gama landed in India (Fernandes and Dutta, 1999). As they sought to establish trade links with Africa, Asia and the Americas, the 17th century saw the creation of the French colonial empire and the Dutch Empire, as well as the English colonial empire, which later became the British Empire. In the 18th century, the Industrial Revolution made European nationalism aggressive and expansionist, promoting international trade and colonization of Asian and African countries. The European nation-states, in vantage positions to increase the productive capacities of their own economies, acquired command over the resources as also the people of the colonies, and thus reinforced their home economies (Sharma, 1998). They began to establish extensive trading networks in Latin America and Asia. By the 19th century, the European Empires and/or European-derived powers controlled nine-tenth of the entire globe (Young, 2003). The exceptions were China, Japan, Nepal, Bhutan and Thailand but they were also subjugated by these powers.

Such unprecedented international event of colonization disturbed many huge civilizations and pulled them back in several ways. As Osterhammel (2005) notes, in colonialism an entire society was robbed of its historical line of development, externally manipulated and transformed according to the needs and interest of the colonial rulers. It led to collapse of civilizations, genocide, enslavement, capture of resources, and subservience of economies (Sharma, 1998). Specifically, it led to disturbance in their economic systems (industrial and agricultural systems), political systems (imposition of the state), and cultural systems (through Eurocentrism, individualism and homogenization).

Disturbance to the Economic Systems

The production machines in the imperial nation-states devoted increasingly to industrial goods, whereas other essential commodities and raw materials were obtained from the colonies (Sharma, 1998). The economies of the colonies were not developed beyond the small but important sectors needed by the European economies, for which the colonial rule was imposed (Smith, 2009). Colonial policy, which ensured capital and raw material flew from the colonies, aimed at developing natural resources in a planned manner, to facilitate the generation of revenues and growth of capital. Nature's transformation into natural resources needed to go hand in hand with the transformation of culturally diverse people into 'skilled human resources' (Shiva, 2010). The international trade of these countries with adjacent countries or with those far away was replaced by the colonizers' economic interests with reference to their own countries.

In India, the chief business of the British East India Company was to carry Indian manufactured goods, textiles, spices, and so on from the East to Europe, where there was a great demand for these articles. With the developments in industrial techniques in England, a new class of industrial capitalists rose there, demanding a change in this policy. The decision taken was to close the British market to Indian products and open the Indian market for British products. This was followed by vigorous attempts to restrict and crush Indian manufacturers by preventing the flow of Indian goods within the country itself. As a result, the Indian textile industry and other industries collapsed leading to wide scale unemployment. The unemployed drifted to agriculture which became more and more the sole business of the people because of the lack of occupations and wealth-producing activities. Inspired by the British pattern, the British rulers allowed the revenue farmers to become the landlords who deprived the village community of all control over their land and its produce. This led to the breakdown of the corporate character of the community. The British East India Company's policy of replacement of food crops with cash crops and heavy taxation resulted in the Bengal Famine of 1770s. The profit earned by the company is supposed to have supported the Industrial Revolution from about 1760 to sometime between 1820 and 1840 (Nehru, 1945). The colonizers preserved the outmoded forms of agricultural practices to maintain a class hierarchy of the local people so as to facilitate governance. As a result, throughout the 19th century and till the mid-20th century, agriculture in Asia remained primitive, exploitative and involutive (Acharya, 1987).

According to Tan (2000), South Korea and Taiwan had benefitted from the Japanese colonizers and Singapore had benefitted from the British colonizers with reference to investments and infrastructure, education, industrial development and public administration during colonization. However, the Dutch, the Spanish and the French colonizers had done relatively little to develop their colonies in South East Asia, namely, Indonesia, the Philippines, Cambodia, Laos and Vietnam.

Disturbance to the Political Systems

For a long time, countries had been thought of as kingdoms and the inhabitants as subjects of the kings. The bourgeois revolutions in Europe laid the foundation of 'modern nation-states', based on the liberal ideology, which accompanied a transition of power to the industrialist commercial group (Ram, 1999). During the colonial rule, this alien system of rational, centralized state of the colonizers was imposed on the complex and heterogeneous realities of developing societies (Srinivasan, 1994), ruled by empires. These empires had changing boundaries and limited authority. They had military power but lacked an administrative apparatus for governing what had been conquered (Martell, 2010). On the other hand, the colonial state had clear boundaries and governed the people through an administrative state. It was the source of legitimate violence which was the base line of the control of the territory. In places, a distinction was drawn between direct and indirect rule with the latter system leaving in place local rulers who acted as a buffer between the colonizers and the colonized. The colonial powers tried wherever possible to concentrate finance and decision-making in the capital and raised taxes. They provided the basic infrastructure of metropolitan life and this included a communication system (ports, roads, railways, telegraphs and so on), an economic system (supporting traders, merchants, manufacturers and financiers), a social system (housing, health, police and recreation) and a cultural system (Preston, 1996: 146).

The emergence of the nation-states in the former colonies thus stands in stark contrast to the emergence of the nation-states in the countries of the colonizers. In the former, the state came into existence as an expression of colonial rule, rather than of endogenous processes of socio-economic transformation. Its interest was in commercial gains and not in any goals of redistribution or citizenship

(Kabeer, 2004). In countries like India, the centralized state destroyed the decentralized autonomous village assemblies (Nehru, 1945).

Colonialism was responsible for development of such a global state system around the world based on Western models (Haynes, 2008). According to Samir Amin (1999), colonization started the building of the modern global system and the destruction of a pre-existing global exchange system where the distribution of income between the parts of the system was not very unequal. It brought a degree of polarization at the global level which was never seen before in the history of humanity. The old global system was destroyed and replaced by the modern capitalist globalization (Amin, 1999).

Disturbance to the Cultural Systems

Eurocentrism

Preston (1996: 138) noted that at the outset in the earliest periods of European trade, non-European peoples were regarded as exotic cultural equals. Later, as trade and commerce grew, non-Europeans were taken to represent innocence, and ideas of the noble savage were presented. Later in the 19th century, as European holdings in the colonies started to become extensive and increasingly integrated into metropolitan patterns of production, trade and finance, the imagery shifted and ideas of 'uncivilized savages' were presented. Eurocentrism is not a banal ethnocentrism; it claims that imitation of the Western model by all peoples is the only way to progress, justifying colonization. Not only that, it destroyed the peoples and civilizations who resisted its spread (Amin, 2008). It is a tendency to view the European cultural practices as superior to all others, providing an ideological justification for their dominance. Its focus on human behaviour in terms of norms or average behaviours, led to the concepts of normal and abnormal (Richard, 1996, cited in Schriver, 2004).

Fernandes and Dutta (1999) noted that aiming to convert them, Christianity played a significant role in the process of colonization; from creating a body of social and political allies to producing educated persons to work at various levels in the administration. Moreover, they noted that the introduction of the British educational and legal structures devalued the local systems of knowledge and jurisprudence and shaped new terms of discourse about society and about what is good and bad.

Homogenization

Conventionally development has been a modern Western mono-cultural project (Pieterse, 2010). According to Bhargava (1999), the modern ideology concerned itself with freedom, equality and justice, given a pronounced individualist coloring. The framework of material welfare and a culturally-neutral universalism underscores the importance of individual choice, the compulsion of a more equitable distribution of material resources and the need to belong to a wider social and political universe, where neither one's class or status nor cultural inheritance was a source of advantage or disadvantage. Here, the dominant cultures generate stereotypes of the dominated which they get their victims to accept, which results in the loss of confidence and pervasive self-images of inferiority. People then lose respect for their own cultures and hasten the progress of homogenization, induced by dominant cultures (Bhargava, 1999).

Individualism

Cultural determinism argues that cultural values condition modes of social and economic organization, including patterns of political relationships, political participation, citizenship and government (Inoguchi and Newman, 1997). Before colonialism, the cultural system in the agriculture-based economy of the colonies was collectivistic. Colonization brought the individualistic culture of the industrialized Western colonizers, to these collectivistic societies. Table 4.1 shows the comparison between the two types of cultures.

Table 4.1
Comparison between the Individualistic Culture of the Colonizers and the Collectivistic Culture of the Colonies

Individualistic Culture of the Colonizers	Collectivistic Culture of the Colonies
Masculinity	Femininity
High degree of separation between men's and women's roles	Overlapping roles for men and women
Importance of challenge and recognition at work	Importance of cooperation at work
Higher job stress	Lower job stress
Centrality of work in life	Centrality of relationships in life
Values of mastery, ambition and independence	Values of well-being and service
Children taught to fight back	Children taught to avoid aggression
Importance of money and things	Importance of quality of life

Source: Hamilton, 2007

Decolonization

Throughout the period of colonial rule, colonized people contested the colonial domination through many forms of active and passive resistance. It was only towards the end of the 19th century that such resistance developed into coherent political movements (Young, 2003). The process of colonialism had involved the importation of Western ideas, including nationalism, which was born in Europe. During the 20th century, the doctrine of nationalism spread throughout the globe as the peoples in the colonies rose in opposition to the colonial rule. They came to resist the established domination of the European colonists, also because they had the vitality and capacity for self-renewal which Europeans had far too easily dismissed as uncivilized. The European powers responded initially with a variety of strategies to delay the inevitable; the overall process saw repression, accommodation, war and, finally, withdrawal after the Second World War (Preston, 1996).

In the wake of the upheavals of the First World War (1914–1918), the notion of eventual decolonization came to be accepted by the colonial powers. The stability of the empires was undermined as colonial resources and personnel were used in the War. There was a slow movement away from colonial ideologies towards ideas of freedom (Young, 2003). The Second World War (1939–1945) brought unparalleled levels of death, devastation, privation, and disorder. It left not only much of Europe and Asia in ruins but the old international order as well (McMahon, 2003). In the Second World War's early months, the Japanese conquered the Western colonial systems in Singapore, Malaya, Burma, the Philippines, Indo-China, the Dutch East Indies (today's Indonesia), Brunei and elsewhere. Japan unconditionally surrendered after the atomic bombings of Hiroshima and Nagasaki by the US in 1945. The vacuums of power left by the surrender of Japan after its defeat in the Second World War, gave aspirant nationalists to mobilize indigenous alternatives to Western and Japanese domination (Preston, 1996). It was these greater upheavals of the Second World War which made decolonization of the colonies by the colonizers inevitable (Young, 2003).

Neocolonialism and the Cold War

Decolonization was a relatively minor move from direct to indirect rule. Recognition that achievement of constitutional independence and sovereignty did not give total freedom to the governments of the newly formed nation-states led to the realization of the existence of neocolonialism. Behind the façade of political autonomy lurked the continuing presence of powerful Western economic interests. Those subtle and indirect forms of domination had, as their root cause, the economies bequeathed by the colonial powers at the time of constitutional independence. The new rulers of the former colonies found that the major proportion of the resources available to them was controlled from metropolitan centres that hitherto had ruled their countries directly. Development aid in the context of the Cold War was the main form of neocolonialism (Young, 2003).

As the Second World War moved into its final phase, the US and the Soviet Union held most of the military, economic and diplomatic power. For most US civilians, the war meant not suffering and privation but prosperity. From the War, it emerged the most powerful nation in the world. The US planners viewed the establishment of a freer and more open international economic system as indispensable to the new order. Soviet Union, three times larger than the US, was number one problem for the US. Soviets and Americans each saw themselves acting out of noble motives, with mirror-opposite ideological values (McMahon, 2003). Other countries were forced to take sides. The widespread conflict, later known as the Cold War (1947–91), divided the world as follows:

- 'First World' comprised the industrialized democracies of Europe and North America plus Australia, New Zealand and Japan, represented by the US.
- 'Second World' comprised the communist countries of Eastern Europe and their ideological allies in Asia and Cuba, represented by the Soviet Union.
- 'Third World' comprised the remaining countries most of which were former colonies.

The Cold War impacted the politics in developing countries significantly through military and other development aid.

The Soviets and Americans identified crucial strategic, economic, and psychological interests in the developing areas of Asia, Latin America and Africa, and sought to gain resources, bases, allies, and influence in these places. The US planners recognized that the resources and markets of Third World countries were essential to the health of the world capitalist economy. The Soviets made a concerted bid for friends and allies among the Third World's uncommitted nations in order to dilute the Western strength. Their Marxist development model appealed to many Third World intellectuals. The process of decolonization and emergence of dozens of newly independent countries not only coincided with the Cold War but were shaped by it. Third World soil was the focal point of Soviet-American competition; virtually all the wars that erupted during the Cold War era were waged on this soil. All but 200,000 of the estimated 20 million people who died in these wars belonged to the Third World. The Cold War, thus, significantly affected the shape, cohesion, and vitality of the Third World states; the international configurations of power within them; their ability to command international attention and prestige; their leaders' prospects for securing external resources, capital and technical assistance to meet economic development priorities or for garnering military assistance to bolster needs (McMahon, 2003).

The Cold War impacted Asia in a significant way due to the emergence of Mao's socialist regime in China, the Sino-Soviet alliance, Soviet and Chinese support for North Korea, the intervention of the US and UN forces, the subsequent entry of Chinese troops, and the presence of communist elements within South East Asia's nationalist movements. During the Cold War, the US provided military and economic aid to the anti-communist allies in the newly independent countries to fight civil wars with their own people to combat communism (Chan, 1993). As a result, the Cold War fragmented China into China and Taiwan, Korea into North and South Korea and Vietnam into North and South Vietnam and supported military rule in many countries. Protected by the US military power, the autocratic states in Asia also promoted state capitalism (Thompson, 2004). The Cold War resulted in communist rule in the South East Asian countries of Laos, Vietnam and Cambodia.

At the height of the Cold War, a Non-Aligned Movement (NAM) sought to influence world affairs without affiliating with either of the two Cold War blocs (Karns and Mingst, 2010). In 1955, the governments of some Asian countries, namely, Burma (now Myanmar), Ceylon (now Sri Lanka), India, Indonesia and Pakistan called a conference in Bandung, Indonesia, with the aim of developing a common development policy. The proceedings of the conference comprised sharp criticism of colonialism, the demand for the independence of all colonial countries, the request for UN membership and so on. It marked the beginning of collective demands of the Third World countries in the field of development, most of which were repeatedly taken up in UN resolutions, and gradually won acceptance. NAM came out of this conference and was formally established in 1961 (Rist, 2008). The NAM leaders set up a South Commission in 1987 to explore policy options and areas for cooperation for the countries of the South. Its final report of 1990, *The Challenge to the South,* identified climate change as a priority and underscored challenges of poverty, social exclusion and the widening gap between rich and poor. It also looked closely at the then-emerging South-South cooperation in aid, trade and other aspects of international policy-making (United Nations Development Programme, 2013).

Diversity in Political Background of Social Development in Asian Sub-Regions

Political Background of East Asia

The sub-region with the highest level of social development, East Asia, did not face colonization by the European countries; however, they were strongly influenced by their domination. They were also the focus of the Cold War, as a result of which, the US allies received enormous aid from the US which promoted their development. The Cold War also split China into China and Taiwan and Korea into North and South Korea.

Japan

Until the 1850s, Japan resisted almost all contact with the West. In the 1850s, the new royal family, the Meiji, began a policy of Westernization. From 1868 onwards, Japan began to learn as much as possible from the West. Industrialization and a strong centralized bureaucratic government were introduced. Since 1918, Japan developed into a leading military and economic force within Asia. In the 1930s, it invaded the European colonies in Asia which initially gave the impression that it was liberating them from the European colonizers. It shattered the omnipotence of the European powers but their barbarity created more hostility from the local peoples (Black,

1999). The US defeated Japan in the Second World War, after which Japan as well as the territories occupied by Japan came under the control of the Americans (Tan, 2000). Almost all of Japanese cities were ravaged by relentless US bombing, with 40 per cent of its urban areas nearly destroyed. The US used its power to remake Japanese society by destroying all vestiges of militarism while helping to foster the development of liberal, democratic institutions. A stable, economically vibrant, pro-American Japan was strategic for the US in Asia in the context of the Cold War (McMahon, 2003).

China and Hong Kong

China came increasingly into contact with the West in the 19th century. The initial reaction of the West was to resist foreign interference, but Britain and France used military force to compel China to open its ports to Western trade (Black, 1999). By the early 19th century, the British Empire trade was heavily dependent upon the importation of tea from China. While the British exported to China luxurious items like clocks and watches, there remained an overwhelming imbalance in trade. The counterbalance of trade came with exports of opium to China, opium being legal in Britain and grown in significant quantities in the UK, and later in far greater quantities in India. The Chinese opposition to the opium trade resulted in the First Opium War, which led to British victories over China and the cession of Hong Kong to the United Kingdom (UK) via the enactment of the new treaties in 1842. In 1997, the UK handed over Hong Kong to the People's Republic of China. It is now a Special Administrative Region (SAR) of China, retaining its laws and a high degree of autonomy. Macau that was colonized by the Portuguese until 1999, is since then also an SAR of China.

China and Taiwan

Inspired by the Soviet Revolution, a Marxist party was formed in China in 1921, under the political leadership of Mao. A revolutionary peasant movement was organized with the support of the rural masses, and the communists won a civil war in 1949 with the support of the Soviet Union. Since then, Mainland China is administered by the People's Republic of China, under the leadership of the Chinese Communist Party (Hudelson, 1993). The Chinese Nationalist Party backed by the US that lost in the civil war set up the Republic of China in Taiwan and surrounding islands. Communism in China signified a fundamental shift in the nature and locus of the Cold War. By the early 1960s, China had in many respects supplanted the Soviet Union as America's most feared adversary as it appeared far more militant, hostile and belligerent than the Soviet Union (McMahon, 2003). China and Taiwan, both states claim to be the sole legitimate ruler of all of China. Taiwan had maintained official diplomatic relations with most states around the world, but by the 1970s, a shift had occurred in international diplomatic circles and China gained the upper hand in international diplomatic relations and recognition count.

Korea

Korea was under Japanese colonial rule from 1910 until 1945. After the Second World War, it was temporarily divided into the north under Soviet occupation and the south under the occupation of other allied countries. The temporary division hardened and North Korea was established as a Soviet-style socialist regime, while South Korea was established as a western-style republic. The Korean War broke out in 1950 when Soviet and China-backed North Korea invaded South Korea which was supported by the US. It dragged on until 1953 and ended inconclusively. The Korean War was the first armed confrontation of the Cold War. Both the US and the Soviet Union inaugurated major arms build-ups following the outbreak of this War. It created the idea of a proxy war, where the two superpowers would fight in another country, forcing the people in that nation to suffer the bulk of the destruction and death involved in a war between such large nations (McMahon, 2003).

Political Background of South East Asia

All the South East Asian countries (except Thailand) faced colonization by diverse European countries namely, the British, French, Dutch, Spanish and Americans. Of these, the Dutch, the Spanish and the French colonizers had done relatively little to develop their colonies in South East Asia, namely, Indonesia, the Philippines, Cambodia, Laos and Vietnam. The anti-colonial struggles in the Philippines, Burma and Vietnam gained momentum by the early decades of the 20th century as the rate of their alienation from the colonial structure was high. However, in Laos and Cambodia, where the French kept the monarchy intact and isolated the peasants from global system, the freedom struggle grew much later (Fernandes and Dutta, 1999). Thus diversity in colonizers was another factor responsible for diversity of development in South East Asia.

As the US actively discouraged Japan from trade with China, Japan needed alternate overseas market for its survival. Moreover, in the context of the Cold War, the US was afraid of China's expansionist activities in that region and so made a series of new commitments in the region (McMahon, 2003). In the context of the Cold War, Indo-China was devastated by the Vietnam War fought by the US on the one hand and the Soviet Union and China on the other, for two decades.

Philippines

The Spanish had colonized the Philippines, which later came under the control of the Americans. During the final stage of the Second World War, 80 per cent of Manila's buildings were razed in savage fighting. The US presided over the orderly transfer of sovereignty to an independent pro-American government in the Philippines in 1946. It retained a visible presence there, demanding extensive base rights which helped secure for the US military a formidable naval and air capacity (McMahon, 2003).

Indo-China

The French had colonized Indo-China (today's Cambodia, Laos and Vietnam). In the context of the Cold War, in 1954, the US showed an open support for the French and the Soviet Union and China supported the communists and nationalists in Vietnam, leading to the First Indo-China War. After this War, the colonial administration ended as French Indo-China was dissolved. According to the Geneva Accords of 1954 the forces of former French supporters and communist nationalists were separated into South and North Vietnam, respectively (McMahon, 2003). The Second Indo-China War, also known as the Vietnam War, was fought between North Vietnam, supported by its communist allies, and South Vietnam, supported by the US and other anti-communist nations for two decades (1955 to 1975). This War Operations spanned borders with Laos and Cambodia heavily bombed. Indo-China was devastated by the Vietnam War. Its own casualties mounting, and facing opposition to the war at home and condemnation abroad, the US began withdrawing from ground combat roles. In 1976, North and South were merged to form the Socialist Republic of Vietnam.

Malaya

The British colonized Malaya (today's West Malaysia and Singapore), North Borneo (today's Brunei) and Sarawak (today's East Malaysia). Within a year, after the Second World War, the loose administration of British Malaya was finally consolidated with the formation of the Malayan Union in 1946. Singapore, however, was not included and was considered a crown colony by itself. The new Union was greeted with strong opposition from the local Malays. The opposition revolved around two issues: loose citizenship requirements and reduction in the Malay rulers' power. Due to the pressure exerted, the Union was replaced with the Federation of Malaya in 1948. The Federation achieved independence in 1957. All Malayan states formed a larger federation called Malaysia together with Singapore, Sarawak and North Borneo. In 1963, Singapore was expelled from the Federation after heated ideological conflict between the state of Singapore's government and the federal government in Kuala Lumpur. Singapore officially gained sovereignty in 1965.

Indonesia

The Dutch had colonized Indonesia. Following the Second World War and Japanese occupation, Indonesian nationalists declared Indonesian independence in 1945. However, after a hard-fought struggle with the Dutch who were supported by the US, Netherlands formally recognized Indonesian sovereignty in 1949 (McMahon, 2003). The first President of independent Indonesia, appointed in 1945, moved the country from democracy towards authoritarianism, and maintained his power base by balancing the opposing forces of the military and the Communist Party of Indonesia. In 1968, a military coup brought military rule supported by the US government that ended in 2004.

Thailand

Thailand was the only Asian country not colonized by any European country. However, the leaders of Thailand sought an American connection and became its ally due to the traditional fear of their huge and potentially menacing neighbour China, whether communist or not. Its military leaders also sought an American connection and its aid to tighten their own grip on power and to silence dissident voices (McMahon, 2003). As with many of the developing nations during the Cold War, Thailand then went through decades of political instability characterized by coups d'état as one military regime replaced another, but eventually progressed towards a stable prosperity and democracy in the 1980s.

Burma

Burma was administered as a province of British India until 1937 when it became a separate, self-governing colony. A brutal combat in Burma during the Second World War had reduced an enormous part of Burma to ruins (McMahon, 2003). After gaining independence from the British in 1948, Burma, now known as Myanmar, shifted from democratic rule to military rule in 1962.

Political Background of North and Central Asia

Russia was the first country to go through a socialist revolution that took place in the wake of the First World War. The Russian Soviet Federative Socialist Republic (SFSR) together with other adjacent countries, including Central Asia, formed the Soviet Union in 1922. The classical Marxist vision of socialism as a planned economy arising out of advanced industrial capitalism offered little help to Soviet Communists who were faced with a largely pre-industrial economy. Lenin responded by putting a ban on all internal factions and introduced a New Economic Policy which promoted the mixed economy through what he called state capitalism. In 1920, a worldwide Marxist movement was split into communists who adopted the ideas of Lenin and socialists (or social democrats) who rejected the ideas of Lenin (Hudelson, 1993). Lenin's successor was Stalin who abandoned the New Economic Policy and adopted a policy of collectivization. He built the Iron Curtain in 1945–46 that ran for 1000 miles cutting Europe into two. The purpose was to prevent any Western influence from reaching the Eastern European countries controlled by the Soviet Union (Black, 1999).

In 1985, Gorbachev became the President of the Soviet Union and announced his policies of Perestroika and Glasnot. Perestroika involved the restructuring of the Soviet economy and Glasnot meant openness. He started the disarmament with the US which made him very popular in the West. In 1989, he and the US President Bush announced that the Cold War was over (Black, 1999). In 1991, the Soviet Union was dissolved and the Commonwealth of Independent States (CIS) was established in its place. Russia is the so called 'continuation state' in exercising the rights and fulfilling the obligations of the former Soviet Union. It is the leading member of the CIS and a recognized global power, inheriting former Soviet foreign representatives and much of Soviet military. CIS Asia includes Russia, Armenia, Azerbaijan, Georgia, Kazakhstan, Kyrgyzstan, Tajikistan, Turkmenistan and Uzbekistan of which this book covers Russia and the Central Asian countries of Kazakhstan, Kyrgyzstan, Tajikistan, Turkmenistan and Uzbekistan. Mongolia, though not part of, was under political protection of and therefore under strong influence of the former Soviet Union.

The changes that followed the collapse of the socialist system have fundamentally redefined people's lives, values and behaviour. Transition has brought freedom and choices to many, but deprived many others of the ability to live long, healthy and productive lives (United Nations Development Programme and Regional Bureau of Europe and CIS, 2011). As North and Central Asian countries have been part of/influenced by the former communist Soviet Union, they lead in equality in social development in Asia.

Political Background of South Asia

The most backward sub-region of Asia, South Asia has been largely influenced by the British colonization and exploitation. In the 18th century, the East India Company expanded its influence in the Indian sub-continent, characterized by dispersed political power. After crushing the first war of independence in 1857, they set up direct administration making India a part of the British Empire (Fernandes and Dutta, 1999). In the former half of the 20th century, India's unique mass-based freedom movement for democracy was led by Mahatma Gandhi through non-violent civil disobedience. Britain offered India post-war independence in return for help during the Second World War. However, the British had encouraged development of the Muslim League comprising of the elites the Muslim minorities of India. This League as well as the Hindu Mahasabha, both were fundamentalist religious organizations and their differences and conflicts were fanned by the British (Nehru, 1945). India's independence from the British in 1947 saw its partitioning into India with a secular constitution and Pakistan (West and East with India in between) with a Muslim constitution. Britain also accomplished peaceful withdrawals from Ceylon (now Sri Lanka) and Burma (now Myanmar).

In the context of the Cold War, the governing elites of Pakistan pursued an American connection, becoming formal US allies in the mid-1950s. The US connection afforded Pakistan protection less from the Soviet Union than from India, its principal regional rival. The alliance with the US bolstered the Pakistani military in particular, distorting the nation's political balance since its inception (McMahon, 2003). On the other hand, although India was an active founding member of the Non-Aligned Movement, it tended to side with the Soviet Union. Following years of political exclusion, ethnic and linguistic discrimination, and economic neglect by the politically dominant western wing, a surge of popular agitation, nationalism and civil disobedience led in 1971 to the Bangladesh Liberation War, resulting in the separation of the region from Pakistan and the formation of an independent Bangladesh.

References

Acharya, S. (1987). *Women and Rural Development in the Third World.* Bombay: Tata Institute of Social Sciences.

Amin, S. (1999). Globalisation yesterday and today. In W. Fernandes and A. Dutta (eds), *Colonialism to Globalisation: Five Centuries after Vasco da Gama. Volume 1: Main Issues around Colonialism and Globalisation* (pp. 22–26). New Delhi: Indian Social Institute.

Amin, S. (2008). *Eurocentrism.* Delhi: Aakar Books.

Bhargava, R. (1999). Introducing multiculturalism. In R. Bhargava, A.K. Bagchi and R. Sudarshan (eds), *Multiculturalism, Liberalism and Democracy* (pp. 1–57). New Delhi: Oxford University Press.

Black, J. (ed.) (1999). *Encyclopedia of World History.* Bath, UK: Parragon.

Chan, S. (1993). *East Asian Dynamism: Growth, Order, and Security in the Pacific Region.* Oxford: Westview Press.

Fernandes, W. and Dutta, A. (eds) (1999). *Colonialism to Globalisation: Five Centuries after Vasco da Gama. Volume 1: Main Issues around Colonialism and Globalisation.* New Delhi: Indian Social Institute.

Hamilton, V.M. (2007). *Human Relations: The Art and Science of Building Effective Relationships.* Upper Saddle River, NJ: Pearson Prentice Hall.

Haynes, J. (2008). *Development Studies.* Cambridge: Polity Press.

Hudelson, R.H. (1993). *The Rise and Fall of Communism.* Oxford: Westview Press.

Inoguchi, T. and Newman, E. (1997). Introduction: 'Asian values' and democracy in Asia. In *'Asian Values' and Democracy in Asia.* Proceedings of a Conference organized by the Shizuoka Prefectural Government and the Oganising Committee of the Asia-Pacific Forum in Japan.

Kabeer, N. (2004). *Imagining 'The Social': Social Policy Analysis for the Poor in Poor Countries.* Brighton, Sussex: Institute of Development Studies.

Karns, M.P. and Mingst, K.A. (2010). *International Organizations: The Politics and Processes of Global Governance.* London: Lynne Rienner Publishers.

Martell, L. (2010). *The Sociology of Globalization.* Malden, MA: Polity Press.

McMahon, R.J. (2003). *The Cold War: A Very Short Introduction.* New York: Oxford University Press.

Nehru, J. (1945). *The Discovery of India.* Calcutta: Oxford University Press.

Osterhammel, J. (2005). *Colonialism.* Princeton: Markus Wiener Publishers.

Pieterse, J.N. (2010). *Development Theory* (2nd ed.). Los Angeles: Sage Publications.

Preston, P.W. (1996). *Development Theory: An Introduction.* Oxford: Blackwell Publishing.

Ram, P.R. (1999). Perversion of Gandhian and national values: The Anti-Gandhi myths of Hindutva – 1. *Facts against Myths,* 5(1).

Rist, G. (2008). *The History of Development: From Western Origins to Global Faith* (3rd ed.). New York: Zed Books.

Schriver, J.M. (2004). *Human Behavior and the Social Environment: Shifting Paradigms in Essential Knowledge for Social Work Practice* (4th ed.). Boston: Pearson Allyn & Bacon.

Sharma, B.D. (1998). The people versus the system. In M. Desai, A. Monteiro and L. Narayan (eds), *Towards People-centred Development* (pp. 44–61). Mumbai: Tata Institute of Social Sciences.

Shiva, V. (2010). Resources. In W. Sachs (ed.), *The Development Dictionary: A Guide to Knowledge as Power* (2nd ed.). (pp. 228–242). New York: Zed Books.

Smith, B.C. (2009). *Understanding Third World Politics: Theories of Political Change and Development* (3rd ed.). New York: Palgrave Macmillan.

Srinivasan, A. (1994). Women and reform of Indian tradition: Gandhian alternative to liberalism. In L. Kasturi and V. Mazumdar (eds), *Women and Indian Nationalism* (pp. 1–15). New Delhi: Vikas Publishing House.

Tan, G. (2000). *Asian Development: An Introduction to Economic, Social and Political Change in Asia.* Singapore: Times Academic Press.

Thompson, M.R. (2004). Pacific Asia after 'Asian values': Authoritarianism, democracy, and 'good governance'. *Third World Quarterly,* 25(6), 1079–1095.

Todaro, M.P. and Smith, S.C. (2009). *Economic Development* (10th ed.). Essex: Pearson Education Ltd.

United Nations Development Programme. (2013). *Human Development Report: The Rise of the South: Human Progress in a Diverse World.* New York.

United Nations Development Programme and Regional Bureau for Europe and the Commonwealth of Independent States. (2011). *Beyond Transition: Towards Inclusive Societies: Regional Human Development Report.* Bratislava.

Young, R.J.C. (2003). *Postcolonialism: A Very Short Introduction.* New York: Oxford University Press.

Chapter 5

Role of State and Civil Society in Social Development in Asia

Introduction

Development systems are systems that influence, formulate and implement development policies. They mainly comprise the state and civil society at the national level and international and regional institutions. This chapter on role of state and civil society in social development in Asia reviews the following:

1. Role of state in Asia with reference to type of state and corruption.
2. Diversity in state role in Asian sub-regions and implications for social development.
3. Role of civil society in Asia with reference to the specific role of non-government organizations in relation to the role of the state.
4. Diversity in role of civil society in Asian sub-regions and implications for social development.

Role of State and Governance in Social Development in Asia

Type of State

Asia has had authoritative, communist and social democratic states, all moving towards democracy today. Asia has mainly had authoritative rules in the form of monarchy, colonial rule, military rule, dictatorship and single-party rule. The great majority of the independent former colonies carried forward the colonial legacy of the nation-states although their peoples were diverse with reference to ethnicity, language and religion. They hoped that the nation-states would bring political stability to their countries that faced economic impoverishment and political instability (Haynes, 2008). They were convinced that the state should assume the major responsibility for economic development and nation-building. They also aimed to enhance their political and economic control. This resulted in an overwhelming concentration of national power in the hands of central governments, as well as a massive accumulation of rules and regulations.

Democratic states provide more space for the social articulation of interests and democracy has, over the years, been used by social movements to push for social policies (United Nations Research Institute for Social Development, 2006). However, as Sen (1999: 148) noted, in developing countries, there is opposition to democracies and basic civil and political freedoms for the following beliefs:

- These freedoms and rights hamper economic growth and development.
- If poor people are given the choice between having political freedoms and fulfilling economic needs, they will invariably choose the latter.
- The emphasis on political freedom, liberties and democracy is a specifically Western priority, which goes, in particular, against Asian values.

According to Thompson (2004), autocrats argued that democracy was an unaffordable luxury until sufficient economic prosperity was achieved. They effectively demobilized civil society. Despite periodic support for democracy movements, the middle class remained primarily concerned with their financial well-being. Dependent on the goodwill of the state for their capitalist accumulation, the industrial bourgeoisie posed little threat to the authoritarian system. The international anti-terrorist campaign further repressed the democratic movements. Todaro and Smith (2009) note that there is a trade-off between democratic versus autocratic states. Under democracy, politicians seeking re-election have an incentive to reflect the will and interests of a majority of the people. On the other hand, a looming election gives an incentive to pursue short-term accomplishments that can be pointed to during a campaign, rather than what is necessarily good for long-term development.

Examples of positive effects of autocracy on growth-enhancing policies are Singapore, South Korea and Taiwan, where the regimes saw that its greatest chance of remaining in power lies in achieving maximum growth rate (Todaro and Smith, 2009). However, as the Asian Human Rights Charter (Asian Human Rights Commission and Asian Legal Resource Centre, 1998) notes, 'Governments have arrogated enormous powers to themselves. They have enacted legislation to suppress people's rights and freedoms and colluded with foreign firms and groups in the plunder of national resources. Corruption and nepotism are rampant and there is little accountability of those holding public or private power. Authoritarianism has in many states been raised to the level of national ideology, with the deprivation of the rights and freedoms of their citizens, which are denounced as foreign ideas inappropriate to the religious and cultural traditions of Asia'.

According to the ADB Report (1999a), the need for greater transparency and accountability in regulating the financial sector in the authoritarian states in East and South East Asia, has been one of the key problems behind the currency turmoil, corporate bankruptcies, and falling stock markets that plagued the region since the Asian Financial Crisis. According to Sen (1999: 184–186) also, undemocratic governance was one of the factors responsible for the Asian Financial Crisis. The region neglected two instrumental freedoms, namely protective security and transparency guarantee. Some of these economies lack transparency in business, in particular the lack of public participation in reviewing financial and business arrangements. Moreover, once the financial crisis led to a general economic recession, the protective power of democracy was badly missed. The newly dispossessed did not have the hearing they needed. Thompson (2004) noted that the 1997 Asian Financial Crisis led to a wave of democratization.

Governance and Corruption

Governance

According to the Human Development Report (HDR) on *Deepening Democracy in a Fragmented World* (United Nations Development

Programme, 2002), governance can be seen as the exercise of economic, political and administrative authority to manage a country's affairs at all levels. The UN report on governance for the MDGs (2007) notes that the following are critical dimensions of good governance needed for the achievement of the MDGs: A pro-poor policy framework, public administration and civil services, accountability and transparency, rule of law, human rights, decentralization and delivery of services and role of civil society.

Corruption

Corruption remains an obstacle to achieve good governance. Transparency International defines corruption as the abuse of entrusted power for private gain. This definition encompasses corrupt practices in both the public and private sectors. The Transparency International's Corruption Perceptions Index (CPI) ranks countries according to the perception of corruption in the public sector on a scale from 10 (highly clean) to 0 (highly corrupt). The CPI is an aggregate indicator that combines different sources of information about corruption, making it possible to compare countries. Broadly speaking, the surveys and assessments used to compile the index include questions relating to bribery of public officials, kickbacks in public procurement, embezzlement of public funds, and questions that probe the strength and effectiveness of public sector anti-corruption efforts (http://www. transparency.org/policy_research/surveys_indices/cpi/2010/in_detail).

According to the UNDP (2008), democracies are better designed to control corruption since citizens can take advantage of regular elections to vote out corrupt politicians, but the quality of democracy determines if this mechanism is actually exercised. However, democracies can also be susceptible to corruption if politicians become beholden to wealthy donors on whom they rely for electoral funds and who will expect favours in return. The following table provides the distribution of Asian countries by the type of state and the Corruption Perception Index.

Diversity in Type of State, Corruption and Social Development in Asian Sub-Regions

Table 5.1 shows that linkage between the type of state, corruption and development in Asian sub-regions.

Table 5.1
Diversity in Type of State, Corruption Perception Index and Social Development in Asian Sub-Regions

Level of HD 2010	Countries in Asia	Type of State	HDI Rank 2010	CPI* Rank 2010
East Asia				
V High	Japan	Monarchy	011	17
V High	South Korea	Long Period of Military Rule	012	39
V High	Hong Kong	Colonized till 1997, now SAR China	021	13
Medium	China	Communist	089	78
South East Asia				
V High	Singapore	Single-Party Rule	027	01
V High	Brunei	Monarchy	037	38
High	Malaysia	Monarchy	057	56
Medium	Thailand	From Monarchy/Military Rule to Democracy	092	78
Medium	Philippines	From Dictatorship to Democracy	097	134
Medium	Indonesia	Long Period of Military Rule	108	110
Medium	Vietnam	Communist	113	116
Medium	Timor-Leste	From Indonesian Occupation to Democracy	120	127
Medium	Laos	Communist	122	154
Medium	Cambodia	Monarchy	124	154
Low	Myanmar	Long Period of Military Rule	132	176
North and Central Asia				
High	Russia	From Communism to Democracy	065	154
High	Kazakhstan	From Communism to Democracy	066	105
Medium	Turkmenistan	From Communism to Democracy	087	172
Medium	Mongolia	From Communism to Democracy	100	116
Medium	Uzbekistan	From Communism to Democracy	102	172
Medium	Kyrgyzstan	From Communism to Democracy	109	164
Medium	Tajikistan	From Communism to Democracy	112	154
South Asia				
High	Sri Lanka	Social Democracy	091	91
Medium	Maldives	From Monarchy to Democracy	107	143

Cont'd...

...Cont'd

Medium	India	Social Democracy	119	87
Medium	Bhutan	From Monarchy to Democracy	132	36
Low	Pakistan	Democracy, Periods of Military Rule	125	143
Low	Bangladesh	Democracy, Periods of Military Rule	129	134
Low	Nepal	From Monarchy to Democracy	138	146

*CPI: Corruption Perception Index prepared by Transparency International (2010) (http://www.transparency.org/policy_research/surveys_indices/cpi/2010/results)

Table 5.1 shows that most of the countries in Asia have had authoritative rule in one form or other and are moving towards democracy. All the countries in Asia at the very high level of human development and most of the countries at high level of human development have authoritative rule. Instead of democracy, it is authoritarianism that has led to high level of human development in East and parts of South East Asia. As far as corruption is concerned, countries in Asia which are at the very high or high level of human development are generally low on corruption or high on transparency and vice versa.

Type of State and Corruption in East Asia

Influenced by Confucius respect for authority, most of the East Asian countries have had authoritarian states. Japan is a parliamentary constitutional monarchy (in which the monarch does not personally exercise powers). Khong (1997) noted that as East Asian societies are exposed to the full brunt of globalizing forces, issues transcend national frontiers. Governments therefore have to justify themselves to people who are increasingly becoming politically aware. Notably in Taiwan and South Korea, growing prosperity under authoritarian rule gave rise to democratic transition led by an emergent middle class. For South Korea, the process was characterized by mass social mobilization and violent confrontation spearheaded by radical students and labour groups. The political process was opened up, but this led to an immediate concern for stability and government efficiency. After a long period of military rule until 1987, South Korea has become a full presidential republic. North Korea is a one-party communist country.

China is a one-party communist country. In China, direct elections at the village level stemmed the pervasive influence of the

Communist Party, which is increasingly under pressure from populist grassroot democracy. Through the 1980s, Taiwan was governed in a state of Martial Law. In Taiwan, the process of democratization was more low-key and involved bargaining and compromise between key political groups. The overriding concern again was to restore the stability of the system. Taiwan is now a democratic multi-party state. Repressed feelings of a distinct Taiwanese identity then found political expression and the independence versus reunification debate reached even into families with roots in both camps (Khong, 1997).

Type of State and Corruption in South East Asia

After independence, like East Asia, most of the South East Asian countries that had colonial rule have also had authoritative rule.

Monarchies: The following countries have monarchy rule:

- Cambodia gained independence from France in 1953. It has a parliamentary constitutional monarchy in which the monarch personally exercises powers often alongside a weak parliament.
- Malaysia is a parliamentary constitutional monarchy in which the monarch does not personally exercise powers.
- Brunei is an absolute monarchy since independence from the British in 1984.
- Thailand is a parliamentary constitutional monarchy (in which the monarch does not personally exercise powers); however it is under military rule since 2006.

Single-Party Rule: Singapore exited Malaysia in 1965 to be a British parliamentary republic, but is ruled by one party since then.

Communist Rule: Vietnam is a single-party communist country since 1992.

Long Periods of Military Rule: The following countries have had long periods of military rule:

- Myanmar has military rule since 1962.
- Indonesia had military rule from 1968 to 2004, and is being democratized since then as a full presidential republic.

Democracy: The Philippines and Timor-Leste have developed as full presidential republics. Countries that have formally adopted liberal democratic institutions but in practice remain authoritarian are Indonesia, Malaysia and Singapore (Blondel, Inoguchi and Marsh, 1999).

Table 5.1 shows that in Asia, Myanmar has the highest and Singapore has the least level of corruption in Asia, and both these countries belong to South East Asia. Thus, this sub-region is diverse with reference to state governance. Corruption is also very high in Laos, Cambodia, Philippines and Timor-Leste.

Type of State and Corruption in North and Central Asia

Since the dissolution of the Soviet Union in 1991, the former Soviet Union countries have moved from communist state to democracy. The North Asian countries of Russia and Mongolia are functioning as semi-presidential republics. The Central Asian countries of Kazakhstan, Turkmenistan, Uzbekistan, Kyrgyzstan and Tajikistan are functioning as full presidential republics. However, being in transition, these countries are grappling with redefining the role of the state, shifting the balance between central and local power, and providing civil service employees with appropriate skills for managing a market economy (Asian Development Bank, 1999a). The UNDP Regional Bureau of Europe and the Commonwealth of Independent States (2011) note that decentralization policies though intended to improve efficiency, can also undermine social inclusion. Assigning spending mandates to local governments needs to be accompanied by resource transfers and capacity building to ensure that decentralization policies do not exacerbate sub-national inequalities.

Table 5.1 shows that all the former communist countries in North and Central Asia are high on corruption or low on transparency. The post-Soviet super-presidential systems, drawing on their Soviet experience of rule, have minimized or eliminated the accountability and transparency mechanisms of the independent judiciary, media, civil society or independent parties that might expose and check individual, family, clan or regional interests from influencing, capturing or dominating state policy and resources (UNDP Regional Bureau for Europe and the Commonwealth of Independent States, 2005).

Type of State and Corruption in South Asia

Since achieving independence from the British since 1947 India continues the British parliamentary republic system as the world's largest democracy and since 1948, Sri Lanka is a semi-presidential republic. Social democracy that is characteristic of South Asia is a democratic and parliamentary oriented politics that arose out of socialism, although its socialist content has been diluted over time (Martell, 2010). All the South Asian countries are social democracies today but some have had periods of military rules or monarchy. Pakistan and Bangladesh both have had periods of military rule but military rule has played a more prominent role in Pakistan than in Bangladesh due to the former's long-standing rivalry with India. In the latter, the military's withdrawal from politics and government after 1990 is probably a factor in the country's subsequent progress (Todaro and Smith, 2009). Pakistan is now a semi-presidential republic and Bangladesh has the parliamentary republic system. After being decolonized from the British in 1965, Maldives had monarchy rule and has shifted to being a presidential republic in 2008. Bhutan and Nepal, that were not colonized, have moved from monarchy rules to parliamentary republic systems in 2007 and 2008, respectively.

Transition to democracy, although important, is not sufficient. The Mahbub ul Haq Human Development Centre's HDR of 1999 noted that the South Asian governments were high on governing and low on serving; parliamentarians elected by the poor but aiding the rich; and societies asserting the rights of some people while perpetuating the exclusion of others. According to the Mahbub ul Haq Human Development Centre's HDR of 2001, the primary ingredient of free and fair elections eludes most South Asians with the exception of India and Sri Lanka. Bangladesh, Pakistan and Nepal continue to have a chequered record of holding free and fair elections. Recently, the Mahbub ul Haq Human Development Centre's HDR of 2012 still observes that lack of effective governance has emerged as one of the most fundamental human development challenges in South Asia. The success of economic growth in the sub-region shows that some part of the state machinery works efficiently. Active civil society engagements in dealing with such issues as education, health, access to credit and population growth are examples of successful participation of civil society in bringing change. However, governance in most countries has failed to adequately address such issues as reducing poverty, ensuring equality of access to public services, and so on. In every country, bureaucracy has become increasingly politicized so that the quality of administration has deteriorated. Transparency in governance has remained poor and accountability weak.

Table 5.1 shows that the only two countries that have had democracy in Asia are Sri Lanka and India which are at high and medium level of development, respectively. These democratic countries seem to have moderate level of corruption. Democracies are supposed to be necessary for development and control of corruption. However, these democratic countries have not had high level of transparency or human development. It is the quality or strength of democracy that is probably inadequate in these countries. Corruption is very high in Nepal, Maldives and Pakistan.

Implications for Policy for Governance

Good governance comprising a pro-poor policy framework, public administration and civil services, accountability and transparency, rule of law, human rights, decentralization and delivery of services and role of civil society, is an imperative for social development. Towards transparency in governance, eight Asia-Pacific countries, including China and India, now have right to information (RTI) legislation. This defines key categories of information that all public bodies are required to publish, and establishes citizens' rights to receive specific information on request (United Nations Development Programme, 2008).

Crouch (2007) notes that disillusionment with democracy has emerged, as powerful minority interests have become far more active than the mass of ordinary people, political elites have learned to manage and manipulate popular demands, people have to be persuaded to vote by top-down publicity campaigns and so on. According to him, post-democracy goes beyond the idea of democracy as people's rule and challenges the idea of rule at all. This is reflected in the collapse of deference to government, the insistence on total openness by government, and the reduction of politicians to something more resembling shopkeepers than rulers, anxiously seeking to discover what their customers want in order to stay in business.

According to White (1995, cited in Lewis and Kanji, 2009), true participation that is empowering in a political sense, is when people have direct access to make decisions and take action on their own terms. The service delivery systems should follow the direct participatory approach through local self-governance systems. The critical thinkers of social policy suggest that social welfare needs to be restructured to achieve an emancipatory social welfare that would be built from the ground up, rather than from a centralist plan dictated by those in positions of power. In the proposed emancipatory concept, social welfare is visualized as a process rather than a plan that is not exclusionary, respects diversity and diverse ways of meeting human needs, is not subordinated to old or new kinds of domination, or expert power, and calls for the participation of people to determine their own welfare (Iatridis, 2000).

Role of Civil Society in Social Development in Asia

Concepts and Role of Civil Society

Civil society is usually taken to mean a realm or space in which there exists a set of organizational actors that are not part of the household, the state or the market. The civil society organizations form a wide-ranging group which includes associations, people's movements, citizens' groups, consumer associations and NGOs (Lewis and Kanji, 2009). Collectively, such entities are thought to help maintain a check on state power and its totalizing tendencies (Stepan, 1988, cited in Haynes, 2008).

The secular ideologies of post-colonialism, multiculturalism and post-colonial Third World feminism that guide social development have their roots in the civil society social movements of the former colonies, including Asia. The UN Report of 2007 stresses that an active civil society contributes to strengthening and deepening good governance in the following ways:

- Undertaking policy analysis and advocacy.
- Monitoring state performance and the action and behaviour of public officials.
- Building social capital through community organization and enabling citizens to identify and articulate their values, beliefs and norms.

- Mobilizing the vulnerable and marginalized sections of society to participate more fully in public affairs.
- Undertaking development works to improve their well-being and that of other communities.

Haynes (2008) identifies three broad categories of civil societies in relation to democratization in the developing world:

- Weak civil societies are ineffective as a counterweight to state power. This is frequently linked to inadequate popular participation and lack of governmental transparency and accountability.
- Relatively strong civil societies are democratized relatively recently.
- Strong civil societies are found in established democracies.

Bebbington, Hickey and Miltin (2008: 6) caution that the treatment of civil society is often excessively normative rather than analytical: it is seen as a source of 'good', distinct from a 'bad' imputed to the state and market. Such approaches understate the potential role of the state in fostering progressive change while also downplaying the extent to which civil society is also a realm of activity for racist organizations, business-sponsored research NGOs or other organizations that may not be benign.

Concepts and Role of Non-Governmental Organizations

Concept of Non-Governmental Organizations

The term, 'non-governmental organization' or NGO, came into use in 1945 because of the need for the UN to differentiate in its Charter between participation rights for intergovernmental specialized agencies and those for international private organizations. At the UN, virtually all types of private bodies can be recognized as NGOs. They only have to be independent from government control, not seeking to challenge governments either as a political party or by a narrow focus on human rights, non-profit-making and non-criminal (Willetts, 2006). The OECD (1988, cited in Kennett, 2001) suggested that the term NGOs may include profit-making organizations, foundations, educational institutions, churches and other religious groups and mission, medical organizations and hospitals, unions and professional organizations, cooperative and cultural groups as well as voluntary agencies.

Samuel (1998) criticized the term NGO as a blanket term that appropriates diverse ideological, cultural, ethical, and institutional initiatives under an all-encompassing stereotype. It exemplifies the homogenizing tendency of globalization as it homogenizes the whole social change spectrum. It sucks up various shades of experience into a dominant discourse dictated by a handful of multilateral developmental institutions in a handful of rich countries.

Resurgence of Non-Governmental Organizations

From 1980 onwards, ideas about civil society began to be increasingly invoked within development policy as part of wider debates about politics and democratization, public participation and improved service delivery (Lewis and Kanji, 2009). According to Lewis and Kanji (2009), the rise of prominence of NGOs in the 1980s was driven by the following interrelated factors:

- There was a theoretical impasse within development theory as the modernization as well as the dependency theories had lost their appeal. NGOs came to be seen as sources of alternative ideas and useful new organizational actors that might open up new theory and practice such as people-centred development.
- Development agencies concluded that governments had performed poorly in the fight against poverty and had contributed to growing levels of bureaucracy and corruption.
- NGOs themselves actively contributed through bringing in new ideas to development such as environment, gender and social development.

In 1980s, the neoliberal agenda of rolling back the state advocated diverting funds away from the government control. For different reasons grassroot movements of the Left also supported the growth of the NGO sector, seeing in its goals of participation and empowerment, potential for a change in social structures (Agg, 2006). As neo-liberalism shifted the state's position from provider to enabler, donors sought non-state mechanisms (Lewis and Kanji, 2009). Funding by international NGOs (INGOs) that function as policy advocates as well as agents for the delivery of aid in developing countries (Deacon, 2007) proliferated local NGOs.

By the 1990s, the NGO sector was increasingly seen as a key actor in development policy. There was a growing perception that non-governmental was preferable to governmental development in the South, particularly the provision of social services such as health and education. Development discussion during the period implicitly portrayed NGOs as innovative, value-driven organizations with access to the people who needed help the most, in comparison to governments, which were seen as bureaucratic, inherently inefficient, and possibly corrupt. In this environment, state structures, which were facing considerable obstacles in providing basic services to their citizens, were not considered suitable conduit for development aid (Agg, 2006). Hall and Midgley (2004) note that the advantages that the NGOs have over the public sector is that they are supposed to be based on principles of voluntarism and local participation and their small scale and lack of red tape make them more flexible and responsive, with the freedom to challenge official development priorities as appropriate.

The ADB (1999b) Report on NGOs in nine countries of Asia notes that growth in the number of NGOs has tended to occur most rapidly where government capacity is limited, for example, in South Asia, Philippines and Indonesia. The tasks of the NGOs range from income-generating projects, education and literacy programmes, organization of cooperatives and credit systems, organizing communities, raising consciousness, to lobbying governments for changes in development policy and practice. Strategic alliances are being forged among groups representing a broad range of concerns such as environment, social justice, women's participation, labour and land issues, in order to influence the direction of development internationally and nationally (Heyzer, 1995).

According to Heyzer (1995), vast differences exist among NGO sponsors, approaches, and levels of work, roles, and capabilities in Asia:

- They may be classified according to whether they are government-initiated, donor-organized, independent local NGOs, or foreign NGOs.
- Some are part of the government's service delivery systems, some are small independent service organizations, and others are experimenting with a range of new options.

Some have chosen to work at the national level, others in provinces/states, districts, sub-districts and villages.

Non-Governmental Organizations and the State

According to the UN Report (2001) on the emerging role of the private sector in delivering social services, states in developed countries are likely to partner with private for-profit service providers and developing countries are likely to partner with NGOs that do not work for profit. Moreover, in developing countries, a weak state together with strong INGOs supported by foreign aid agencies may lead to strong civil society. On the other hand, strong states are likely to have a weak civil society. Thus, depending on the strength of the state, market and civil society supplement and compensate it with reference to delivery of social services.

Lewis and Kanji (2009) observe that as non-governmental organizations, NGOs are conditioned by, and gain much of their legitimacy from their relationships with government, and by the nature of the state in any given context. They cite Clark (1991) who pointed out the reality faced by all NGOs: they oppose, complement, or reform the state but they cannot ignore it. Kabeer (2009) stresses three ways in which strong civil society organizations have sought to promote economic and social rights:

1. One is through collaboration with the state, working alongside the state in various programmes in order to reap the benefits of comparative advantage.
2. The second is to act as intermediary between the state and marginalized citizens, lobbying on their behalf, engaging in advocacy roles and taking the state to court for failure to respect rights.
3. The third is to empower poor people to mobilize on their own behalf.

The ADB Report on NGOs in nine countries of Asia (1999b) identified that the activities of NGOs are often poorly coordinated with the government and among themselves. Governments across the region are still searching for ways to define working relationships with NGOs. Heyzer (1995) observes that governments in Asia have generally been ambivalent about the growing role of NGOs in national development. While some governments have voiced official support for a larger role for NGOs in national development, they have also increased the regulations and controls on these organizations. They classify all NGOs in the same category, and then define structure and regulate them, often restricting their activities. To influence the mainstream agenda and the political process, NGOs need to develop viable strategies to get greater political space. Asian governments are more skilled at limiting rather than expanding political space (Heyzer, 1995).

Issues and Limitations of Non-Governmental Organizations

The ADB Report on NGOs in nine countries of Asia (1999b) identified the following five critical issues that characterize the NGO community across Asia:

1. The uncontrolled growth of small NGOs which are weak in institutional and managerial capacities raises questions about the capacity and sustainability of NGOs as a whole.
2. The activities of NGOs are often poorly coordinated with the government and among themselves. There is a need for effective NGO coordinating bodies that do not discourage initiative or experimentation with innovative solutions.
3. NGOs can never be financially sustainable as they are supposed to not work for profit.
4. Accountability and credibility of NGOs through a code of ethics for self-regulation or regulatory legislation is an issue.
5. Governments across the region are still searching for ways to define working relationships with NGOs.

The UNRISD (2000, cited in Agg, 2006) draws the following conclusions about impact of NGOs:

- *Reaching the Poorest:* Most NGO projects do reach the poor but not necessarily the poorest.
- *Coverage:* The scale of operations is limited and the coverage patchy. Moreover, NGOs are not very good at coordinating with each other or with the state.
- *Policy Direction:* NGOs cannot provide a broader framework for action. Only a government can develop clear policy and regulation in fields like health and education.
- *Quality:* There is little evidence that NGOs provide better quality services than the state. What seems to matter more is which of the two has more money.

- *Cost-effectiveness:* There is little evidence that NGOs are inherently more cost-effective than the state. Small projects may be more efficient than larger ones, regardless of who is running them.

Hall and Midgley (2004) identified that NGOs are heavily dependent on financial support from government or international agencies, compromising their autonomy. Their diversity and contrasting philosophies lead to competition and rivalry rather than collaboration and, as they offer better salaries than the government agencies, result in a drain of qualified personnel from the public sector.

Regovernmentalization

According to Kabeer (2004), the state is the only institution that has the capacity and is obliged to respond to claims for welfare entitlements, unlike either the market or the NGOs. In 2005, the Paris Aid Donor Conference laid out a set of new principles on aid harmonization that stressed donor coordination in place of disparate projects, priorities and programmes. It led to 'regovernmentalization' of aid away from NGOs. The recent international initiatives have stressed the need to work with recipient governments to reduce poverty. This includes emphasizing the responsibility of the government to provide social services (Agg, 2006). Lessons from the UN Research Institute for Social Development (UNRISD, 2006) also show that the state is a key institution as an organizer, if not necessarily a provider, of social protection and provisioning. The state not only makes direct provision of social services through public expenditure, but also regulates and stimulates non-state actors in the fulfillment of requirements in social sectors. Hickey and Mitlin (2009) note that growing importance of the rights-based approach also placed the state back at the forefront of development debates.

Diversity in Role of Civil Society in Social Development in Asian Sub-Regions

Civil Society in East and South East Asia

In East and South East Asia (except in Philippines) NGOs are a very recent phenomenon as in the past they have been discouraged by authoritarian regimes (Yamamoto, 1999, cited by Gough, 2000). In these countries the middle class is created under state-sponsored capitalism, so it is generally beholden, even compliant, to the state, lacking the instinctive desire for democratization as demonstrated by its European counterpart (Chong, 2005). However, Wong (2004, cited by Cook and Kwon, 2007) argues that democratization accounted to a large extent for the expansion of the welfare state in South Korea and Taiwan. In Korea, a group of policy makers, experts and civil society activists who wanted an inclusive health care system formed an effective policy coalition and consequently carried out the reform successfully. In Taiwan, the privatization of National Health Insurance was blocked by civil society groups. According to Wong, democratization opened up institutional spaces for the different political actors to participate in social policy-making (Cook and Kwon, 2007).

According to China's Human Development Report (UNDP China and the China Institute for Reform and Development, 2008), the role of non-state actors, including civil society organizations, communities and the private sector, is quite underdeveloped in providing services, weakening effectiveness. The previous state dominance in service delivery has been sharply cut back through market liberalization, privatization and decentralization, but clear delineation of the roles of new non-state actors has not yet been formulated, even as the role of these new types of service providers grows steadily. In the aftermath of SARS, the state has moved to strengthen capacities to manage sudden outbreaks of the contagious disease, for example, by allowing civil society organizations to play a role in grassroots service delivery, public education and outreach to difficult-to-reach groups in the population.

In South East Asia, NGOs are encouraged and are expanding fast. In Indonesia, the Philippines and Thailand, non-profit organizations play significant roles in identifying issues, pro-poor advocacy, delivering services, and mediating issues between the government and local communities (Suwannarat, 2003). However, Gough (2004) notes that the lessons from the Philippines, with its extensive, diverse and dynamic NGOs, are not encouraging. So much progressive energy had very little to show for in terms of poverty reduction and alleviation of suffering. In Vietnam, indigenous non-profit organizations remain more closely linked with government agencies than their counterparts elsewhere (Suwannarat, 2003).

Civil Society in Central Asia

According to the *Central Asia Human Development Report* (UNDP Regional Bureau for Europe and the Commonwealth of Independent States, 2005), civil society became active in Central Asia in the 1980s, and played a major role in ending communism and forcing a political transition to democratic regimes. Although the levels of political and civic freedom have varied across Central Asia over time, civic space has remained generally constrained. Labour unions were strongly under party control before 1991, but have almost disappeared in post-Soviet Central Asia or remain vehicles for state control. With the collapse of industry and lack of government financing, unions have few members and little power. The governments closely monitor private farmers' associations. While the governments have increasingly recognized and allowed civic organizations that work on social issues, such as HIV/AIDS prevention or gender equality, organizations that promote political transparency, better governance and economic reform are vulnerable to interference and risk being shut down. Moreover, civic organizations of all kinds face great difficulties in operating on a regional level; national governments generally oppose transnational civic groups that attempt to put pressure on government policy. From the limited political space that civil society had in the 1990s in Central Asia, the ability of civil society organizations to function has narrowed further over the last few years. The Central Asian governments have largely subdued, coopted or in some cases eliminated the civic actors that could help them foster good governance. They have commonly operated on the assumption that all of these groups are anti-governmental (UNDP Regional Bureau for Europe and the Commonwealth of Independent States, 2005).

Part of the weakness of civil society may be attributed to tight political control in the region during the 1980s and even during the era of Gorbachev's 'perestroika'. Civil society leaders also had less access to Western democratic institutions and less financing for their organizations. Still, a grassroot civil society has developed in the past 15 years:

- In Kyrgyzstan, initial political liberalization fostered the growth of a democratic civil society and a free media.
- In Tajikistan, numerous civic organizations flourished in the wake of the civil war, as they engaged in prevention of renewed conflict.

- In Kazakhstan, civil society has been particularly active in the environmental sphere.
- In Uzbekistan and Turkmenistan, civil society has been strictly under the control of the state and NGOs work mostly on less politically sensitive issues (UNDP Regional Bureau for Europe and the Commonwealth of Independent States, 2005).

Civil Society in South Asia

The Mahbub ul Haq Human Development Centre's (2008) 10-year review of human development in South Asia notes that civil society organizations help fill the void that is left by the public sector in the provision of basic social services. It also helps the poor and other disadvantaged groups to participate and act collectively on fundamental issues. South Asia is home to one of the most vibrant civil society in the world. Over the past decade, civil society organizations have made impressive gains in their expanding areas of influence. In particular, they have played an increasingly proactive role in the fields of education, poverty alleviation, social mobilization, capacity building, provision of various social services, community development, environmental protection and health and sanitation. Micro-finance institutions, in particular, have gained much greater credibility and have expanded their outreach in providing small loans to the poor especially women. In Bangladesh, micro-finance has now reached more than one-third of Bangladeshi households and around 60 per cent of poor households. The total number of branches and disbursements by such institutions has also exhibited an astounding growth in the recent past. In Pakistan, legislation has been put in place to allow the private sector to enter the field of micro-finance.

Civil society in South Asia is also attempting to reform the political arena by informing people about their civil and political rights. It has also been engaged in concerted efforts to compel their governments to enact laws that facilitate a more open and transparent governance. Civil society groups are advocating that governments implement and be faithful to the rights accorded in their constitutions, many of which remain on paper, but not in practice. There has been mass mobilization by civil society against curbing rights in many parts of South Asia. In Pakistan, in local government elections of 2005, civil society organizations played a very important role in training both the voters and councillors, mobilizing the voters, and observing the election process. In India, there has been a proliferation of NGOs. These groups make demands on the system for redistribution of political power, economic resources, and social status (The Mahbub ul Haq Human Development Centre, 2008).

South Asia is also the home of some influential civil society organizations, professional groups and the media that have gender-specific agendas, have identified the problems faced by women in South Asia, and have specific programmes of action. Most of these groups, having flexible organizational structures, are able to react quicker than governments in situations of crisis. They have developed valuable experience in a number of areas that benefit poor women. Some work to alleviate poverty and to enable economically marginal women to earn a living; some provide information, education and vocational training; others pressure governments to meet national and international commitments on women's rights and to enact gender-sensitized labour legislation (The Mahbub ul Haq Human Development Centre, 2008).

Implications for Policies for Civil Society Organizations

Haynes' (2008) framework of three broad categories of civil societies in relation to democratization is modified when applied to Asia as shows in the following table:

Table 5.2
Strength of Civil Society with reference to Type of State in Asia

Type of State	Strength of Civil Society	Countries in Asia
Authoritarian states	Non-existent civil societies	North Korea
		Myanmar
Partly democratized and strong states	Mild civil societies	East Asian Countries except North Korea
		South East Asian Countries except Myanmar and the Philippines
		North and Central Asian Countries
		South Asian Countries except India, Bangladesh and Sri Lanka
Democratic but weak states	Strong civil societies	The Philippines
		India, Bangladesh and Sri Lanka

The limitations of NGOs lead us to consider importance of the more natural systems of community-based organizations (CBOs) and cooperatives. The CBOs are representatives of their community, that is membership-based but consequently tend to vary dramatically in size and focus. CBOs are rarely self-sufficient in terms of service provision but typically work in partnership with external support organizations and service providers, including local government, private sector, NGOs and central government agencies (Slaymaker and Christiansen, 2005). Slaymaker and Christiansen (2005) identified four broad overlapping categories of objectives of CBOs: empowerment, improving efficiency, effectiveness and sustainability, building organizational capacity, and strengthening local government.

Throughout the developed world, cooperatives have been, and continue to be, a significant economic force. In many countries co-ops are among the largest major enterprises in diverse fields of agricultural marketing, savings and credit, rural electricity, insurance, information/communications technologies and housing. The cooperative business model helps low income developing country individuals:

- *Economically* by improving incomes and creating value and investment opportunity along product supply chains in today's global economy.
- *Democratically* by providing first-hand experience with democratic governance, transparency and member participation.
- *Socially* by increasing trust and solidarity, leading to stability in the face of adversity and conflict (US Overseas Cooperative Development Council, 2010).

References

Agg, C. (2006). *Trends in Government Support for Non-governmental Organizations: Is the 'Golden Age' of the NGO Behind Us?* Geneva: United Nations Research Institute for Social Development.

Asian Development Bank. (1999a). Governance in Asia: From crisis to opportunity. Retrieved 17 May 2010 from http://www.adb.org/Documents/Reports/Governance/default.asp?p=gvrnance

——. (1999b). A Study of NGOs: Regional Overview Report.

Asian Human Rights Commission and Asian Legal Resource Centre. (1998). Asian Human Rights Charter, Kwangju. Retrieved 11 September 2011 from http://www.kekidatabank.be/docs/Instrumenten/Regional_organisations/1998%20Asian%20HR%20Charter.pdf

Bebbington, A.J., Hickey, S. and Miltin, D.C. (2008). Introduction: Can NGOs make a difference? The challenge of development alternatives. In A.J. Bebbington, S. Hickey and D.C. Mitlin (eds), *Can NGOs Make a Difference? The Challenge of Development Alternatives* (pp. 3–37). London: Zed Books.

Blondel, J., Inoguchi, T. and Marsh, I. (1999). Economic development versus political democracy. In I. Marsh, J. Blondel and T. Inoguchi (eds), *Democracy, Governance, and Economic Performance: East and Southeast Asia* (pp. 1–20). Tokyo: The United Nations University Press.

Chong, T. (2005). *Modernization Trends in Southeast Asia.* Singapore: Institute of Southeast Asian Studies.

Cook, S. and Kwon, H. (2007). Economic reform and social protection in East Asia, paper presented at the RC19 Annual Conference at Florence University. Retrieved 15 May 2009 from https://docs.google.com/viewer?url=http://www.unifi.it/confsp/papers/pdf/Kwon_Cook.doc&pli=1

Crouch, C. (2007). *Post-Democracy*. Alden, MA: Polity Press.

Deacon, B. (2007). *Global Social Policy and Governance.* Los Angeles: Sage Publications.

Gough, I. (2000). Globalisation and regional welfare regimes: The East Asian case, paper presented at the Conference on Social Security, organized by the International Social Security Association, Helsinki.

——. (2004). Welfare regimes in development contexts: A global and regional analysis. In I. Gough and G. Wood (eds), *Insecurity and Welfare Regimes in Asia, Africa and Latin America* (pp. 15–48). Cambridge: Cambridge University Press.

Hall, A.L. and Midgley, J. (2004). *Social Policy for Development.* Thousand Oaks, CA: Sage Publications.

Haynes, J. (2008). *Development Studies.* Cambridge: Polity Press.

Heyzer, N. (1995). Toward new government-NGO relations for sustainable and people-centred development. In N. Heyzer, J.V. Riker and A.B. Quizon (eds), *Government-NGO Relations in Asia* (pp. 1–14). New York: St. Martin's Press.

Hickey, S. and Mitlin, D. (2009). The potential and pitfalls of rights-based approaches to development. In D. Mitlin and S. Hickey (eds), *Rights-based Approach to Development: Exploring the Potential and Pitfalls* (pp. 209–230). Sterling, VA: Kumarian Press.

Iatridis, D.S. (2000). Critical social policy. In J. Midgley, M.B. Tracy and M. Livermore (eds), *The Handbook of Social Policy* (pp. 393–410). London: Sage Publications.

Kabeer, N. (2004). *Imagining 'The Social': Social Policy Analysis for the Poor in Poor Countries.* Brighton, Sussex: Institute of Development Studies.

——. (2009). A review of social protection in South Asia. SPA Working Papers. Retrieved 16 March 2011 from http://www.socialprotectionasia.org/pdf/Naila-Kabeer_draft-May09.pdf

Kennett, P. (2001). *Comparative Social Policy: Theory and Research.* Philadelphia: Open University Press.

Khong, C.O. (1997). Asian values: The debate revisited. In *'Asian Values' and Democracy in Asia.* Proceedings of a Conference organized by the Shizuoka Prefectural Government and the Oganising Committee of the Asia-Pacific Forum in Japan.

Lewis, D. and Kanji, N. (2009). *Non-Governmental Organisations and Development.* London: Routledge.

The Mahbub ul Haq Human Development Centre. (1999). *Human Development in South Asia 1999: The Crisis of Governance.* Oxford: Oxford University Press.

——. (2001). *Human Development in South Asia 2001: Globalisation and Human Development.* Oxford: Oxford University Press.

——. (2008). *Human Development in South Asia 2007: A Ten-year Review.* Oxford: Oxford University Press.

——. (2012). *Human Development in South Asia 2012: Governance for People's Empowerment.* Lahore: Oxford University Press.

Martell, L. (2010). *The Sociology of Globalization.* Malden, MA: Polity Press.

Samuel, J. (1998). Who's afraid of NGOs? *Humanscape,* 5(10), 34–35.

Sen, A. (1999). *Development as Freedom.* New York: Random House.

Slaymaker, T. and Christiansen, K. (2005). Community-based approaches and service delivery: Issues and options in difficult environments and partnerships. Overseas Development Institute. Retrieved 24 June 2012 from http://www.odi.org.uk/resources/docs/3822.pdf

Smith, B.C. (2009). *Understanding Third World Politics: Theories of Political Change and Development* (3rd ed.). New York: Palgrave Macmillan.

Suwannarat, G. (2003). Southeast Asia: Learning from crisis. In S. Cook, N. Kabeer and G. Suwannarat (eds), *Social Protection in Asia* (pp. 200–260). New Delhi: Har-Anand Publications.

Thompson, M.R. (2004). Pacific Asia after 'Asian values': Authoritarianism, democracy, and 'good governance'. *Third World Quarterly,* 25(6), 1079–1095.

Todaro, M.P. and Smith, S.C. (2009). *Economic Development* (10th ed.). Essex: Pearson Education Ltd.

United Nations. (2001). The emerging role of the private sector in delivering social services in the ESCAP region. Retrieved 8 April 2010 from http://www.unescap.org/esid/psis/publications/spps/04/2166.pdf

——. (2007). Governance for the Millennium Development Goals: Core issues and good practices. Retrieved 24 May 2010 from http://unpan1.un.org/intradoc/groups/public/documents/un/unpan025110.pdf

United Nations Development Programme. (2002). *Human Development Report: Deepening Democracy in a Fragmented World*. New York: Oxford University Press.

——. (2008). *Tackling Corruption, Transforming Lives: Accelerating Human Development in Asia and the Pacific.* Colombo: Macmillan.

United Nations Development Programme China and the China Institute for Reform and Development. (2008). *Human Development Report China 2007/08: Access for All.* Retrieved 1 November 2010 from http://hdr.undp.org/en/reports/national/asiathepacific/china/China_2008_en.pdf

United Nations Development Programme Regional Bureau for Europe and the Commonwealth of Independent States. (2005). *Central Asia Human Development Report – Bringing Down Barriers: Regional Cooperation for Human Development and Human Security.* Bratislava, Slovakia.

——. (2011). *Beyond Transition: Towards Inclusive Societies: Regional Human Development Report.* Bratislava.

United Nations Research Institute for Social Development. (2006). *Transformative Social Policy: Lessons from UNRISD Research*. Geneva.

United States Overseas Cooperative Development Council. (2010). Cooperatives: Pathways to economic, democratic and social development in the global economy. Retrieved 24 June 2012 from http://www.acdivoca. org/site/Lookup/OCDC_Pathways_Paper/$file/OCDC_Pathways Paper.pdf

Willetts, P. (2006). What is a non-governmental organization? London: City University. Retrieved 21 December 2009 from http://www.staff.city.ac.uk/p.willetts/CS-NTWKS/NGO-ART.HTM#Top

CHAPTER 6

Economic Policy Approaches and Role of Regional Institutions in Social Development in Asia

Introduction

This chapter on economic policy approaches and role of regional institutions in social development in Asia aims to review the following:

1. The economic policy approaches in Asia with reference to state economic planning, process of industrialization, and causes and effects of the Asian Financial Crisis and the American Financial Crisis.
2. Diversity in economic policy approaches in Asian sub-regions with reference to development state approach, centrally planned economy approach and mixed economy approach.
3. Role of regional and sub-regional institutions for social development in Asia.
4. Diversity in role of sub-regional institutions in social development in Asian sub-regions.

Economic Policy Approaches and Social Development in Asia

The Overall Economic Policy Approach

State Economic Planning

Todaro and Smith (2009) cite Keyfitz and Dorfman who have identified the following institutional and cultural requirements for the operation of effective private markets for economic development:

1. Trust (in banks, insurance companies, suppliers, etc.)
2. Law and order (enforcement of contracts)
3. Security of persons and of property
4. Balancing competition with cooperation (for a safe workplace and a cleaner environment)
5. Division of responsibility and diffusion of power (an independent judiciary)
6. Community altruism (a social safety net for the impaired, chronically unemployed, elderly, etc.)
7. Social mobility, legitimation of ambition, and toleration of competitiveness
8. Materialistic values as a stimulus to greater production
9. Deferring gratification to generate private saving
10. Rationality unconstrained by tradition
11. Honesty in government
12. Efficient forms of competition, as opposed to monopolistic control
13. Freedom of information (along with protection of privacy)
14. Flows of information without restrictions of favouritism

Todaro and Smith (2009) note that such a well-functioning market system is often absent in developing nations. According to them, proponents of economic planning for developing countries claimed that the market economy is not geared to the principal operational task of poor countries that is, mobilizing limited resources in a way that will bring about the structural change necessary to stimulate a sustained and balanced growth of the entire economy. They note that economic planning came to be accepted, therefore, as an essential and pivotal means of guiding and accelerating economic growth in almost all developing countries.

In the capitalist countries, the state has played a regulatory role in industrialization, which means the government refrains from interfering in the marketplace, except to ensure its regulation (Chan, 1993). However, in Asia, economic planning may be described as a deliberate governmental attempt to coordinate economic decision-making over the long run and to influence, direct, and in some cases even control the level and growth of a nation's principal economic variables (income, consumption, employment, investment, saving, exports, imports etc.) to achieve a predetermined set of development objectives. Most development plans have been formulated and carried out within the framework of the mixed economies of the developing world. These economies are characterized by the existence of an institutional setting in which some of the productive resources are privately owned and operated and some are controlled by the public sector (Todaro and Smith, 2009).

Process of Industrialization

The process of industrialization in Asia is characterized by the shift in the state economic planning from import-substitution to export-oriented strategies, colonization of the rural, integration into the global economy and developmental aid.

Import-Substitution Policies

Since gaining independence, many Asian countries diversified their economies away from agriculture to industry, following the colonizer's liberal paradigm of economic development, based on production and consumption of physical goods. In the 1950s and 1960s, industrialization was accomplished by implementing import-substitution policies. This was done by preventing the imports of certain manufactured products, and producing these products domestically. Trade barriers were imposed which would raise the price of imports in the domestic markets. This policy led to rapid growth of industrial production in the beginning. However, within a decade or so, the small domestic market became saturated. Thus, import-substitution turned out to be a self-terminating industrialization strategy (Tan, 2000).

Shift to Export-Oriented Policies

In order to convert import-substituting firms into export-oriented firms, tariffs would have to be reduced, high-cost, inefficient firms would have to be closed down, and only those that are able to compete effectively in world markets would be allowed to remain. The shift of most Asian countries to export-oriented industrialization was often accompanied by a movement away from centralized, state-dominated economies towards decentralized, market-oriented economies. This would necessarily create considerable unemployment in the short to medium term, and is often politically and socially unacceptable (Tan, 2000).

Colonization of the Rural

The rural production system became a colonized base for the extraction of surplus for the urban-industrial economy (Saldanha, 1995). The new hierarchical dichotomy broadly assumed the form of 'urban-organized' versus the 'rural-unorganized', the urban elite assuming the aura and the role of the imperialists (Sharma, 1998).

Integration into the Global Economy

Since the 1970s, the rising cost of labour in industrialized countries, together with rapid advances in information technology and transportation systems, have allowed production processes to be broken down and their labour-intensive stages relocated to different regions of the world. The scale of integration into the global economy explained the spread of development as well as exposure to the vagaries of the global capital markets (Kabeer, 2008).

Development Aid

The MDG Report of Asia-Pacific (UNESCAP, ADB and UNDP, 2009–10) notes that historically, most development aid has come from the developed countries. Increasingly, however, more is arriving as a result of South-South cooperation from other developing countries in the region, notably China, India and Thailand. Generally, these regional donors are helping their immediate neighbours, though they do also support other countries:

- China's aid, for example, flows mostly to Cambodia, North Korea, Indonesia, Laos, Myanmar, Pakistan, Philippines and Vietnam. China is Cambodia's and Myanmar's biggest donor.
- India's aid goes mostly to Afghanistan, Bangladesh, Bhutan, Myanmar and Nepal. India is the largest donor for Nepal and Bhutan.

- Thailand's aid flows mostly to Cambodia, Laos, Myanmar, Maldives, and Vietnam. Thailand is the largest donor to Laos.

Causes and Implications of the Asian Financial Crisis

The Asian Financial Crisis of 1997–98 began in early July 1997, when the Thai baht was floated, and spread into a virulent contagion, leaping from Thailand to South Korea, Indonesia, the Philippines, and Malaysia. It led to severe currency depreciations and an economic recession that threatened to erase decades of economic progress for the affected East and South East Asian nations. Financial liberalization in the region led to surges in capital flows to domestic banks and firms, which expanded bank lending, ultimately resulting in a rapid accumulation of foreign debt that exceeded the value of foreign exchange reserves. As international speculation on dwindling foreign reserves mounted, the regional currencies came under attack (Muchhala, 2007). However, in several countries of South East Asia such as Malaysia and South Korea, the relatively rapid recovery from the crisis of 1997–98 has added to the general perception of inherent economic dynamism in the region as a whole (Ghosh, 2005). China was not affected by the crisis; on the contrary, maintenance of its exchange rate during the crisis reinforced the view of China as a stabilizing force in the regional economy (Cook, 2003).

Implications of the American Financial Crisis

The American financial crisis of 2007 was triggered by a liquidity shortfall in the US banking system. It resulted in the collapse of large financial institutions, the 'bail out' of banks by national governments and downturns in stock markets around the world. It is considered by many economists to be the worst financial crisis since the Great Depression of the 1930s. It contributed to the failure of key businesses, declines in consumer wealth estimated in trillions of US dollars, substantial financial commitments incurred by governments, and a significant decline in economic activity.

Since many Asian nations have witnessed rapid growth and wealth creation in recent years, they have made investment in Western countries. In addition, there was increased foreign investment in Asia, from the West. Many Asian countries have, therefore, seen their stock markets suffer and currency values going on a downward trend due to this crisis. Asian products and services are also global, and a slowdown in wealthy countries means increased chances of a slowdown in Asia and the risk of job losses and associated problems such as social unrest (Shah, 2009). South Asia is less integrated in the global economy than East Asia and South East Asia, so is less affected by this crisis (Asian Development Bank, 2009).

O'Neill and Stupnytska (2009) note that while overall the NICs in Asia saw much sharper contractions than the developed countries, they also saw much stronger rebounds. A number of countries are already back to their pre-2007 levels on a number of metrics, while others are recovering more slowly. In terms of the differentiation, they identify three broad groups:

- One group comprises those that have displayed remarkable resilience during the global financial crisis. This group of 'winners' includes China, India, Indonesia and the Philippines: they have experienced a relatively mild slowdown, and have shown an impressive rebound in growth and activity.
- At the other end of the spectrum, Pakistan and Russia have suffered more from the crisis. They stand out given the depth of their recessions and sluggishness of recoveries.
- In between the two groups lies another group that includes South Korea and Vietnam, which have also seen impressive rebounds despite relatively sharp contractions.

Type of State and Economic Policy Approaches

Instead of liberal democratic state and strong civil society to support the industrialization, Asia has had authoritative, communist and social democratic states. Depending on the type of state, the prominent development policy approaches in Asia have been the following:

- Development state approach in the authoritative East and South East Asian countries,
- Centrally planned economy approach in former and current communist countries,
- Mixed economy approach in the social democratic South Asian countries.

All the three regions have moved towards market economy since globalization in the 1990s.

Social development is maximum in the development states and minimum in the countries that have had mixed economy. Most of the former or current communist countries, which have had planned economy, fall under the medium level category.

Developmental State Approach

Chan (1993) notes that, instead of the market, the authoritative state has played a developmental role in the Asian countries that achieved fast economic growth. A developmental state intervenes actively in the economy directly and indirectly. Directly the government owns, maintains and operates various public enterprises deemed essential for industrial development. Indirectly, developmental states use easy credits, low taxes, and secure cheap supply of raw materials, guaranteed government purchases and trade discrimination against foreign imports. These governments have been strong and capable in nurturing and promoting those domestic industries that are internationally competitive, in marshaling resources for advantageous economic undertakings, in seeking out profitable niches in international markets and products, in regulating the economic and political influences of foreign companies, and in guiding the activities of the private sector and managing the demands of this sector (Chan, 1993).

The following authoritative states in East and South East Asia have generally been known as developmental states:

- Monarchies: Japan, Malaysia, Indonesia, Thailand
- Long Periods of Military Rule: South Korea, Taiwan
- Single-Party Rule: Singapore

Japan

By the middle of the 19th century, Japan was a highly commercialized and entrepreneurial society but not yet an industrial one. After Japan's 19th century revolution, the Meiji Restoration, industrialization was directed by the state as part of a programme to build a strong and independent country that could stand up to the western empires that were encroaching upon Japan. A distinctive feature of Japanese industrialization was the emergence of the large industrial groupings known as *zaibatsu*, owned by families which controlled them through holding companies. The *zaibatsu* were closely connected with the state (Fulcher, 2004). After the Second World War, the US used its power to remake Japanese society by helping to foster the development of liberal, democratic institutions as a stable, economically vibrant, pro-American Japan was strategic for the US in Asia in the context of the Cold War (McMahon, 2003). Japan recovered quickly from the Second World War and has been prominent since the late 1960s. It was the first country in East Asia to develop economically and, thus, serve as a model in East and South East Asia. According to Thompson (2004), capitalist growth that would fend off the communist danger was successfully spread from Japan to other countries through an expanding regional financial network.

Fulcher (2004) notes that in the early 1970s, rapprochement between the US and China changed the American view of Japan, from a bulwark against East Asian communism to industrial competitor that engaged systematically in unfair trade practices. When in the 1990s, a stock-market crash led to economic stagnation, the institutions that had enabled growth began to attract criticism and undermined the developmental state, he observed.

Asian Tigers

According to Tan (2000), South Korea and Taiwan had benefitted from the Japanese colonizers and Singapore had benefitted from the British colonizers with reference to investments and infrastructure, education, industrial development and public administration during colonization. After decolonization, the shift from agriculture to industry was fastest in South Korea, while Singapore and Hong Kong had very small agricultural sectors anyway. Hong Kong, which never implemented import-substitution, South Korea, Singapore and Taiwan were the first of the less-developed countries in Asia to make the transition from import-substitution to export-oriented industrialization in the 1960s (Tan, 2000).

Kwon (2004) notes that the authoritarian governments in South Korea and Taiwan attempted to legitimize their rule by focusing on economic development. According to Tan (2000), the painful measures needed for the transition from import-substitution to export-oriented industrialization were possible to be undertaken under strong authoritarian governments without much opposition. South Korea, Singapore and Taiwan did not develop as completely free market economies. The state orchestrated the export-oriented industrialization strategy in these countries through the operation of markets. These countries were the first to experience an acceleration of growth rates in the 1960s, based on manufactured exports (Tan, 2000). South Korea, Singapore, Hong Kong and Taiwan were, therefore, collectively known as the newly industrialized countries (NICs) or the Asian Tigers in the 1970s and the 1980s.

Amsden (1989, cited by Kwon, 2004) argued that the South Korean state had intervened in the market mechanism and deliberately distorted market prices in order to compete internationally. It imposed performance standards on private firms, and once these standards were met, the state provided various kinds of subsidy, for example low-interest capital, allowing businesses to enter new markets or consolidate their monopoly status. The other side of the industrial policy in South Korea during the period of rapid economic growth was the harsh suppression of trade unions and labour movements. Political suppression was not, however, the only measure used to ensure industrial stability and workers' loyalty. It established a range of policies to enhance the welfare of industrial workers. A cheap but well-trained labour force was an essential requisite for the export-oriented industrialization strategy. In this context, vocational training and occupational welfare programmes for workers were promoted by the state, which private firms perceived as orders rather than guidelines. These occupational welfare benefits were very often workplace-based and consequently non-transferable, so that workers' loyalty to firms was ensured. Flynn (1999) noted that lifetime employment and mutual loyalty between employers and employees contributed to hard work, loyalty, flexibility and productivity in Japanese and Korean corporations. However, when layoffs and cost reduction were required, such loyalties were forgotten.

All four Asian tiger countries have since graduated into advanced economies and high-income economies, surpassing the ranks of many developed countries. All four economies are classified as high-income economies by the World Bank. Hong Kong and Singapore have become world's leading international financial centres, while South Korea and Taiwan have become world leaders in information technology.

Malaysia and Indonesia

In the 1980s, the Japanese moved their relatively inefficient industries offshore where wages were low, exchange rates were more favourable and productivity was relatively high. The NICs moved their labour-intensive industries to other countries with the same criteria. The Dutch, the Spanish and the French colonizers had done relatively little to develop their colonies in South East Asia, namely, Indonesia, the Philippines, Cambodia, Laos and Vietnam. Political instability, breakdown of law and order, poor infrastructure and natural disasters made the Philippines an favourable destination for foreign investment. Authoritarian governments in Malaysia and Indonesia controlled all the levers of power but intervened less pervasively in economic affairs than the NICs. These countries were, therefore, found to be ideal for the purpose, which resulted in large inflows of foreign investment in these countries which propelled them into export-oriented industrialization (Tan, 2000).

The Human Development Report (HDR) of 2013 notes that from the mid-1970s, supported by revenues from newfound oil wealth, Indonesia complemented import-substituting industrialization with a major thrust in agriculture and rural development. This strategy of balanced growth increased the demand for labour, thus reducing unemployment and increasing real wages. Then in the mid-1980s, as oil income began to decline, Indonesia shifted from import substitution to outward-oriented industrialization, drawing in surplus labour from agriculture to work in manufacturing, which offered higher wages (United Nations Development Programme, 2013).

The East Asian Miracle

The World Bank (1993) study of the fast growth achieved by the eight economies of Japan, Hong Kong, South Korea, Taiwan, Singapore, Indonesia, Malaysia and Thailand between 1965 and 1990 was published under the title *The East Asian Miracle*. Anderson (1998, cited by Gough, 2004) identified the maximum military, economic and political aid to Japan, South Korea and Taiwan from the US, during the Cold War, as one of the factors responsible for the 'Asian Miracle'. According to Chan (1993), instead of interpreting them as a 'miracle', these countries are proof of the need for the role of the state. According to Schech and Haggis (2000) the following Confucian cultural features are most prominent in cultural explanations of East Asian economic development:

same as that of the capitalistic world. Production and consumption of goods and services had been accepted as the measure of development. The decision regarding production, use and distribution, however, was not in the arena of market forces but under the command of the political system (Sharma, 1998).

A review of literature by Szelenyi (1992) shows that the socialist countries secured a number of major achievements such as industrialization, advancement of science and technology, full employment, price stability, and so on. After achieving decrease in inequalities in income in the first stage, the second stage of the experiment of socialism was marked by the emergence of new privileges and crystallization of new inequalities. Intellectual or bureaucratic elite emerged under state socialism to take the place of the old capitalist class. They did not formally own the means of production but they controlled the production of goods and the allocation of valued resources while managing others (Grusky and Takata, 1992).

Fulcher (2004) notes that the Soviet economy collapsed largely because it could not compete with the more dynamic capitalist economies of the West, and the burden of the Cold War was insupportable. Once state direction ceased, economic paralysis followed. The 'shock therapy' recommended by the US and the IMF administered to the economy in 1991 freed prices from state control and privatized Russia's medium and large enterprises, creating mass poverty. According to Mahubani (2008), Russia's mistake was that it tried to make a leap from communist rule to democracy without reforming the economic system first. The 1997 HDR (United Nations Development Programme, 1997) states that the transition from socialism to democracy and market economies in these countries has proved more difficult and costly than anyone imagined. The costs have been not only economic, from the dramatic decline in GDP; they have also been human, from falling wages, growing crime and loss of social protection. In some countries life expectancy has fallen by five years or more.

Central Asian Countries

The *Central Asia Human Development Report* (UNDP Regional Bureau for Europe and the Commonwealth of Independent States, 2005) notes that during 70 years of Soviet rule, when the Central Asian republics were largely shut off from the rest of the world, their economies were closely linked with the rest of the Union. Living standards improved as a result of heavy investments in physical infrastructure and human capital. However, despite the growth of industry in Central Asia, especially during the Second World War, the region's economy remained predominantly based on agriculture and natural resources, with relatively low productivity even by Soviet standards. Because of high transfers from the Soviet Government and artificial price supports, Central Asia was able to maintain a higher level of development than its productivity would have supported, even as its standard of living indicators were the lowest in the Soviet Union.

The UNDP Regional Bureau for Europe and the Commonwealth of Independent States (2005) notes that in 1991, the disintegration of the Soviet Union produced the new countries in Central Asia with new borders that interrupted trade and other human links, and weakened critical but vulnerable region-wide water and energy systems. The severing of supply connections for industry and agriculture, the flight of many skilled Russians, the drying up of subsidies from Moscow, and the disappearance of the central administrative apparatus of the Soviet Union led to a dramatic economic collapse. This brought about a significant increase in poverty, severely weakening the region's human development and human security. As far as the economic systems are concerned, Uzbekistan and Turkmenistan approximate the former Soviet command economies, while Kazakhstan, Kyrgyzstan and even Tajikistan with its recently enhanced reform efforts increasingly have adopted the institutions of modern market economies (UNDP Regional Bureau for Europe and the Commonwealth of Independent States, 2005).

According to the UNDP Regional Bureau for Europe and the Commonwealth of Independent States (2011), the unbalanced capital city-centred growth models have created new exclusionary structures in some Central Asian countries. These have been exacerbated by the legacy of centralized planning that left mono-company towns with very limited economic alternatives and excluded whole communities from economic, social and civic opportunities. While people under socialism lacked the freedom to fully participate in society, many now lack the ability or interest in the opportunities offered by transition.

China and Vietnam

Rather than following the Soviet communist policies of capital-intensive industrialization and centralized economic planning, Mao favoured a decentralized development model in China in which each county and prefecture would become self-sufficient economic units. He sought to combine tradition with development to achieve an egalitarian society, using the country's indigenous technologies, as against Western ones (Schech and Haggis, 2000). Mao encouraged in Chinese peasants an enormous sense of pride and equal citizenship, destroying the feudal mindset. He took China from an agrarian to a modern industrial economy through the Great Leap Forward, and attempted to remove the capitalist elements through the Cultural Revolution. However, both of these failed. After Mao's death, since 1980, Deng Xiaoping led China to the modern economy through modernization of agriculture, industry, science and technology, and the military (Mahubani, 2008).

By the early 1990s, the communist regimes abandoned central-planning and embraced market-oriented economic reforms. As part of this process, they became more closely integrated into the world economy through trade and investment. Because of the quickening space of market-oriented reforms in China, many multinational companies from Western countries as well as from Japan started operations in China in the hope of capturing market shares in the large domestic market. This resulted in rapid economic growth in China (Tan, 2000). Lo (2011: 255–256) notes that China has gone through a classic process of industrialization and development with peculiar features of its own. The country has had high ratio of savings, the formation of an urban and industrial workforce, out of rural and agricultural origins, the expansion of both domestic and export markets, the upgrading of technology and so on. According to him, China has three lessons to offer:

1. Adjustment to changed global circumstances at a national level inevitably involves state intervention to facilitate and promote economic activity both across and within the divides between internal and external markets (and in supporting social provision through domestic mobilization of resources).
2. There is a need to wrest control from finance so that it serves the economy rather than vice versa.

3. There is a need for total reform of the world financial and trading systems in which two pillars of the US dollar as reserve currency and the US trade deficit as a major element of global demand are fundamentally transformed, if not abolished.

China's evolution from an agricultural to an industrial society and from a closed to an open society has brought unprecedented change and mobility. The relatively simple social structures associated with the traditional planned economy are evolving into complex structures as a result of the development of a market economy. These changes have inevitably introduced new challenges characterized by polarization, special interest groups and conflicts of interest (UNDP China and the China Institute for Reform and Development, 2008).

Vietnam's process of Renovation (*Doi Moi*), from 1986, prioritized economic growth with social and redistributive objectives being largely neglected during the first two decades of reform. Just as China's rural decollectivization paved the way for a dramatic increase in agricultural productivity stimulating growth, Vietnam's *Doi Moi* policy also started in the agricultural sector to address the serious inability to recover from war, produce sufficient food and overcome the reduction of aid from Soviet Russia (Cook and Kwon, 2007).

In China and Vietnam, these liberalizing policies brought about impressive improvements in growth as well as major reductions in poverty. However, unlike the growth of the Asian NICs, in the pre-crisis period, this current phase of rapid growth has not been equalizing, and is characterized by a sharp rise in inequality. While a move away from the strict egalitarianism of the planned economy was a necessary component of growth, the extent of inequality is beginning to raise concerns among policy makers. The communist leaderships in both China and Vietnam have continued to emphasize their pursuit of a socialist market economy, a seemingly paradoxical notion which implies that the communist party will maintain its political power while pursuing economic development based on market principles. Despite emerging social tensions, both countries continue to reaffirm the policy rationale of maintaining political stability to ensure continued economic growth (Cook and Kwon, 2007).

North Korea

Cook and Kwon (2007) note that the North Korean economy experienced a serious contraction in the 1990s. In particular, the agricultural and manufacturing sectors registered a constant decline. North Korea suffered from a massive scale of famine in the early 1990s and many people died of starvation. From the late 1990s, agricultural sector recovered to some extent, but North Korean people found it hard to maintain their already minimum level of livelihood. This disastrous economic failure was caused by the loss of capital stock, lack of technological innovation and policy mistakes. The most direct shock to the economy came from the collapse of the Soviet Union which was the source of aid and partners of trade for North Korea. In particular, North Korea suffered from a shortage of petroleum, which used to be imported from the Soviet Union. It led to a sharp decline in the domestic production of fertilizers, most of which was petroleum-based, and then to agricultural failure. Despite a number of attempts to reform the economy following the Chinese open-door policy, the nuclear stand-offs with the US in 1993 and 2002 prevented North Korea from making any meaningful progress. While agricultural production in North Korea continues to fall short of the required amount for minimum subsistence, its people remain highly vulnerable (Cook and Kwon, 2007).

Mixed Economy Approach

Social democracy that is characteristic of South Asia is a democratic and parliamentary oriented politics that arose out of socialism, although its socialist content has been diluted over time (Martell, 2010). It implies a mixed economy consisting of both private enterprise and publicly owned or subsidized programmes of education, universal health care, child care and related social services for all citizens. The South Asian HDR (The Mahbub ul Haq Human Development Centre, 2001) noted that following independence, most countries in South Asia favoured development strategies which limited the region's participation in the global economic system. Historical circumstances clearly played a role, as South Asia's colonial heritage fostered the sentiment that a more open economy, as under British rule, would lead to exploitation. India led the way in pursuing inward-oriented policies that accorded the state a dominant role in directing economic development and limited the development of the private sector. A vast network of government controls and subsidies emerged to manage economic decision-making as well as economic assets, comprising the well-known panoply of overvalued exchange rates, quantitative restrictions and tariffs, and industrial regulations associated with import-substitution industrialization. Although Pakistan initially pursued more outward-oriented policies based on private sector development, it eventually followed suit, as did other countries in the region. By the 1970s, all South Asian countries were pursuing inwardly-focussed development strategies.

By the late 1980s, however, the situation was fundamentally altered. Confronted by lagging growth rates and external payments crises, the majority of South Asian countries adopted a more outward-oriented development strategy, emphasizing greater integration with the world economy. The system of import-substitution based on controls and incentives was gradually replaced by near current account convertibility, reductions in the level of quantitative restrictions and tariffs, as well as more uniform rates of protection, improved incentives for exports, and a more hospitable environment for foreign investors (The Mahbub ul Haq Human Development Centre, 2001).

Bangladesh and Sri Lanka began reforming first during the late 1970s; while Pakistan and India began last, starting in 1991. By the early 1990s, all South Asian countries had begun reforms to make their economies more open (The Mahbub ul Haq Human Development Centre, 2001). A later South Asian HDR (The Mahbub ul Haq Human Development Centre, 2008) observed that since then, drastic economic reforms, including trade and market liberalization, were undertaken across the region. As a result of these reforms, South Asia is much more liberalized, much more open and integrated with the rest of the global economies, and much more market oriented than it was 10 years ago. Some of the benefits of this impressive economic growth have also touched the lives of the ordinary people in terms of some reduction in poverty and improvement in human development indicators. But by and large it is the rich, the educated and the skilled class, mostly based in urban areas, that has benefitted the most with the result that income inequality and wealth disparities continue to show a rising trend throughout the region (The Mahbub ul Haq Human Development Centre, 2008).

The HDR of 2013 notes that during the inward-focussed strategies, India had a deliberate policy of building human capabilities and invest in world-class tertiary education (though perhaps neglecting primary education). These investments paid off when following the reforms in the 1990s, India was unexpectedly able to capitalize on its stock of skilled workers in emergent information technology-enabled industries, which by 2011–12 were generating $70 billion in export earnings. Bangladesh experienced a rapid decline in poverty in the 1990s due to the expansion of labour-intensive exports and increase in employment in the rural non-farm sector, for example, small and cottage industries (United Nations Development Programme, 2013).

Role of Regional and Sub-Regional Institutions for Social Development in Asia

Karns and Mingst (2010) note that states within a given geographic area are presumed to share some background and approaches and can more easily and effectively address common economic and security problems.

Role of Regional Institutions

Economic and Social Commission for Asia and the Pacific

The Economic and Social Commission for Asia and the Pacific (UNESCAP) is the regional development arm of the UN for the Asia-Pacific region. With a membership of 62 Governments, 58 of which are in the region, and a geographical scope that stretches from Turkey in the West to the Pacific island nation of Kiribati in the east, and from Russia in the north to New Zealand in the south, UNESCAP is the most comprehensive of the UN five regional commissions. Established in 1947 with its headquarters in Bangkok, Thailand, UNESCAP carries out work in the following areas that are most effectively addressed through regional cooperation: Macroeconomic policy and development, sub-regional activities for development, environment and sustainable development, information and communications technology and disaster risk reduction and social development.

The Social Development Division of UNESCAP helps strengthen cooperation among countries in the region in order to build more inclusive societies, through social and financial policies and measures promoting social protection, social inclusion, gender equality and development. The UNESCAP (2002) report notes that it has forged the landmark regional cooperation agreement among its members in the Agenda for Action on Social Development in the ESCAP Region, adopted by the Commission in 1995. It has also forged other regional plans of action for cooperation regarding women, human resources development, disabled persons and ageing. The UNESCAP has advocated specific collaboration agreements among governments with common borders to prevent the spread of HIV/AIDS and drug abuse.

The UNESCAP (2005) recommends regional cooperation in pursuit of what might be termed 'international public goods', such as monetary cooperation and environmental security, goods that once provided can be shared by everyone across the region. By analogy, countries can also work together to eliminate 'international public bads' such as pollution, communicable diseases or trafficking in persons. The Report suggests gaining more resources through trade, foreign direct investment and official development assistance, encouraging Asian monetary cooperation, regularizing labour migration, creating an Asia-Pacific grain security system, agreeing to compacts to tackle the HIV/AIDS pandemic, aiming for green growth, improving governance by fighting corruption and promoting e-governance, and strengthening cooperation between regional institutions.

Asia-Pacific Economic Cooperation

The idea of Asia-Pacific Economic Cooperation (APEC) was firstly publicly broached by former Prime Minister of Australia, Mr Bob Hawke, during a speech in Seoul, Korea, in January 1989. Later that year, 12 Asia-Pacific economies met in Canberra, Australia, to establish APEC. The founding members were: Australia, Brunei Darussalam, Canada, Indonesia, Japan, Korea, Malaysia, New Zealand, the Philippines, Singapore, Thailand and the United States. In 1998, the full membership reached 21. Between 1989 and 1992, APEC met as an informal senior official and Ministerial level dialogue. Since 1993, the APEC Economic Leaders' Meeting is held annually. Today, APEC is the premier Asia-Pacific economic forum with the goal to support sustainable economic growth and prosperity in the Asia-Pacific region. It drives to build a dynamic and harmonious

Asia-Pacific community by championing free and open trade and investment, promoting and accelerating regional economic integration, encouraging economic and technical cooperation, enhancing human security, and facilitating a favourable and sustainable business environment.

Asian Development Bank

The ADB is an international development finance institution committed solely to Asia and the Pacific. Its mission is to help its developing member countries reduce poverty and improve the quality of life of their people. Headquartered in Manila, and established in 1966, ADB is owned and financed by its 67 members; of which 48 are from the region and 19 are from other parts of the globe. ADB's main partners are governments, the private sector, NGOs, development agencies, community-based organizations, and foundations. Under Strategy 2020, a long-term strategic framework adopted in 2008, ADB will follow three complementary strategic agendas: inclusive growth, environmentally sustainable growth, and regional integration. In pursuing its vision, ADB's main instruments comprise loans, technical assistance, grants, advice, and knowledge. Although most lending is in the public sector, and to governments, ADB also provides direct assistance to private enterprises of developing countries through equity investments, guarantees, and loans. In addition, its triple-A credit rating helps mobilize funds for development (http://adb.org/About/).

The ADB development model favours private arrangements, notably commercial provision and family support, as social protection systems of the first resort, bolstered by philanthropic and voluntary efforts to compensate for withdrawn or pared-down public provision. All but the critically poor are supposed to make their own private arrangements, and public schemes are relegated to little more than a residual role for groups for whom private commercial schemes are not available and/or who are unable to rely solely on informal sources of support. This model does not consider as a legitimate goal the promotion of a more egalitarian income distribution, be it achieved through tax-transfer mechanisms or comprehensive pubic good provision (Holzmann and Jorgensen, 2000 and World Bank, 2001, cited by Yeates, 2005). The 2013 HDR notes that prior to the global financial crisis, the ADB was already lending more in the region than the World Bank. The crisis accelerated this trend (United Nations Development Programme, 2013).

Diversity in Role of Sub-Regional Institutions

Association of South East Asian Nations

The Association of South East Asian Nations (ASEAN) is the oldest sub-regional institution in Asia, established in 1967, with the signing of the ASEAN Declaration (Bangkok Declaration). Concerns about the outcome of the war in Vietnam, the future of the US commitment to regional security, Chinese-supported communist insurgencies, and separatist movements, united these diverse countries (Karns and Mingst, 2010). The aims and purposes in the ASEAN Declaration comprise cooperation in the economic, social, cultural, technical, educational and other fields, and in the promotion of regional peace and stability through abiding respect for justice and the rule of law and adherence to the principles of the UN Charter. The motto of ASEAN is 'One Vision, One Identity, One Community'. In the 1990s, ASEAN played an important role in establishing the ASEAN Regional Forum (ARF) and the Asia Pacific Economic Cooperation (APEC).

Yeates (2005) observes that the ASEAN originated as a Western-sponsored political alliance to counteract the communist threat (from China) in the region. The development of a more substantial trading bloc has been its priority and is currently evolving into a trade liberalization project. According to Deacon (2001), the ASEAN has no regional social or labour regulations or redistributive mechanisms and is confined to cross-border educational exchanges and cross-border trade in health services and insurance. There are very real cross border issues such as HIV/AIDS, drug trafficking, child trafficking and prostitution and the forced labour policy of Myanmar, but these have received little attention at a regional level. ASEAN has adopted a policy of non-interference in its members' internal affairs. Combined with the ASEAN way of organizing, which emphasizes relationship-building rather than institution-building, with a strong preference for pragmatism and flexibility over programme formation, attempts to raise social development issues onto the group's political agenda would anyhow have been frustrated by members' internal authoritarian political structures, the absence of a tradition of civil society political involvement, and by their markedly different levels of development and types of welfare arrangements (Yeates, 2005).

In 2002, ASEAN convened a conference in Jakarta on 'Social Development in the National Development Agenda' that focused specifically on social policy challenges. The central conclusion of the participants of this conference was that the challenge is less to integrate social sectors into countries' national agendas; practically all have done so, but rather to determine how governments can reach social development goals in a context of globalization and market liberalization, economic cycles and financial crises, and demographic transitions. However, Yeates (2005) observes that hopes that ASEAN might play a stronger political role in the region and push for a social dimension to the trade liberalization project are dampened by the regional dominance of the ADB. According to Deacon (2001), ADB has been unresponsive toward the emergence of ASEAN as a lead (rival) player in the region. The institutional weakness of ASEAN is regrettable because of the power of the more influential ADB.

Chiang Mai Initiative Multilateralization

ASEAN Plus Three (APT) is a forum that functions as a coordinator of cooperation between ASEAN and the three East Asian nations of China, Japan and South Korea. The first meeting of APT was held in 1997 and the group's significance and importance was strengthened by the Asian Financial Crisis. The grouping was institutionalized by 1999. ASEAN Plus Three, in establishing the Chiang Mai Initiative, has been credited as forming the basis for financial stability in Asia, the lack of such stability being a contributing factor to the Asian Financial Crisis. The APT cooperation is now being pursued in 20 areas, covering political and security, transnational crime, economic, finance and monetary, agriculture and forestry, energy, minerals, tourism, health, labour, culture and arts, environment, science and technology, information and communication technology, social welfare, rural development and poverty eradication, disaster management, youth, women, and other tracks. In early 2009, the initiative was multilateralized and renamed the Chiang Mai Initiative Multilateralization.

South Asian Association for Regional Cooperation

The South Asian Association for Regional Cooperation (SAARC) was established when its Charter was formally approved in 1985 by the heads of Governments of Bangladesh, Bhutan, India, Maldives, Nepal, Pakistan and Sri Lanka. Afghanistan became a member of SAARC during the Fourteenth SAARC Summit in 2007. SAARC aims to promote the welfare of the peoples of South Asia and to improve their quality of life through accelerated economic growth, social progress and cultural development in the region. The key issues emphasized by SAARC are telecommunication, energy, climate change, transport, poverty alleviation, science and technology, trade, education, food security and tourism. Cooperation in SAARC is based on respect for the five principles of sovereign equality, territorial integrity, political independence, non-interference in internal affairs of the member states and mutual benefit.

The SAARC Social Charter of 2004 commits South Asian governments to ensure that every member of society is enabled to satisfy their basic human needs and to realize their personal dignity, safety and creativity. It also goes on to declare: 'State Parties agree that access to basic education, adequate housing, safe drinking water and sanitation and primary health care should be *guaranteed in legislation, executive and administrative provisions,* in addition to ensuring of adequate standard of living, including adequate shelter, food and clothing. State parties underline the imperative for providing a better habitat to the people of South Asia as part of addressing the problems of the homeless'.

In 2007, the SAARC member countries signed an agreement to establish a SAARC Food Bank. This would act as a regional food security reserve for the SAARC member countries, to help them address food shortages and emergencies. It would also provide regional support to national food security efforts and foster inter-country partnerships and regional integration. The Food Bank would commence with a reserve of 241,580 metric tons of foodgrains. The Food Bank is to be administered by a board. Each member country has an earmarked share of the reserve, which would remain the property of the member. Members are required to inform the board of the location of these reserves. The Agreement contains broad principles for determination of price, including the cost of procuring and maintaining the grain stocks and of transportation.

The prices, terms and conditions of payment in respect of the foodgrains would be the subject of direct negotiations between the concerned member countries based on the guidelines for price determination. The Agreement contains detailed specifications for the quality of grains, procedures for the withdrawal and release of foodgrains (UNESCAP, ADB and UNDP, 2009–10).

Regional Associations in North and Central Asia

The *Central Asia Human Development Report* (UNDP Regional Bureau for Europe and the Commonwealth of Independent States, 2005) notes that Central Asian countries, their neighbours and their international partners have begun the process of cooperation by setting up regional organizations. They started just after independence in 1992 with the creation of:

- The Commonwealth of Independent States (CIS), involving the participation of all the former Soviet countries except for the three Baltic nations.
- The Eurasian Economic Community (EEC and various predecessors) followed, with Kazakhstan, Kyrgyzstan and Tajikistan as members besides Belarus and Russia.
- The Central Asian Cooperation Organization (CACO), with Kazakhstan, Kyrgyzstan, Russia, Tajikistan and Uzbekistan as members.
- The Shanghai Cooperation Organization (SCO), involving China, Kazakhstan, Kyrgyzstan, Russia, Tajikistan and Uzbekistan.
- Economic Cooperation Organization (ECO), which includes Afghanistan, Azerbaijan, Iran, Kazakhstan, Kyrgyzstan, Pakistan, Tajikistan, Turkey, Turkmenistan and Uzbekistan.
- The Central Asia Regional Economic Cooperation programme (CAREC) comprising the Central Asian countries and Azerbaijan, China and Mongolia, together with the multilateral institutions led by the ADB.

According to the *Central Asia Human Development Report* (UNDP Regional Bureau for Europe and the Commonwealth of Independent States, 2005), these organizations so far have had a limited impact on Central Asian regional integration and cooperation, for a number of reasons:

- The membership is generally not complete (Turkmenistan, for example, only belongs to the CIS and ECO, and generally has not been an active participant even in these organizations).
- The mandates and objectives of the organizations are generally unclear and overlapping, and change over time.
- The organizations have only very limited financial resources and weak organizational capacities, and lack mediation or enforcement authority for the agreements reached.
- They have not been systematically supported by the international community as a vehicle for channelling financial and technical support for regional cooperation and integration (UNDP Regional Bureau for Europe and the Commonwealth of Independent States, 2005).

Implications for Policies for Regional Institutions

The sub-regional institutions in Asia so far have had a limited impact on social development. The MDG Report of Asia-Pacific (UNESCAP, ADB and UNDP, 2009–10) notes that the regional cooperation mechanisms in the Asia-Pacific region have been much more active in signing agreements on trade than in other areas. Karns and Mingst (2010: 189–190) identified the following characteristics of the Asian and Asia Pacific institutions compared to the regional organizations of Europe:

- The Asian regional institutions are informal, having few specific rules, no binding commitments, small secretariats, consensus decision-making, and a strong emphasis on process over substance and outcomes. Informal processes include extensive meetings, consultations, and dialogues; informal outcomes typically refer to agreements on general principles and non-binding codes of conduct.
- Since many Asian countries gained their independence only after World War II, they have been strongly nationalistic, attached to state sovereignty, and suspicious of other forms of dependency on perceived domination. As a result, the norm of non-intervention in states' internal affairs is a strong component of Asian regionalism.

According to Girvan (2005), regionalism's epistemic dimension relates to accumulation of local diagnostic and prescriptive capacities for development policy-making, linked to democratic participation in decision-making at the national and regional levels. Many countries are, therefore, recognizing the need to work more closely with each other in managing the globalization process, to reduce the threats to social stability and to seize the opportunities inherent in their increasing interdependence for sustainable social development (UNESCAP, 2002).

According to Deacon (2001), the potential advantages for developing countries of building a social dimension to regional groupings of countries in relation to the rest of the world are the potential afforded for protection from global market forces that might erode national social entitlements, and a louder voice in the global discourse on economic and social policy in UN and other forums. He further noted that through intergovernmental agreement, regionalism would make possible the development of regional level social redistribution mechanisms, social and labour regulation, sectoral social policies in health, education and so on, food and livelihood cooperation, recognition of social security entitlements and social empowerment mechanisms that give citizens a voice to challenge their governments in terms of human and social rights. Other advantages of regionalism are regional strategies for transnational issues such as combating human trafficking, HIV/AIDS prevention and mitigating any negative social impact of international labour migration and resource mobilization for social development, enabling and encouraging domestic tax reform which would otherwise be avoided for fear of competition from other countries (UNESCAP, 2002).

The MDG Report of Asia-Pacific (United Nations Economic and Social Commission for Asia and the Pacific et al., 2009–10) argues that the Asia-Pacific countries have the resources, the capacity and the know-how to address the basic problems affecting human development. It recommends that the regional cooperation has to go beyond trade and investment issues to cover social areas such as health, food security, water and sanitation, labour migration and development assistance, and the environment. Stronger cooperation on these issues could make the region more resilient to future crises and bolster the capacity of many of the poorest countries to achieve the MDGs.

References

Asian Development Bank. (2009). Outlook 2009 Update. Retrieved from: http://www.adb.org/Documents/Books/ADO/2009/update/subregional.pdf

Chan, S. (1993). *East Asian Dynamism: Growth, Order, and Security in the Pacific Region.* Oxford: Westview Press.

Cleaver, H. (2010). Socialism. In W. Sachs (ed.), *The Development Dictionary: A Guide to Knowledge as Power* (2nd ed.). (pp. 260–278). New York: Zed Books.

Cook, S. (2003). After the Iron Rice Bowl: Extending the safety net in China. In S. Cook, N. Kabeer and G. Suwannarat (eds), *Social Protection in Asia* (pp. 57–128). New Delhi: Har-Anand Publications.

Cook, S. and Kwon, H. (2007). Economic reform and social protection in East Asia, paper presented at the RC19 Annual Conference at Florence University. Retrieved 15 May 2009 from https://docs.google.com/viewer?url=http://www.unifi.it/confsp/papers/pdf/Kwon_Cook.doc&pli=1

Deacon, B. (2001). The social dimension of regionalism: A constructive alternative to Neo-liberal globalization? Globalism and Social Policy Programme, Occasional Paper No. 8/2001. Retrieved 12 January 2009 from http://gaspp.stakes.fi/NR/rdonlyres/02A8960F-764F-4E8C-9477-B0CECCFC3478/0/gaspp82001.pdf

Flynn, N. (1999). *Miracle to Meltdown in Asia: Business, Government, and Society.* New York: Oxford University Press.

Fulcher, J. (2004). *Capitalism: A Very Short Introduction.* New York: Oxford University Press.

Ghosh, J. (2005). Globalisation and economic empowerment of women: Emerging issues in Asia. In *UNESCAP, Asia and the Pacific Beijing+10: Selected Issues.* New York. Retrieved 13 May 2010 from http://www.unescap.org/esid/gad/PDF/AsiaandPacificBeijing+10.pdf

Girvan, N. (2005). *The Search for Policy Autonomy in the South.* Geneva: United Nations Research Institute for Social Development.

Gough, I. (2004). Welfare regimes in development contexts: A global and regional analysis. In I. Gough and G. Wood (eds), *Insecurity and Welfare Regimes in Asia, Africa and Latin America* (pp. 15–48). Cambridge: Cambridge University Press.

Grusky, D.B. and Takata, A.A. (1992). Social stratification. In E.F. Borgatta (ed.), *Encyclopedia of Sociology*, Volume 4 (pp. 1955–1970). New York: Macmillan.

Hudelson, R.H. (1993). *The Rise and Fall of Communism.* Oxford: Westview Press.

Kabeer, N. (2008). *Mainstreaming Gender in Social Protection for the Informal Economy.* London: Commonwealth Secretariat.

Karns, M.P. and Mingst, K.A. (2010). *International Organizations: The Politics and Processes of Global Governance.* London: Lynne Rienner Publishers.

Kwon, H. (2004). *Transforming the Developmental Welfare States in East Asia.* Geneva: United Nations Research Institute for Social Development.

Lo, D. (2011). The Washington consensus and the China anomaly. In K. Bayliss, B. Fine and E.V. Waeyenberge (eds), *The Political Economy of Development: The World Bank, Neo-liberalism and Development Research* (pp. 239–262). London: Pluto Press.

The Mahbub ul Haq Human Development Centre. (2001). *Human Development in South Asia 2001: Globalisation and Human Development.* Oxford: Oxford University Press.

——. (2008). *Human Development in South Asia 2007: A Ten-year Review.* Oxford: Oxford University Press.

Mahubani, K. (2008). *The New Asian Hemisphere: The Irresistible Shift of Global Power to the East.* New York: Public Affairs.

Martell, L. (2010). *The Sociology of Globalization.* Malden, MA: Polity Press.

McMahon, R.J. (2003). *The Cold War: A Very Short Introduction.* New York: Oxford University Press.

Muchhala, B. (2007). Introduction. In B. Muchhala (ed.), *Ten Years After: Revisiting the Asian Financial Crisis.* Washington, DC: Woodrow Wilson International Center for Scholars, Asia Program.

O'Neill, J. and Stupnytska, A. (2009). The long-term outlook for the BRICs and N-11 post crisis. Goldman Sachs, Global Economics Paper No. 192. Retrieved 4 April 2010 from http://www2.goldmansachs.com/ideas/brics/brics-at-8/BRICS-doc.pdf

Saldanha, D. (1995). State, society and voluntary intervention: Reflections of some action groups. In M. Savur and I. Munshi (eds), *Contradictions in Indian Society* (pp. 189–209). Jaipur: Rawat Publications.

Schech, S. and Haggis, J. (2000). *Culture and Development: A Critical Introduction.* Oxford: Blackwell Publishers.

Shah, A. (2009). Global financial crisis. Retrieved 3 April 2010 from http://www.globalissues.org/article/768/global-financial-crisis#Thefinancialcrisisandthedevelopingworld

Sharma, B.D. (1998). The people versus the system. In M. Desai, A. Monteiro and L. Narayan (eds), *Towards People-centred Development* (pp. 44–61). Mumbai: Tata Institute of Social Sciences.

Szelenyi, S. (1992). Socialism. In E.F. Borgatta (ed.), *Encyclopedia of Sociology,* Volume 4 (pp. 1858–1863). New York: Macmillan.

Tan, G. (2000). *Asian Development: An Introduction to Economic, Social and Political Change in Asia.* Singapore: Times Academic Press.

Thompson, M.R. (2004). Pacific Asia after 'Asian values': Authoritarianism, democracy, and 'good governance'. *Third World Quarterly,* 25(6), 1079–1095.

Todaro, M.P. and Smith, S.C. (2009). *Economic Development* (10th ed.). Essex: Pearson Education Ltd.

United Nations Development Programme. (1997). *Human Development Report: Human Development to Eradicate Poverty*. New York: Oxford University Press.

——. (2013). *Human Development Report: The Rise of the South: Human Progress in a Diverse World.* New York.

United Nations Development Programme China and the China Institute for Reform and Development. (2008). *Human Development Report China 2007/08: Access for All.* Retrieved 1 November 2010 from http://hdr.undp.org/en/reports/national/asiathepacific/china/China_2008_en.pdf

United Nations Development Programme Regional Bureau for Europe and the Commonwealth of Independent States. (2005). *Central Asia Human Development Report – Bringing Down Barriers: Regional Cooperation for Human Development and Human Security.* Bratislava, Slovakia.

——. (2011). *Beyond Transition: Towards Inclusive Societies: Regional Human Development Report.* Bratislava.

United Nations Economic and Social Commission for Asia and the Pacific. (2002). *Sustainable Social Development in a Period of Rapid Globalization: Challenges, Opportunities and Policy Options.* Bangkok.

——. (2005). *A Future within Reach: Reshaping Institutions in a Region of Disparities to Meet the Millennium Development Goals in Asia and the Pacific.* Retrieved 30 November 2006 from https://docs.google.com/viewer?url=http%3A%2F%2Fwww.mdgasiapacific.org%2F2ndMDG Report%2FMDG-PDF-I.pdf

United Nations Economic and Social Commission for Asia and the Pacific, Asian Development Bank and United Nations Development Programme. (2009–10). *Achieving the Millennium Development Goals in an Era of Global Uncertainty: Asia-Pacific Regional Report.* Retrieved 9 January 2010 from http://www.mdgasiapacific.org/regional-report-2009–10

World Bank. (1993). *The East Asian Miracle: Economic Growth and Public Policy.* Washington, DC.

Yeates, N. (2005). *'Globalization' and Social Policy in a Development Context: Regional Responses.* Geneva: United Nations Research Institute for Social Development.

CHAPTER 7

Social Policy Approaches and Social Development in Asia

Introduction

Concept of Social Policy

Gough (2004) provided the following broad working definition of social policy: A public policy that is an intentional statement of action within the public sphere to achieve:

- Social welfare goals, that is some negative conception of avoiding harm and suffering, or some positive conception of human well-being.
- Which operates through a wide variety of policy instruments across a number of sectors.
- Is formulated and implemented by a wide range of actors, state and non-state and national and international.

Chapter Objectives

This chapter on social policy approaches and social development in Asia reviews the following:

1. The overall social policy approaches in Asia with reference to history of social policy, policy approach for social protection and policy approach to human rights.
2. Diversity of social policy approaches and social development in Asian sub-regions.

Overall Social Policy Approaches in Asia

History of Social Policy

The colonial rulers introduced the first social services in the form of formal education, health and other social services. The provision at this time was minimal, residual and discriminatory, generally benefitting the expatriate communities and those members of the local community who were considered beneficial to the colonial mission. Moreover, these services were generally staffed with specialists/experts from the colonizers whose values permeated the welfare institutions. As a result, colonial societies experienced extreme inequalities with a small privileged elite gaining access to these services (Kennett, 2001).

Due to the colonial legacy, the post-colonial social policy was biased towards formal employment in the urban economy, when the majority of the labour force lived in rural areas and worked in the informal sector. However, social policy initiatives played an important role in legitimizing postcolonial governments, with major programmes in education, housing, urban planning, health, and price subsidies and controls (Kennett, 2001). The UNRISD Report (2010) notes that during the 1960s and 1970s, public expenditure on social services grew rapidly in many developing countries, with social policies treated as integral to development objectives of creating a modern economy, national identity and social cohesion. However, for many countries, the crises and trends towards market liberalization from the 1980s led to severe cuts in social sector spending, with varying effects on social policies and outcomes. Neo-liberalism shifted the state's position from provider to enabler.

Policy Approach for Social Protection

Concept of Social Protection

Since the 1980s, social protection is emerging as a key social development policy that reflects attempts to integrate concerns with social security and poverty reduction within a unified conceptual and policy framework in response to the perceived increase in the vulnerability of populations across the world (Cook and Kabeer, 2009). According to Devereux and Sabates-Wheeler (2006: 1), 'Social protection describes all public and private initiatives that provide income or consumption transfers to the poor, protect the vulnerable against livelihood risks, and enhance the social status and rights of the marginalized; with the overall objective of reducing the economic and social vulnerability of poor, vulnerable and marginalized groups.'

Studies on Social Protection in Asia

Cook, Kabeer and Suwannarat (2003) carried out a study of social protection in Asia, covering the communist countries of China and Vietnam, Thailand, Indonesia and the Philippines in South East Asia, and India and Bangladesh in South Asia. It found that formal social protection measures cover roughly 10 per cent of the population across the region. These measures are largely limited to government and state enterprise officials, and to very thin level of employees in large private sector businesses. Of the 90 per cent of the population falling outside formal systems, those with most limited access to social protection tend to be those marginalized on the basis of ethnicity (and caste in India), gender, age and migrant status, as well as by their economic status.

Sponsored by the Asian Development Bank (ADB), Wood (2009) created an inventory of social protection programmes for 31 Asian and Pacific countries to formulate a Social Protection Index (SPI) comprising four summary social protection indicators (cost, coverage, distribution and impact) for these countries. He found the following:

- On an average, the Asian and Pacific countries spend just under five per cent of their GDP on social protection and achieve an overall average coverage level of 35 per cent of the key target groups.
- The average proportion of the poor (using national poverty lines) who receive some social protection benefits is 57 per cent implying that the majority of Asia's poor receive some social protection.
- Per capita expenditure on the poor, however, averages less than 25 per cent of the poverty line; it, thus, brings only limited benefits to most recipients. These averages mask substantial variations. At the top end of the scale, two distinct groups of countries can be identified:

1. First, Japan and Korea, by virtue of their status as developed high income countries; achieve the highest values on most of the social protection summary indicators (SPSIs).
2. Second, the Central Asian countries (including Mongolia) have generally high levels of social protection resulting from the comprehensive social protection systems introduced in these countries during the Soviet era.

- In most Asian and Pacific countries, the majority of expenditure on social protection is provided through formal social insurance systems. Countries with below average proportions of expenditure on social insurance tend to be those with less developed social insurance systems but with substantial other social protection expenditures. The programmes that provide the greatest coverage of and greatest benefits to the poor are the targetted programmes: educational assistance, subsidized health care, food for work programmes, and micro-credit finance schemes, which are a very important component of social protection in countries with such diverse characteristics as Bangladesh, Kyrgyzstan, Laos and Philippines. Conversely, formal means-tested social assistance programmes involving direct cash hand-outs are rarely important and are usually targetted only at the poorest and the most vulnerable.
- Coverage levels for the key target groups vary widely both within and between countries with the highest ratios tending to be for poor children (educational assistance programmes), social assistance to the poor, and the elderly (pensions and targeted health and social welfare schemes).

Welfare Regimes

Gough (2004) observes that Esping-Andersen's welfare state regimes, with liberal, conservative-corporatist and universalist/social democratic state types are less applicable to the developing and transitional countries. In applying the regime model to the developing world, he recommended that the welfare state regimes, that privilege the state, have to be replaced by 'welfare regimes' where state is only one of the players. He defined welfare regimes as the entire set of institutional arrangements, policies and practices affecting welfare outcomes and stratification effects in diverse social and cultural contexts. He classified welfare regimes into welfare state regimes, informal security regimes and insecure welfare regimes. Instead of welfare state regimes, developing countries generally have informal security regimes or insecure welfare regimes.

Most of the countries in Asia have informal security regimes where residual welfare is the dominant form of welfare. Bevan (2004) conceptualized an insecurity regime, which reflects a set of conditions, which generate gross insecurity and block the emergence of stable informal mechanisms. These regimes arise in areas of the world where powerful external players interact with weak internal actors to generate conflict and political instability, for example, some countries in Africa. No Asian country has an insecure welfare regime.

Informal Security Regimes

Gough (2004) and Wood (2004) identified the eco-political context of such regimes comprising:

- The dominant mode of production not being capitalism as other forms of production interact with capitalism.
- Livelihoods and employment in the informal sector dominate employment in the formal sector.
- Besides class, ethnicity, regional origin, religion, caste, clan or kinship groups can all form the basis of identity and mobilization.
- States are weakly differentiated from surrounding social and power systems so social policy cannot act as an independent countervailing force and reinforces privilege, private short-term gain, exclusion or domination.
- Welfare pluralism is the main mode for welfare where besides the state, the informal actors such as family and community play a dominant role in meeting social needs. With large rural economies, the family plays an extensive role in providing security, housing, shaping livelihood strategies and funding private education and health in this regime.

However, throughout this region, a slow decline is predicted in family's ability to continue performing these functions due to demographic changes, challenges from women's changing roles and expectations and inherent limits in its ability to ensure acceptable levels of security (Gough, 2004). Moreover, the informal security regimes lead to several barriers in service delivery systems in Asia as discussed below.

Non-Availability of Services

The 2007 report by the UNESCAP, UNDP and ADB discusses the following problems with availability and quality of services in the Asia-Pacific region. Availability of basic services differs widely within a country, and affects different groups in a multitude of ways. Overall, those in rural areas tend to face more limited availability and lower quality of services than other poor people. Particularly in remote areas such as economically underdeveloped landlocked regions, upland areas away from major roads and urban centres, and small islands, primary education and health care, clean drinking water and reliable sanitation are often unavailable or only available at a considerable distance. Planning the geographical distribution of facilities is a matter of economic efficiency. Limited resources compel the government to set priorities, taking into account the range (i.e. the maximum distance people are prepared to travel for the service) and the threshold (the minimum number of users for a viable centre). Moreover, the presence of a facility in a location does not mean that a service is actually provided. Reports of empty schools and abandoned clinics are numerous. Construction may require a substantial one-time investment, but funding for operation and maintenance of services is often more problematic, especially if users contribute little or nothing.

Financial Barriers

Hidden and Opportunity Costs

The poor in developing countries may simply not be able to afford the services. Even when ostensibly free at the point of use (like many education, health and welfare services), there is a hidden cost, for example, of transport to the service, time lost from work, costs of childcare, and costs of prescribed medicines (UNESCAP, 2002). They face high opportunity costs such as time spent in going to and waiting for free medical treatment, going to a distant well, spring or river, waiting in line at a public water tap or simply going to school can be considerable for a poor family (UNESCAP, UNDP and ADB, 2007).

Corruption

Because these services are expensive and demand tends to exceed supply if it is provided free of charge, the service provider may ration access by asking for additional payments. Teachers, often poorly paid, may ask parents for payments before admitting a child, and nurses or doctors may insist on payment before treating a patient. These payments, essentially bribes, create access barriers for the poor to free services. Corruption in the form of diverting money allocated for the purchase of teaching equipment, demanding bribes from parents for school admission and better exam results and selling school material that should be distributed free, can have a particularly severe impact. The poor cannot pay the bribes, thus, corruption denies them their right to equal access to education, and consequently to one of the most powerful mechanisms to escape poverty (UNESCAP, UNDP and ADP, 2007).

Socio-Cultural Barriers

When services in principle are available to all, certain groups typically get inferior treatment, or are excluded altogether: Women, ethnic minorities, people living with HIV/AIDS, people with disabilities, socially unaccepted or illegal groups and others. The reason is that planning of these systems is based on a set of assumptions that apply to the average rural male. Gender discrimination remains a major barrier to accessing services that is still prevalent throughout the region and affects most people. Men tend to enjoy greater access than women to essential education and health services, water and sanitation. Access barriers to health and education for women and girls are major obstacles to poverty reduction. Many users of health services are women, but decision makers tend to be men who are often also urban-based. Beliefs, norms and practices concerning appropriate behaviour in matters related to reproductive health may stop a woman from seeking health care. The availability of female staff can make a crucial difference to a woman's access to health care, if she is reluctant to be examined by a male physician (UNESCAP, UNDP and ADB, 2007).

Ethnic minorities, people living with HIV/AIDS and people with disabilities are often also subjected to systematic stigmatization, discrimination and marginalization and this has a significant impact on their health and education. People with disabilities have the same or greater needs for health and educational services as other people, but they face more challenges in securing access due to physical and social barriers, despite improvements in disability legislation. Women with disabilities are often the most marginalized, as they have multiple disadvantages through their gender and disability (UNESCAP, UNDP and ADB, 2007).

Other Barriers

Poor Quality

Given the need to use limited resources efficiently, it is difficult to increase access to services and simultaneously improve the quality of the service. If the public sector cannot, or does not want to, provide a service to the poor, the private (informal) sector may step in. Many urban poor buy water from informal water vendors and pay rates many times higher than other income groups pay for municipal water. The poor may turn to traditional healers who treat them immediately and charge them less, but do not solve their problem. As a result, the poor may have to seek further treatment incurring additional costs (UNESCAP, UNDP and ADB, 2007).

Problems with Training and Motivation of Staff

The staff needs to be trained and motivated, but many teachers and nurses in rural areas come from the city or have been trained there. They may have problems understanding and communicating with the local population and may lack the motivation to provide adequate services, due to difficult working conditions and low salaries (UNESCAP, UNDP and ADB, 2007).

Administrative Formality

The use of social services often requires a certain amount of administrative formality. For instance, users may need some form of identification, insurance numbers, identity cards, or registration with a specific facility. This inevitably entails paperwork and can disadvantage some groups of people, especially illiterate persons, some very old people or those with mental or psychological problems who do not live with caring relatives (UNESCAP, 2002).

Legal Barriers

Non-availability of legal documents often becomes a barrier to access to services. Governments can review the regulations on service provision to identify those elements – whether laws, regulations, standards or procedures – that tend to exclude the poor (UNESCAP, UNDP and ADB, 2005).

Emergency Situations

During wars or civil conflicts and natural disasters, social service delivery systems are often disrupted or even abandoned in the case of some war zones, or the civil aid functions usurp the wider welfare aspects following natural disasters (UNESCAP, 2002).

Policy Approach to Human Rights

Importance of the Human Rights Policy Approach

Human rights bring principles of accountability and social justice to the process of human development (United Nations Development Programme, 2000). The existence of international human rights conventions means that development policy is no longer simply a matter of charity, or morality, or social preference, or economic or social benefit, as it is legally enforceable (Munro, 2009). According to Jolly, Emmerji, Ghai and Lapeyre (2004, cited in Munro, 2009), human rights have universal international legitimacy as an organizing framework; states have legal obligations to respect, protect and help fulfill rights; rights are universal, so their use draws attention to the most marginalized groups whose rights are least respected; human rights, having legal force, bring with them the possibility of legal redress; and the realization of rights is not just of mere instrumental value for the fulfillment of other objectives, rights are end in themselves. The transformative approach to social protection based on activist ideology recommends universal social protection as a minimum level of income or consumption granted as a right by the state to all citizens and residents of a country, requiring the state to assume key responsibilities (United Nations Research Institute for Social Development, 2010).

According to the UNRISD Report (2010), lessons from successful democracies suggest that effective strategies to combat poverty require that:

- Rights are institutionalized to allow citizens to organize and contest public policies as autonomous actors.
- Political parties are embedded within broad social coalitions that include the active participation of the poor, women and other disadvantaged groups.
- Bargaining regimes or social pacts are constructed that give groups voice and influence in holding corporations and states to account and in shaping development policies and outcomes.
- The democratic regime is sufficiently competitive to create uncertainties in electoral outcomes, allow for periodic changes in power and prevent ruling parties from becoming complacent.

Asian State Human Rights Approach against Western Interference

Colonized populations achieved national independence as socially-embedded members of kinship, community, lineage and clan rather than as rights-bearing citizens (Kabeer, 2004). In spite of the growing importance of human rights issues in world politics, Asian states prefer to deal with human rights within their own domestic jurisdiction, resisting international monitoring. They are reluctant to sign major instruments of international human rights protection. Countries such as China, Indonesia, Malaysia, Singapore and Thailand are not signatories to the International Covenant on Civil and Political Rights and the International Covenant on Economic, Social and Cultural Rights. If many Asian states have resisted committing themselves to international human rights regimes they have displayed even less interest in the establishment of a regional human rights system (Tang, 1997).

According to Tang (1997), human rights were usually accorded low priority by Asian states, which devoted their energy to efforts in developing their economies, and creating national identities. Culturally, they assert that the Western approach ignores the specific cultural traditions and historical circumstances of Asian societies, whose interpretations of human rights are different from the Western tradition. Economically, they maintain that the priority of developing Asian societies has to be the eradication of poverty: the right to survival must come first. Therefore, political stability under the capable leadership of good government is essential. They also question the motives of the Western countries by accusing them of having double standards and using human rights merely as an instrument for advancing Western economic or security interests (Tang, 1997).

Tang (1997) noted that the Asian regional preparatory meeting for the World Conference on Human Rights in 1993, which took place in Bangkok, provided an opportunity for Asian governments to put forward their definition of human rights on the global agenda. The Bangkok Declaration (World Conference on Human Rights, 1993: 5), signed by over 40 Asian governments, did not reject universal human rights. However, the Declaration suggested that universality should be considered 'in the context of a dynamic and evolving process of international norm-setting, bearing in mind the significance of national and regional particularities and various historical, cultural and religious backgrounds'. The Asian states also sought to link development issues with human rights questions and emphasize the importance of non-interference. The division between Asian and Western governments at the World Conference was clear: Western governments criticized the human rights conditions in the Asian region and maintained that universal standards in human rights should be observed; East Asian states accused the West of using human rights to interfere with the domestic affairs of other countries, and ignoring the different economic, social and cultural conditions in the developing world (Tang, 1997).

Asian Human Rights Non-Government Organizations

If there is an absence of governmental support for establishing region-wide human rights protection systems in Asia, the same definitely cannot be said of the non-governmental groups in Asia. Since the 1970s, Asian NGOs have been more and more active in promoting human rights protection in the region. Most of today's Asian NGOs are national organizations, but some are organizations with wider, regional concerns. These NGOs include the Law Association for Asia and the Pacific (Lawasia), the Asian Coalition of Human Rights Organizations, the ASEAN-based Regional Council on Human Rights in Asia, the Asian Human Rights Commission and the Asian Legal Resource Centre. These are not the only human rights NGOs with a regional focus. The Asian Centre for the Progress of Peoples and the Asian Regional Exchange for New Alternatives, for example, have been actively involved with human rights promotion in the region. The considerable number of regional organizations which attended the Bangkok NGO conference in 1993 is also indicative of the interest in human rights issues at the regional level. Many of these groups, however, may have different agendas, and a sub-regional focus. The Asia Pacific Forum on Women, Law and Development and the Asian Students Association have a specific focus. In terms of resources and activities they may also have significant differences, but they have all been involved in the promotion of human rights with a regional focus (Tang, 1997).

Asian Human Rights Charter

In 1998, the Asian Human Rights Commission, with support of several NGOs, created the Asian Human Rights Charter Draft. The Charter embodies universally applicable rights that arise from an 'Asian' perspective and incorporates many of the rights supported by most Asian states under various other treaties. By defining specific rights and outlining enforcement mechanisms that can be used to protect these rights, the Charter creates a strong foundation for a human rights structure. The Preamble of the Charter (p. 3) states that 'For long, especially during the colonial period, the peoples of Asia suffered from gross violations of their rights and freedoms .... Increasingly the people realize that peace and dignity are possible only when the equal and inalienable rights of all persons and groups are recognized and protected. They are determined to secure peace and justice for themselves and the coming generations through the struggle for human rights and freedoms. Towards that end they adopt this Charter as an affirmation of the desire and aspirations of the peoples of Asia to live in peace and dignity.'

Following are some extracts from the Background of the Charter:

1.1 The Asian struggle for rights and freedoms has deep historical roots, in the fight ... for the establishment or restoration of democracy .... Asia is passing through a period of rapid change, which affects social structures, political institutions and the economy...

1.3 Asian development is full of contradictions. There is massive and deepening poverty in the midst of growing affluence of some sections of the people .... At the same time valuable resources are wasted on armaments, Asia being the largest purchaser of arms of all regions. Our governments claim to be pursuing development directed at increasing levels of production and welfare but our natural resources are being depleted most irresponsibly...

1.6 In contrast to the official disregard or contempt of human rights in many Asian states, there is increasing awareness among their peoples of the importance of rights and freedoms .... They believe that political and economic systems have to operate within a framework of human rights and freedoms to ensure economic justice, political participation and accountability, and social peace. There are many social movements that have taken up the fight to secure for the people their rights and freedoms.

Thus, the Charter seems to be based in the ideology of post-colonialism and confronts the state for their anti-human rights stand and the contradictions of inequalities created by the Asian development.

Diversity in Social Policy Approaches in Asian Sub-Regions

Social Policy Approaches in East and South East Asia

Confucian Familism

Within these overall economic strategies, social protection for vulnerable people in society was left to families (Kwon, 2004). According to Jones (1990, 1993, cited by Croissant, 2004), low levels of government investment in social policy, underdeveloped formal systems of social security and the fundamental importance of the family and community-based social safety nets are explained as the consequences of a culturally bounded view of state and society, based on the continuous relevance of Confucian social ethics in these countries. Culture, thus, provides the foundations for a model of the family-based 'Confucian Welfare State'. The notion of Confucian familism, involving a strong reliance on the family as the site of social welfare and service delivery is often considered a core feature of East Asian welfare states. Social arrangements are based on the assumption of the family as the main provider of care. The traditional image of the family is of a unit composed of three generations where household work, including homemaking and care-giving, is produced by 'housewives' (Goodman and Peng, 1996, cited by Cook and Kwon, 2007). Women were doubly burdened in the export-oriented industrialization in both Korea and Taiwan, since they were the main providers of cheap labour for industry as well as of welfare for their families (Kwon, 2004). Cook and Kwon (2007) note that despite the rapid changes across East Asia in family structure, and the demise of the 'ideal-typical' family, the welfare state still falls short in providing alternative care needs, and the underlying assumption of family care responsibility remains.

Productivist Welfare Regimes

According to Gough (2004), all the countries in East and South East Asia (except for Philippines), identified as developmental states, can be described as productivist welfare regimes. He described the following characteristics of these regimes:

1. Social policy is not an autonomous agent in society; rather it is subordinated to economic policy and the pursuit of economic growth.
2. Social policy is concentrated on social investment, notably in education and basic health rather than social protection.
3. Social policy has largely been driven by the imperatives of nation-building and regime legitimation.
4. The state is mainly confined to regulation rather than provision and plays only a contributory role to the broader welfare mix, which is sustained by strong families and household strategies, high savings and marketized provision.

According to Goodman and White (1998, cited by Kwon, 2004), in East Asia, the state developmental strategy discouraged dependence on the state, promoted private source of welfare, and diverted the financial resources of social insurance to investment in infrastructure. Kwon (2004) calls it developmental welfare state. He notes that in East Asia the state provided social insurance programmes for industrial workers, in which people were required to pay contributions prior to entitlement to social benefits. As a result, only selected groups of people had access to social protection, while leaving the vulnerable section of the population outside the system. To avoid a demand for universal entitlement, the state did not provide funding for the welfare programmes, but enforced the rules, formal and informal, which regulated the payment of contributions for social benefits by companies and their employees. The social insurance programmes were operated by quasi-governmental agencies. Since social policy programmes in East Asia covered mainly industrial workers, it tended to reinforce socio-economic inequalities. Some social insurance programmes, such as unemployment insurance, were never on the agenda since they were perceived as discouraging the work ethic and encouraging dependency on the state.

Lee and Ku (2007) empirically test the thesis of developmental welfare states in order to see whether East Asian welfare regimes, Japan, Korea and Taiwan, are distinctive from Esping-Andersen's three welfare state regimes. They introduce 15 variables developed for factor and cluster analyses of 20 countries. The variables include governmental social expenditure, social investment, non-coverage of pensions, gender discrimination, family support, and contribution from employers. As a result, they conclude that Korea and Taiwan establish a unique fourth model, different from Esping-Andersen's three worlds, though they share features of liberal (low-coverage) and conservative regimes (welfare stratification). By contrast, Japan contains various characteristics of different regimes, but can be located between developmental regimes and Esping-Andersen's conservative regimes.

Implications of the Asian Financial Crisis

The Asian Financial Crisis of 1997–1998 exposed the weaknesses of the productivist welfare regime approach for people's welfare. For example, during the economic crisis in South Korea, one of the hardest-hit countries, it was very clear that the welfare state could not cope with the sudden rise in unemployment, because it had been based on the assumption of full employment and, therefore, minimal support for the unemployed. While the economy grew fast, the number of the unemployed was small, and those who were unemployed relied on their families or on their savings as a safety net. During the economic crisis, the welfare state that had focused on workers employed in the formal sectors did not help those who lost their jobs. As in Taiwan and Singapore, the public assistance programmes, which were based on a very low level of means-tested criteria, were not available to them in times of need (Kwon, 2004).

Croissant (2004) notes that East and South East Asian countries can be divided into two groups with reference to their social policy response to the Asian Financial Crisis.

1. Democratic progress in the East Asian countries of South Korea and Taiwan and, to some degree, Thailand, was already creating pressures for greater attention to social policy, and the economic crisis accelerated these trends. The transition to democracy in the late 1980s or early 1990s had created a new political environment and raised the political costs for neglecting public demands for greater government social spending. In these three countries, all major parties discovered social policy as an important issue for mobilizing electoral support. The governments in all three countries passed legislation to strengthen their social security systems.
2. The governments of the South East Asian countries namely, Singapore, Malaysia, Indonesia and the Philippines believed that the restoration of economic growth and traditional values of self-reliance and mutual support were the best way to solve the social crisis. They sought to strengthen established patterns of welfare residualism, and relied on familialism, communitarianism and traditional norms of subsidiarity and mutual support.

Suwannarat (2003) noted that the Thai Constitution incorporated rights to a number of social services and decentralization in its constitution in 1997. However, the status and implications of constitutional guarantees of access to free basic education and health services remain contested and political conservatives fear decentralization as a threat to Thai unity.

Outcome

According to Gough (2003), in terms of welfare outcomes, East and South East Asia achieved high scores in public health, education and poverty reduction. However, persistent gaps and inequalities remain in areas such as morbidity, school dropout rates, working conditions, and patterns of exclusion from society of specific social groups. According to the social protection study by Wood (2009), Japan and

Korea, by virtue of their status as developed high income countries have achieved the highest values on most of the social protection summary indicators. Thus, addition of the social security element in the productivist social policy approach in East Asia seems to have contributed to highest level of human development in the sub-region.

Social Policy Approaches in Transition Countries

Cook, Kabeer and Suwannarat (2003) noted in their study of social protection in Asia that the two communist countries of China and Vietnam are dismantling the socialist system that guaranteed security. They are going through a shift from universal access for health and education to an effectively privatized fee-for-service system where most social relief is ad hoc and uncertain.

China

China's formal system of welfare provision, that was developed since the 1950s, was an integral part of the economic policy and planning, rather than a separate residual sector. It comprised an egalitarian system of income distribution, collective organization of production and distribution, combined with an institutional system of relief which acted as a guarantee of minimal economic and social needs for much of the population. This approach to some extent underpinned the country's success in providing a basic level of welfare to its population. However, China used a differential approach to the rural and the urban population, with the former having less generous programmes (Cook, 2003).

After China began to open up, this mode became increasingly problematic and was unable to keep up with market-oriented reforms. In the 1990s, China began to reform the public service sector by introducing a multiple-contribution mechanism. Over time, the actual execution of this mechanism involved a low ratio of government contributions, while the ratio of personal contribution has risen year after year. For example, individuals have assumed the main responsibility for paying for medical care and education. At times, the rising prices of public services, especially for education and health care, outpaced the income growth of urban and rural residents, making the reform of public services an issue for attention among people from all walks of life (UNDP China and the China Institute for Reform and Development, 2008).

Central Asia and Mongolia

According to the study by Wood (2009), the Central Asian countries and Mongolia have generally high levels of social protection resulting from the comprehensive social protection systems introduced in these countries during the Soviet era. However, this is inadequate and changing as employment rate is falling and cost of living is rising. Muller (2003) notes that in Soviet times, the subsidized or free supply of the most important everyday goods and services (primarily foodstuffs, rents and electricity) in Central Asia had largely replaced social assistance to specific target groups. In the 1990s, on the other hand, the cost of living rose sharply. In view of the shortage of financial resources social assistance payments are currently restricted to a relatively small group of beneficiaries. Targetting is a basic challenge in this context. Income testing in Central Asia is difficult because of the variety and lack of transparency of the types and sources of income.

According to Muller (2003), the old-age security schemes that exist in Central Asia are a further source of monetary transfers within the usually multigenerational households of Central Asia. He observed that retirement pensions currently make a far larger contribution to household incomes than social assistance payments. In the course of the 1990s, however, the purchasing power of pensions fell sharply. The greatest challenge for the contribution-funded systems in the Central Asian context is the steady fall in employment in the formal sector, which will result in a sharp rise in system dependency rates and the erosion of what has hitherto been an almost universal entitlement. The United Nations Development Programme and Regional Bureau of Europe and the Commonwealth of Independent States (2011) notes that the unfinished social policy reforms represent a critical gap in social inclusion tools.

Social Policy Approaches in South Asia

According to a review of social protection in South Asia by Kohler, Cali and Stirbu (2009), all countries in this sub-region have established some components of social protection, but social protection is not yet a broadly-based notion in the sense of an entitlement that people claim as citizens. No government in the region has as yet established a full-fledged, comprehensive and interlinked social protection system per se.

Contributory Social Security

Formal, contributory social security is available in all eight countries for government civil service, staff in public sector enterprises and large-scale private enterprises when applicable. This is in the form of a guaranteed pension, and other coverage such as health coverage for this group. Such formal social security, however, excludes the vast majority of people in South Asia, who are not connected to government or formal employment. Therefore, in most instances, households and individuals in South Asia primarily rely on informal social protection networks of family, community, women's groups, or savings cooperatives such as rotating chit funds and informal credit markets (Kohler, Cali and Stirbu, 2009).

Social Assistance

Kabeer (2009) noted that in South Asia, unconditional transfers tend to be confined to those who are perceived to be unable to fend for themselves: elderly, disabled and destitute. The idea of social security as a right has very shallow roots across much of the sub-continent. According to Kohler, Cali and Stirbu (2009), many social transfers are long-term, established programmes; others are ad hoc responses to immediate needs and demands, of which some reflect political opportunism as opposed to a strategic approach to providing social protection as a right. Some schemes are localized, while others are national in outreach. In terms of design, some social protection programmes are subject to means tests or proxy means tests; others use geographical or categorical targetting. Among the categorical targetting programmes, some are universal for an age group or gender, such as the old-age pensions in Bangladesh, India, Maldives and Nepal or the girls' secondary school stipends in Bangladesh. Most are conditional on action by the recipient, usually related to working, to school enrolment, or to utilizing a health-care facility. There are also a number of ad hoc or programme-based emergency transfers to cope with conflict and natural disasters, and even housing loans (Kohler, Cali and Stirbu, 2009).

Employment Generation

In South Asia, there has been far less emphasis on unconditional transfers and much greater emphasis on employment generation (Kabeer, 2009). According to Kohler, Cali and Stirbu (2009), six of the eight countries have some form of employment generating public works programmes providing either cash or food in return for work. These have traditionally been offered as a last resort to those stricken by absolute poverty (often seasonally reinforced), and have been a widespread policy tool in India, Bangladesh, Nepal and Pakistan. In India, the Integrated Rural Development Programme is probably the world's largest rural credit programme that provides a package of assistance including a subsidized bank loan that enables households below the poverty line to acquire productive assets which will allow viable self-employment. Similarly, the self-employment programme for the urban poor provides assistance to the urban households. Other employment-generating programmes in India are Jawahar Rozgar Yojana that encourages microenterprises and the National Rural Employment Programme that is the first large scale rural wage employment programme in India (Kabeer, 2003).

Microfinance Interventions

The idea of microfinance started in Bangladesh around 1976 with Muhammad Yunus, who was awarded the Nobel Peace Prize in 2006 for his work with the Grameen Bank. The microfinance sector emerged in response to the failure of formal providers of financial services to reach the poor and to the limitations of the informal alternatives that the poor use for life cycle expenditures and to deal with emergencies. Personal savings can be stolen from slum dwellings or village huts, informal money-lenders charge excessive interest rates and informal cooperatives provide little protection in times of generalized scarcity (Kabeer, 2008). The Grameen Bank, Bangladesh Rural Advancement Committee (BRAC) and other microfinance NGOs together disburse more than the public sector financial institutions in Bangladesh (Kabeer, 2003).

Limitations

Cook, Kabeer and Suwannarat (2003) noted in their study that India and Bangladesh in South Asia remain characterized largely by chronic poverty and limited formal social protection measures. Kohler, Cali and Stirbu (2009) identified the following shortcomings in social protection interventions across South Asia:

- Many programmes remain piecemeal and ad hoc. The various causes and manifestations of socioeconomic insecurity are not addressed, and programmes often overlap.

- Many initiatives are inspired by political opportunities, or are donor-driven. This creates an ad hoc, disparate set of programmes that do not cohere.
- There is a lack of objective, transparent and coherent criteria to establish and communicate eligibility and targetting for the individual social protection schemes. Many of the programmes reviewed lack equity considerations in targeting.
- Because of their unsystematic nature, the fiscal sustainability of individual programmes is at risk. This is especially the case in smaller, more aid-dependent countries, where donors have substantial influence.
- Government agencies appear to have devoted limited resources and built insufficient capacity for social protection policy analysis, delivery monitoring, or impact evaluation.
- There is great variation within individual countries.

Implications for Social Policy Approach in Asia

Table 7.1 shows the importance of social policy for social development in the Asian sub-regions.

Table 7.1
Diversity in Social Policy Approaches and Social Development in Asian Sub-Regions

Social Policy Approach	Characteristics		Level of Human Development	Limitations
Social Policy Approaches in East and South East Asia	Social policy subordinate to economic policy, focusing only on health and education Confucian familism	After the Asian financial crisis some countries in East Asia strengthened their social protection policy besides focus on health and education	High level of social development	
		Some countries in South East Asia continue to focus only on health and education	Diverse levels of social development	Rapid changes in the family structure

Cont'd...

...*Cont'd*

Social Policy Approaches in Transition Countries	Dismantling of the socialist system of comprehensive social protection	Shift toward privatized fee-for-service system	High and medium levels of social development	Most social relief is ad hoc and uncertain rising cost of living
Social Policy Approaches in South Asia	Continues formal, contributory social security of colonial times	Emphasis on employment generation	Medium and low levels of social development	Ad hoc, disparate set of programmes for those in the informal sector

According to Wood (2009), there is a clear positive association between the SPI and both the HDI and the GDP. Countries with high human development levels have average SPI values that are 2.3 to 6.3 times those of low human development countries. This disparity indicates that low development countries provide little in the way of substantive social protection to their poor populations even where coverage is quite high. This general relationship is as one would expect: higher levels of development are associated with increased social protection activities, as firstly higher GDP enables greater expenditure on social protection; and secondly better education and health indicators permit governments to devote more attention to social protection issues. Yet in both cases, there is substantial variation in SPIs for countries with similar HDI or GDP per capita values. Furthermore, the pro-poor targetting of this assistance is uncorrelated with both the HDI and GDP per capita. What this means is that, if governments are willing, virtually every country has scope for providing some level of social protection to its vulnerable populations (Wood, 2009).

Universal social protection as a human right is thus far from reality in Asia. The Concept Note of the World Bank's (2005) Social Policy Flagship Conference argued that the social policy approach borrowed from OECD countries assumes state capacity, legitimacy of public institutions, and clearly established citizenship rights and obligations that do not exist in many parts of the developing world. The social development approach is more important in developing countries than the welfare approach. Findings of the UNRISD (2007) research on social policy in a development context challenged the residual role given to social policy in public policies concerned with stabilizing the economies of developing countries and pushing them onto a growth path. The report of a workshop organized by the UNRISD in 2007 noted that social policy is not something to be engaged in only after reaching a certain development threshold, nor is it an exclusive domain of advanced welfare states; rather, it is a key instrument for development, including social development. Social policy must be designed not only residually, to cater to social casualties, but also integrated as a central component of policies, to ensure the wherewithal for their sustainability.

Note

Part of this chapter is a modified version of my article published as 'Social Policy Approaches, Human Rights and Social Development in Asia', for the Special Issue of *Social Development Issues* on 'Social Development, Democracy and Human Rights', in 2013.

References

Asian Human Rights Commission and Asian Legal Resource Centre. (1998). Asian Human Rights Charter, Kwangju. Retrieved 11 September 2011 from http://www.kekidatabank.be/docs/Instrumenten/Regional_organisations/1998%20Asian%20HR%20Charter.pdf

Bevan, P. (2004). Conceptualising in/security regimes. In I. Gough and G. Wood (eds), *Insecurity and Welfare Regimes in Asia, Africa and Latin America* (pp. 88–118). Cambridge: Cambridge University Press.

Cook, S. (2003). After the Iron Rice Bowl: Extending the safety net in China. In S. Cook, N. Kabeer and G. Suwannarat (eds), *Social Protection in Asia* (pp. 57–128). New Delhi: Har-Anand Publications.

Cook, S. and Kabeer, N. (2009). Socio-economic security over the life course: A global review of social protection, prepared as the final report of a social protection scoping study funded by the Ford Foundation. Institute of Development Studies. Retrieved 12 May 2010 from http://www.ids.ac.uk/go/idspublication/a-global-review-of-social-protection

Cook, S., Kabeer, N. and Suwannarat, G. (2003). Introduction. In S. Cook, N. Kabeer and G. Suwannarat (eds), *Social Protection in Asia* (pp. 13–56). New Delhi: Har-Anand Publications.

Cook, S. and Kwon, H. (2007). Economic reform and social protection in East Asia, paper presented at the RC19 Annual Conference at Florence University. Retrieved 15 May 2009 from https://docs.google.com/viewer?url=http://www.unifi.it/confsp/papers/pdf/Kwon_Coo k.doc &pli=1

Croissant, A. (2004). Changing welfare regimes in East and Southeast Asia: Crisis, change and challenge. *Social Policy and Administration*, 38(5), 504–524.

Devereux, S. and Sabates-Wheeler, R. (2006). Transformative social protection. *IDS in Focus*. Retrieved 12 May 2010 from http://www.ids.ac.uk/go/ idspublication/transformative-social-protection

Gough, I. (2003). Welfare regimes in East Asia and Europe compared. In K. Marshall and O. Butzbach (eds), *New Social Policy Agenda for Europe and Asia: Challenges, Experience and Lessons* (pp. 27–44). Washington, DC: World Bank.

——. (2004). Welfare regimes in development contexts: A global and regional analysis. In I. Gough and G. Wood (eds), *Insecurity and Welfare Regimes in Asia, Africa and Latin America* (pp. 15–48). Cambridge, England: Cambridge University Press.

Kabeer, N. (2003). Safety nets and safety ropes: Addressing vulnerability and enhancing productivity in South Asia. In S. Cook, N. Kabeer and G. Suwannarat (eds), *Social Protection in Asia* (pp. 129–199). New Delhi: Har-Anand Publications.

——. (2004). *Imagining 'The Social': Social Policy Analysis for the Poor in Poor Countries*. Brighton, Sussex: Institute of Development Studies.

——. (2008). *Mainstreaming Gender in Social Protection for the Informal Economy*. London: Commonwealth Secretariat.

——. (2009). A review of social protection in South Asia. SPA Working Papers. Retrieved 16 March 2011 from http://www.socialprotection asia.org/pdf/Naila-Kabeer_draft-May09.pdf

Kennett, P. (2001). *Comparative Social Policy: Theory and Research*. Philadelphia: Open University Press.

Kohler, G., Cali, M. and Stirbu, M. (2009). Social protection in South Asia: A review. UNICEF. Retrieved 16 March 2011 from http://www.unicef.org/socialpolicy/files/social_protection_in_south_asia_-_a_review_-_unicef_rosa_2009.pdf

Kwon, H. (2004). *Transforming the Developmental Welfare States in East Asia*. Geneva: United Nations Research Institute for Social Development.

Lee, Y. and Ku, Y. (2007). East Asian welfare regimes: Testing the hypothesis of the developmental welfare state. *Social Policy and Administration*, 41(2), 197–212.

Muller, K. (2003). *Poverty and Social Policy in the Central Asian Transition Countries*. Bonn: German Development Institute.

Munro, L.T. (2009). The 'human rights-based approach to programming': A contradiction in terms? In D. Mitlin and S. Hickey (eds), *Rights-based Approach to Development: Exploring the Potential and Pitfalls* (pp. 187–208). Sterling, VA: Kumarian Press.

Suwannarat, G. (2003). Southeast Asia: Learning from crisis. In S. Cook, N. Kabeer and G. Suwannarat (eds), *Social Protection in Asia* (pp. 200–260). New Delhi: Har-Anand Publications.

Tang, J.T.H. (1997). A clash of values? Human rights in the post-cold war world. Proceedings of a Conference organized by the Shizuoka Prefectural Government and the organizing committee of the Asia-Pacific Forum in Hamamatsu, Shizuoka, Japan. Retrieved 2 March 2010 from http://archive.unu.edu/unupress/asian-values.html#CLASH

United Nations Development Programme. (2000). *Human Development Report: Human Rights and Human Development.* New York: Oxford University Press.

United Nations Development Programme China and the China Institute for Reform and Development. (2008). *Human Development Report China 2007/08: Access for All.* Retrieved 1 November 2010 from http://hdr.undp.org/en/reports/national/asiathepacific/china/China_2008_en.pdf

United Nations Development Programme and Regional Bureau for Europe and the Commonwealth of Independent States. (2011). *Beyond Transition: Towards Inclusive Societies: Regional Human Development Report.* Bratislava.

United Nations Economic and Social Commission for Asia and the Pacific. (2002). *Access to Social Services by the Poor and Disadvantaged in Asia and the Pacific: Major Trends and Issues.* New York.

United Nations Economic and Social Commission for Asia and the Pacific, United Nations Development Programme and Asian Development Bank. (2005). *A Future within Reach.* Retrieved 1 May 2007 from http://www.unescap.org/publications/detail.asp?id=1153

——. (2007). *Access to Basic Services for the Poor: The Importance of Good Governance.* Retrieved 7 August 2012 from http://www.unescap.org/pdd/publications/MDG-access2basic-service/MDG-access-to-basic-services.pdf

United Nations Research Institute for Social Development. (2007). *Conference News: Poverty Reduction and Policy Regimes: Report of the UNRISD Workshop in Geneva.* Geneva. Retrieved 7 May 2010 from http://www.unrisd.org/80256B3C005BCCF9/httpNetITFramePDF?ReadForm&parentunid=77F86E2ED70080E7C1257336003E1378&parentdoctype=newsletter&netitpath=80256B3C005BCCF9/(httpAuxPages)/77F86E2ED70080E7C1257336003E1378/$file/ConfNews17.pdf

——. (2010). *Combating Poverty and Inequality: Structural Change, Social Policy and Politics.* Geneva. Retrieved 17 May 2011 from http://www.unrisd.org/publications/cpi

Wood, G. (2004). Informal security regimes: The strengths of relationships. In I. Gough and G. Wood (eds), *Insecurity and Welfare Regimes in Asia, Africa and Latin America* (pp. 49–87). Cambridge: Cambridge University Press.

Wood, J. (2009). A social protection index for Asia. Retrieved 16 March 2011 from https://www.appam.org/conferences/international/singapore 2009/sessions/downloads/2 301.pdf

World Bank. (2005). Concept note: New frontiers of social policy. Retrieved 5 August 2010 from http://www.egnghana.org/publications/sd/ Concept Note-new frontiers of social policy.pdf

World Conference on Human Rights. (1993). Report of the Regional Meeting for Asia. Bangkok. Retrieved 5 October 2012 from http://graduate institute.ch/faculty/clapham/hrdoc/docs/bangkokdeclaration.pdf

Part 2

Diversity in Social Development Progress in Asia and Implications

Chapter 8

Diversity in Progress in Poverty Eradication and Food Security in Asia

Introduction

Asia is economically the fastest developing region in the world at present. East Asia and some countries in South East Asia have made phenomenal economic progress. Due to India and China's fast economic growth, they now exercise considerable geopolitical and economic power at the global level. However, Asia is diverse as the World Bank classification for economic development in the sub-regions ranges from mainly high income in East Asia, to mainly upper middle income in North and Central Asia, to mainly lower middle income in South East and South Asia to low income in some countries. South Asia lags behind the rest of the sub-regions in Asia with four least developed countries. The contradiction lies in the fact that inequality in income or poverty is prevalent throughout Asia, and cuts across the levels of economic development.

This chapter on diversity in progress in poverty eradication and food security in Asia reviews the following:

1. Concepts and causes of poverty in Asia with reference to the social exclusion profile, fast economic development, environmental degradation and weak social policy.
2. Progress in reduction of poverty in Asia with reference to Human Poverty Index and reduction of poverty as an MDG and

diversity in Asian sub-regions and implications for policy for poverty eradication.

3. Concepts and causes of food insecurity with reference to poverty, barriers in agriculture, market-based food insecurity, speculation and price rise and problems with quality of food in Asia.
4. Progress in reduction of food insecurity as an MDG in Asia with reference to underweight children under-five, malnourishment and Global Hunger Index and diversity in Asian sub-regions and implications for policy for food security.

Progress in Reduction of Poverty in Asia

Concepts of Poverty

Definitions of poverty deployed in the late 19th and early 20th centuries were supposedly 'absolute' in the sense that poverty was said to be understood as lacking sufficient money to meet basic physical needs. At its most basic, absolute poverty is defined in terms of survival or subsistence, linked to a basic standard of physical capacity necessary for production (paid work) and reproduction (the bearing and nurturing of children). Nutrition is central to such definitions (Lister, 2004). Townsend (1979, cited by Lister, 2004) criticized this subsistence notion of needs, as divorced from their social context, upon which absolute definitions of poverty were based. According to his relative definition of poverty, individuals, families and groups in the population can be said to be in poverty when they lack the resources to obtain the types of diet, participate in the activities and have the living conditions and amenities which are customary, or are at least widely encouraged or approved, in the societies to which they belong. Their resources are so seriously below those commanded by the average individual or family that they are, in effect, excluded from ordinary living patterns and activities. Relative poverty places poverty in the context of inequality within societies, between those on lower and higher incomes, women and men, and minority and majority ethnic groups (Lister, 2004).

Amartya Sen (1999: 20–21) sees poverty as a deprivation of basic capabilities, rather than merely low income. This is reflected in premature mortality, significant undernourishment, persistent morbidity, widespread illiteracy and other failures. Similarly, unemployment is not merely a deficiency of income that can be made up through transfers by the state. It is also a source of far-reaching debilitating effects on individual freedom, initiative and skills. Among its manifold effects, unemployment contributes to social exclusion of some groups, and it leads to losses of self-reliance, self-confidence and psychological and physical health. Thus, Sen's perspective concentrates on deprivations that are intrinsically important unlike low income which is only instrumentally important.

According to Chapter 2 of the UN World Summit for Social Development Programme of Action (1995), 'Poverty has various manifestations, including lack of income and productive resources sufficient to ensure sustainable livelihoods; hunger and malnutrition; ill health; limited or lack of access to education and other basic services; increased morbidity and mortality from illness; homelessness and inadequate housing; unsafe environments; and social discrimination and exclusion. It is also characterized by a lack of participation in decision-making and in civil, social and cultural life.' The document notes that poverty occurs in all countries: as mass poverty in many developing countries, pockets of poverty amid wealth in developed countries, loss of livelihoods as a result of economic recession, sudden poverty as a result of disaster or conflict, the poverty of low-wage workers, and the utter destitution of people who fall outside family support systems, social institutions and safety nets.

Causes of Poverty

Social Exclusion and Poverty

Social Exclusion and Poverty

According to the UN Report on the World's Social Situation (United Nations, 2010) on the theme of rethinking poverty, the concept of social exclusion contributes to an understanding of the nature of poverty and helps identify the causes of poverty that may have been otherwise neglected. The Report notes that the social exclusion approach to poverty analysis focuses on the non-material dimensions of deprivation and takes account of the concept of identity and social relations that engender deprivation. Social exclusion exists across all societies in numerous and often compounded forms, affecting people of all ages and backgrounds. The lens of social exclusion allows one to isolate and address those processes which create deprivation in society. By fostering social cohesion and the realization of rights of individuals and groups, the promotion of social inclusion effectively complements other poverty reduction strategies.

The socially excluded groups are:

- Less likely to benefit from the 'normal' processes of economic growth because not only do they own fewer resources of various kinds than other sections of the poor, but they also find it harder to translate their resources into income because of the discrimination they face in markets for labour and commodities.
- More likely to be denied access to 'normal' forms of social provisioning, whether these are provided through private provision or by the state.
- Unlikely to have the means necessary to purchase these services in the market place while the discriminatory attitudes prevalent in society at large are often reproduced by state officials responsible for service provision.
- Less likely to participate in 'normal' models of democracy (Kabeer, 2005).

Social Exclusion Profile and Poverty in Asia

The social exclusion profile of poverty in Asia provides further explanations for poverty in Asia.

Women: According to the IFAD, women are still one of the single-most disadvantaged groups in Asia. In many Asian countries, particularly in South Asia, women and girls are consistently discriminated against regarding their access to health, nutrition and education. In some areas gender disparities are even on the increase, as in parts of China where women are taking over a larger share of agricultural tasks as men migrate to work elsewhere. Poverty is always more severe for women, who face greater hardships in providing for themselves and their children. Women generally have fewer employment opportunities, weaker skills and less access to training. They lack control of and ownership of assets (http://www.ifad.org/operations/projects/regions/pi/poverty.htm). Moreover, development has led to women's vulnerability to poverty as the focus in development policies has been on men and women's work has been undervalued.

Indigenous Peoples: IFAD notes that about 70 per cent of the world's more than 250 million indigenous peoples live in Asia and the Pacific. Indigenous groups form a small proportion of the general population but constitute concentrations of extreme poverty and marginalization. These peoples are isolated in many ways. They often live in remote upland and mountain areas, and their languages, culture and religions set them apart from mainstream societies and economies. The violation of their civil rights, particularly their rights to access land and other resources, has transformed many areas into seats of long-standing rebellion. In addition, in countries like India and Nepal, other socially marginalized groups such as the *Dalits* are among the poorest (http://www.ifad.org/ operations/projects/ regions/pi/poverty.htm).

Rural Population: In spite of fast economic growth, Asia has predominantly a rural population. As of 2007, in Asia, 40.8 per cent of the population live in urban areas and 59.2 per cent live in rural areas. IFAD provides the following profile of rural poverty in the Asia-Pacific region. Across the region hundreds of millions of rural people in less favoured environments struggle to eke out a living and to feed their families. The poorest and most vulnerable communities live in areas with uncertain rainfall, steep slopes and poor soils, where land is marginal, low in natural resources and difficult to farm. Typically these are mountainous and highland areas, or semi-arid zones with acute problems of water scarcity. They are often remote with very limited access to markets, infrastructure and services. Land ownership in many of the region's countries is concentrated in the hands of a few. Widespread poverty is often the direct result of inequitable property rights and unequal distribution of assets. The majority of poor rural households survive by cultivating a small piece of land. The poorest of them are either landless, dependent on piecemeal work as labourers, or else farm tiny plots that are inadequate for feeding a family (http://www.ifad.org/operations/projects/regions/pi/poverty.htm).

Caste System: Caste system is an endogamous hierarchical crystallization of what was originally an economic division of labour in the socio-cultural context of South Asia. The upper castes exploited the labour of the lower castes who had no scope for upward mobility. It is, therefore, responsible for inter-generational poverty among those fixed at the lowest rung of the system. In this sub-region, the caste system exists not only in Hindu-dominated India but also in Muslim-dominated countries of Pakistan and Bangladesh and Buddhist Sinhalese. However, the long historical influence of Hinduism on South East Asian countries did nothing to create a caste system in those countries (Omvedt, 1994).

Development and Poverty

Development and Poverty

The international events that promoted poverty of nations are colonization, World Wars, neo-colonialism through development aid and now globalization. In the social construction of 'underdevelopment' as a lack rather than the result of historical circumstances, the 'underdeveloped' were simply treated as poor without seeking the reasons for their destitution (Rist, 2008). The underdeveloped were also considered deprived of the capacity to define their own interests (Rahnema, 2010). The neoliberal structural adjustment programme of the IFIs discredited, marginalized and dismissed developmentalist theories and policies. Through globalization, the new rules of the game centred on reciprocal market liberalization, which would lead to trade expansion and economic growth (Girvan, 2005). The 'old poor' (unskilled workers, those unable to work, and informal sector workers) were joined by the 'new poor' (newly unemployed middle income households) (Minuchin, 1995, cited by Mitlin and Hickey, 2009).

Fast Economic Development and Poverty in Asia

The fast economic development in Asia has earned itself descriptions such as 'Asian Miracle' and 'the most globally integrated region in the world'. However, it has its downside. As the Asian Human Rights Charter of 1998 notes:

> 1.3 Asian development is full of contradictions. There is massive and deepening poverty in the midst of growing affluence of some sections of the people. Levels of health, nutrition and education of large numbers of our people are appalling, denying the dignity of human life. At the same time valuable resources are wasted on armaments, Asia being the largest purchaser of arms of all regions. Our governments claim to be pursuing development directed at increasing levels of production and welfare but our natural resources are being depleted most irresponsibly and the environment is so degraded that the quality of life has worsened immeasurably, even for the better off among us. Building of golf courses has a higher priority than the care of the poor and the disadvantaged.

A study by the Asian Development Bank (2007) notes that by and large, the increase in inequality in Asia is not a story of the 'rich getting richer and the poor getting poorer'. Rather, it is the rich getting richer faster than the poor. According to this report, it is quite likely that fast growth of incomes among the rich has been driven, to a considerable degree, by the opportunities unleashed by market-oriented reforms, international integration, and new technologies. At the same time, the historical record of today's developed countries does not show declining inequalities to be an automatic outcome of continued economic development. High levels of inequality and/or rapidly increasing inequality can imply slow improvements in the economic well-being of the poor even in a growing economy, and can also undermine both social cohesion and the quality of policies and institutions.

The International Fund for Agricultural Development (IFAD), a specialized agency of the UN, notes that with increased growth have come accelerated industrialization, deforestation and intensified farming in Asia, which present major challenges such as the following:

- Rising disparities between urban and rural areas.
- The spread of unemployment.
- Degradation of the environments (both coastal and inland) and the natural resources on which poor rural people depend (http://www.ifad.org/operations/projects/regions/pi/poverty.htm).

The economic recession that resulted from the Asian Financial Crisis shocked the world with its staggering economic and social costs. Over a million people in Thailand and approximately 21 million in Indonesia found themselves impoverished in just a few weeks, as personal savings and assets were devalued to a fraction of their pre-crisis worth. As firms went bankrupt and layoffs ensued, millions lost their jobs. Soaring inflation raised the cost of basic necessities. Strapped fiscal budgets imposed a financial squeeze on social programmes, and the absence of adequate social safety nets led to grim economic displacement. Poverty and income inequality across the region intensified, as a substantial portion of the gains in living standards that had been accumulated through several decades of sustained growth evaporated in one year (Muchhala, 2007).

Environmental Degradation and Poverty

Environmental Degradation and Poverty in Asia: According to IFAD, poverty in Asia is more severe in areas where agricultural productivity is declining. Where the competition for land is fierce, natural resources are exhausted and degraded and productivity decreases. In areas that are already environmentally fragile, subsistence farming puts pressure on limited resources. The consequences of deforestation, overgrazing of livestock and increased production on marginal soils can be devastating in terms of soil erosion and soil fertility depletion. In the worst cases, communities are forced to migrate or enter into conflict over limited resources. Land degradation, desertification and depleted marine resources are major concerns in many parts of Asia, and they inevitably lead to greater poverty (http://www.ifad.org/operations/projects/regions/pi/poverty.htm).

Weak Social Policy and Poverty

Poverty in Asia can be explained by the fact that most of the countries in Asia have welfare pluralism or residual welfare is the dominant form of welfare. Universal social protection as a human right is far from reality in Asia where the states have generally accorded low priority to human rights. East Asia shows the maximum reduction of poverty probably due to strong social policy after the Asian Financial Crisis. The North and Central Asian countries are dismantling their socialist universal access to social services, and are showing decline in poverty equality. South Asia has the weakest form of social policy and the lowest level of reduction of poverty in Asia.

Progress in Reduction of Poverty

Measures for Reduction of Poverty

Human Poverty Index and the Millennium Development Goal (MDG)–1 are used in this chapter as measures of reduction in poverty. Rather than measure poverty by income, the Human Poverty Index (HPI: the level of human poverty), launched in the 1997 HDR, uses indicators of the most basic dimensions of deprivation: a short life, lack of basic education and lack of access to public and private resources. It concentrates on the deprivation in the three essential elements of human life already reflected in the HDI: longevity, knowledge and a decent standard of living (The Human Development website http://hdr.undp.org/en/humandev/hdi/). The 2010 HDR (United Nations Development Programme, 2010) introduced the Multidimensional Poverty Index (MPI), which complements money-based measures by considering multiple deprivations and their overlap. The index identifies deprivations across the same three dimensions as the HDI and shows the number of people who are poor (suffering a given number of deprivations) and the number of deprivations with which poor households typically contend. It can be deconstructed by region, ethnicity and other groupings as well as by dimension, making it an apt tool for policymakers. The Millennium Development Goal (MDG)–1 to eradicate extreme poverty and hunger has two targets. Target 1 is to halve, between 1990 and 2015, the proportion of people whose income is less than one US dollar a day. This poverty line has fixed purchasing power across countries or areas and is often called an 'absolute poverty line' or measure of extreme poverty.

Reduction of Poverty in Asia

The 2013 HDR (UNDP, 2013: 27) reports that in the 104 countries covered by the MPI, about 1.56 billion or more than 30 per cent of their population are estimated to live in multidimensional poverty. The countries with the highest headcount percentages based on the MPI are in Africa, followed by South Asia. According to the MDG Report of 2012, both the number of people living in extreme poverty and the poverty rates fell in every developing region (United Nations, 2012: 6–7). In China and India combined, the number of people living in extreme poverty between 1990 and 2005 declined by about 455 million, and an additional 320 million people are expected to join their ranks by 2015 (United Nations, 2011). Whole of Asia is expected to meet the MDG target with reference to reduction of extreme poverty and may even far exceed it. However, the table below shows that inequality in income is prevalent throughout Asia, and cuts across the levels of economic development.

Diversity in Reduction of Poverty in Asian Sub-Regions

Table 8.1 shows the diversity in Asian sub-regions by the level of human development, MPI and population below poverty line (PPP USD 1.25/Day) as reported by the Human Development Report (HDR) of 2013 (United Nations Development Programme, 2013).

Table 8.1
Diversity in Human Poverty Indicators in Asian Sub-Regions

Level of Human Development 2012	Countries in Asia	Multi-Dimensional Poverty Index 2002–2011	And of Population below Poverty Line: PPP USD 1.25/Day 2002–2011	Income Gini Coefficient 2000–2010
East Asia				
Medium	China	0.056	13.1	42.5
South East Asia				
High	Malaysia	—	—	46.2
Medium	Thailand	0.006	0.4	40.0
Medium	Philippines	0.064	18.4	43.0
Medium	Indonesia	0.095	18.1	34.0
Medium	Vietnam	0.017	40.1	35.6
Medium	Timor-Leste	0.360	37.4	31.9
Medium	Laos	0.267	33.9	36.7
Medium	Cambodia	0.212	22.8	37.9
Low	Myanmar	—	—	—

Cont'd...

...Cont'd

North and Central Asia				
High	Russia	0.005	0.0	40.1
High	Kazakhstan	0.002	0.1	29.0
Medium	Turkmenistan	0.002	—	—
Medium	Mongolia	0.065	—	36.5
Medium	Uzbekistan	0.008	—	36.7
Medium	Kyrgyzstan	0.019	6.2	36.2
Medium	Tajikistan	0.068	6.6	30.8
South Asia				
High	Sri Lanka	0.021	7.0	40.3
Medium	Maldives	0.018	—	37.4
Medium	India	0.283	32.7	33.4
Medium	Bhutan	0.119	10.2	38.1
Low	Pakistan	0.264	21.0	30.0
Low	Bangladesh	0.292	43.3	32.1
Low	Nepal	0.217	24.8	32.8

East Asia

The MDG Report of 2011 notes that the fastest growth and sharpest reduction in poverty continue to be found in East Asia, particularly in China (United Nations, 2011). In China, after the extreme poverty rate had dropped from 60 per cent in 1990 to 16 per cent in 2005, the incidence fell further to 13 per cent by 2008 (United Nations, 2012). However, Table 8.1 shows that one of the countries with maximum income inequality is China, higher than most of the countries in North and Central and South Asia. The MPI and population below the poverty line is among the lowest in East Asia with the highest level of social development and stronger social protection policy after the Asian Financial Crisis.

North and Central Asia

Table 8.1 shows that North and Central Asia, the former Soviet Union countries have the lowest multi-dimensional poverty and the lowest percentage of people below the poverty line. Kazakhstan, Turkmenistan and Russia are doing the best. However, the one US dollar a day poverty line may not be appropriate for cold climate countries where spending on food, heat, and winter clothing is higher than in other sub-regions (UNESCAP, 2007). On the other hand, Kazakhstan has the minimum income inequality and Russia has the maximum income inequality in this sub-region. Mongolia and Tajikistan are the most problematic with reference to MPI.

South Asia

South Asia is the second-highest sub-region with reference to Multiple Poverty Index in the world. However, India has contributed to the large reduction in global poverty. In India, poverty rates are projected to fall from 51 per cent in 1990 to about 22 per cent in 2015 (United Nations, 2011). Table 8.1 shows that the Northern countries of South Asia have the high level of MPI and high percentage of people below the poverty line. Bangladesh has the maximum percentage of people living below the poverty line (43.3%) in South Asia and Asia as a whole. India follows with almost a third of its population living below the poverty line. As high as 65 per cent of the extremely poor of Asia live in South Asia (Asian Development Bank, 2012). This is due to South Asia having the weakest social policy and low level of human development. The Southern countries of Maldives and Sri Lanka have low level of MPI and population below the poverty line but have high level of income inequality.

South East Asia

Table 8.1 shows that South East Asia is problematic as in whole of Asia, Timor-Leste has maximum MPI, Vietnam has second-largest percentage of people living below the poverty line and Malaysia has maximum income inequality. However, Thailand has minimum MPI (0.006) and the percentage of people living below the poverty line (0.4%).

Implications for Policy for Poverty Eradication

According to the HDR on *Human Development to Eradicate Poverty* (United Nations Development Programme, 1997), the eradication of absolute poverty in the first decade of the 21st century is feasible, affordable and a moral imperative. It recommends the following priorities for action for poverty reduction: Building assets for the poor, gender equality, pro-poor growth, globalization for global equity, enabling environment, and international support.

Since the concept of social exclusion contributes to an understanding of the multiple causes of poverty, Kabeer (2005) recommends that policy responses to social exclusion needs to use a multi-pronged approach to address poverty. According to her, a legal framework can help to ensure that discrimination on the grounds of race, ethnicity, disability, gender, or age, are rendered unacceptable within a society. It can also ensure that rights of excluded groups to land, credit, employment and benefits are secured, given the greater vulnerability of these groups. Policies to address social exclusion may need to incorporate special provisions to address the multiple disadvantages associated with social exclusion and to break the inter-generational transmission of poverty that it has often entailed. Such provisions may entail special attention to geographical or group targetting. It may entail targetting the children of excluded groups to ensure that they face that limited life chances which their parents faced. It may also need addressing gender inequalities within excluded groups so that promoting respect for hitherto marginalized cultures does not necessarily promote the internal inequalities which such cultures may embody (Kabeer, 2005). According to the UNRISD Flagship Report on *Combating Poverty and Inequality* (2010), comprehensive social policies are essential for successful poverty reduction. An effective social policy framework for rapid and sustained poverty reduction must be grounded in universal rights.

Progress in Reduction of Food Insecurity in Asia

Concepts of Food Insecurity

Hunger

Hunger is usually understood to refer to the discomfort associated with lack of food. FAO (2011, cited by International Food Policy Research Institute, 2012) defines food deprivation or undernourishment as the consumption of fewer than about 1800 kilocalories a day, the minimum that most people require to live a healthy and productive life. Undernourishment goes beyond calories and signifies deficiencies in any or all of the following: energy, protein, or essential vitamins and minerals. Undernutrition is the result of inadequate intake of food-in terms of either quantity or quality-poor utilization of nutrients due to infections or other illnesses, or a combination of these factors, which are in turn caused by household food insecurity, inadequate maternal health or child care practices; or inadequate access to health services, safe water, and sanitation (International Food Policy Research Institute, 2012: 20). Malnutrition refers more broadly to both undernutrition and overnutrition (problems of unbalanced diets, such as consumption of too many calories in relation to requirements with or without low intake of micronutrient-rich foods) (International Food Policy Research Institute, 2012: 20).

Food Security

According to the HDR on Human Security (United Nations Development Programme, 1994), 'Food security means that all people at all times have both physical and economic access to basic food.' This requires not just enough food to go round. It requires that people have ready access to food, that they have an 'entitlement' to food, by growing it for themselves, by buying it or by taking advantage of a public food distribution system. The availability of food is thus a necessary condition of security, but not a sufficient one. People can still starve even when enough food is available, as has happened during many famines. The overall availability of food in the world is not a problem. Even in developing countries, per capita food production increased by 18 per cent on average in the 1980s. This led to enough food to offer everyone in the world around 2,500 calories a day, 200 calories more than the basic minimum. However, this does not mean that everyone gets enough to eat. The problem often is the poor distribution of food and a lack of purchasing power. Government and international agencies have tried many ways of increasing food security at both national and global levels. But these schemes have had only a limited impact. Access to food comes from access to assets, work and an assured income. And unless these question are tackled upstream, state interventions can do little for food insecurity downstream (United Nations Development Programme, 1994).

Causes of Food Insecurity

Myths about Hunger

The Institute for Food and Development Policy (2006) notes the following myths about hunger:

1. *Not enough food to go around:* There is abundance of food in the world.

2. *Nature is to blame for famine:* Human-made forces are making people increasingly vulnerable to nature's vagaries.
3. *Too many people:* Birth rates are falling rapidly worldwide. Although rapid population growth remains a serious concern in many countries, nowhere does population density explain huger.
4. *Environmental crisis:* Efforts to feed the hungry are not causing the environmental crisis.
5. *The green revolution is the answer:* Mere revolution in food production cannot alleviate hunger.
6. *We need large farms:* Large landowners do not necessarily use all their land for food production.
7. *The free market and free trade can end hunger:* Even in countries with free market and trade, hunger is not eradicated.

The fact is that many people are too poor to buy the available food. The UNESCAP Report (2009) notes that poverty makes people food insecure, and food insecurity increases the risk of falling into poverty. The poor spend greater proportion of their income on food, up to 60 per cent to 70 per cent. Although poverty rates were reduced significantly across Asia in the late 2000s, the pace of poverty reduction was slowed by rising food prices. This was especially true during the global food crisis, when prices of rice, wheat, and maize spiked to record heights (Asian Development Bank, 2012). The following explanations of poverty in Asia also explain food insecurity in Asia:

- Fast economic development
- Social exclusion profile
- Asian financial crisis
- Weak social policy

Food-Insecure Groups

A UNESCAP Report (2009) identified the following groups as food-insecure in Asia Pacific region:

- Rural children: Rural children are twice as likely to be under-nourished as those living in urban areas.

- Women: In some countries there is a persistent gender bias, as a result of mal-distribution within households, which causes women to be at greater risk of undernourishment than men.
- Migrant workers, tribal peoples as well as people living with HIV and AIDS (UNESCAP, 2009).

The UNESCAP Report (2009) identifies barriers in agriculture, market-based food insecurity, speculation and price rise, problems with quality of food as some of the causes for food insecurity that create a cycle of poverty in Asia and the Pacific.

Barriers in Agriculture

The barriers facing agriculture are not just technical, but also social and political. Many countries still face severe structural constraints, such as inequitable or inefficient land ownership. Many of the agricultural benefits are reaped by the richer farmers. Long-term sustainability is threatened by the overuse of fertilizers and other inputs. Agriculture, like many other forms of development, is further constrained by low levels of human capacity. Farmers often lack the education, training or the necessary health standards to make the best use of available resources and have found it more difficult to get extension services. While some farmers now have cell phone access to market prices, many still neither have access to such information nor to markets. They have also been held back by government policy, which until recently at least, has tended to tax agriculture at the expense of urban consumers. In future, farmers will find things steadily more difficult – faced with environmental degradation, expanding deserts, shrinking forests, competing for water, displaced by bio-fuels, genetically modified crops and climate change. Unless they can produce food not just efficiently, but also in ways that respect the environment, the food security outlook will be bleak (UNESCAP, 2009).

Market-based Food Insecurity

For large numbers of people, the primary source of food security is their income – either from producing non-food goods or from selling their labour. Under these circumstances, much depends on the national terms of trade – on the balance between the prices of food and those of other goods. The problem of food insecurity, like that of poverty, is thus frequently traceable to macroeconomic conditions and market failures. Farming communities and others can also suffer from food insecurity because of the actions of exploitative intermediaries, including landowners, moneylenders and traders. One of the most severe problems is the shortage of affordable credit. Desperate for cash, small and marginal farmers, for example, are forced to sell their crops immediately after the harvest to middlemen or their creditors, only to have to repurchase some of this food later, at a higher price (UNESCAP, 2009).

Speculation and Price Rise

While speculation is not a driver of commodity prices, it can nevertheless accelerate and amplify price movements driven by fundamental supply and demand factors. Given how steeply food prices increased and how fast they fell in 2008, it is likely that the growing presence of financial investors in commodity markets made prices overreact to new market information and deviate from fundamentals. Households that come under pressure, as a result of rising prices or falling food supplies, show a range of coping responses. Typically, they react first by eating less food, or cheaper food. But, if high prices persist, the poorest households will be driven to borrowing money or selling some of their assets (UNESCAP, 2009).

Problems with Quality of Food

Even when food is available in the household, some family members may not be able to take advantage of it – hampered by inadequate water supplies and poor standards of sanitation which reduce the quality of their food or make it hazardous. Without reliable water supplies or basic sanitation, children especially are constantly exposed to infections and diseases that not only threaten their lives directly, but also prevent their absorption of many essential nutrients. People have to be concerned about the ever-present dangers of food contamination, which can arise, for example, through the use of chemical products in food production, as well as from failures in the ways in which food is transported, stored and served (UNESCAP, 2009).

Reduction of Hunger as a Millennium Development Goal

The measure for reduction of food insecurity used is the Target 2 of the MDG–1, which is to halve, between 1990 and 2015, the proportion of people who suffer from hunger. Following are the indicators for this Target:

- Prevalence of Underweight Children Under-Five Years of Age
- Proportion of Population below Minimum Level of Dietary Energy Consumption

One of Asia's most disturbing shortfalls is hunger. The following table provides comparative data on progress of reduction of hunger in Asian sub-regions.

Table 8.2
Diversity in Progress of Reduction of Hunger in Asian Sub-Regions

Level of Human Develop-ment 2012	Country	Reduction of Hunger		
		Underweight Children under-five per cent of Children under-five 2006–2010	% of Population below minimum level of Dietary Energy Consumption 2004–2006	Global Hunger Index 2005–10
East Asia				
V High	Japan	NA	<05%	—
V High	South Korea	NA	<05%	—
V High	Hong Kong	NA	NA	—
Medium	China	03.8%	10%	05.1
Low	North Korea	18.8%	—	19.0
South East Asia				
V High	Singapore	NA	NA	—
V High	Brunei	NA	<05%	—
High	Malaysia	12.9%	<05%	05.2
Medium	Thailand	07.0%	16%	08.1
Medium	Philippines	21.8%	15%	12.2
Medium	Indonesia	18.4%	13%	12.0
Medium	Vietnam	20.2%	11%	24.3

Cont'd...

...Cont'd

Medium	Timor-Leste	11.7%	31%	27.3
Medium	Laos	31.1%	23%	19.7
Medium	Cambodia	28.3%	22%	19.6
Low	Myanmar	22.6%	16%	—
North and Central Asia				
High	Russia	—	—	<05.0
High	Kazakhstan	03.9%	<05%	<05.0
Medium	Turkmenistan	08.2%	06%	06.9
Medium	Mongolia	05.0%	26%	11.7
Medium	Uzbekistan	04.0%	11%	06.9
Medium	Kyrgyzstan	02.2%	10%	05.8
Medium	Tajikistan	15.0%	30%	15.8
South Asia				
Medium	Sri Lanka	21.1%	19%	14.4
Medium	Maldives	17.3%	07%	—
Medium	India	42.5%	21%	22.9
Medium	Bhutan	12.7%	NA	—
Low	Pakistan	31.3%	26%	19.7
Low	Bangladesh	41.0%	27%	24.0
Low	Nepal	38.6%	16%	20.3

Sources: Column 1: United Nations Development Programme, 2013
Column 2: Asian Development Bank, 2011
Column 3: International Food Policy Research Institute, 2012

Reduction of Underweight Children under-Five

Prevalence of (moderately or severely) underweight children is the percentage of children under five years whose weight for their age is less than minus two standard deviations from the median for the international reference population ages 0–59 months. The international reference population was formulated by the National Centre for Health Statistics (NCHS) as a reference for the US and later adopted by the World Health Organization (WHO) for international use (often referred to as the NCHS/WHO reference population). Due to poor performance by India, Asia without India performs better on underweight children – moving from slow to on track (UNESCAP, ADB and UNDP, 2012–13).

Table 8.2 shows that there are no underweight under-five children in the countries with very high human development. The sub-regions show the following variations.

East Asia: East Asia is leading with reference to the lowest percentage of underweight under-five children with only North Korea being a little problematic.

North and Central Asia: After East Asia, North and Central Asia leads in Asia for dealing with this problem. The lowest percentage of underweight under-five children is in Kyrgyzstan and Kazakhstan. Tajikistan is a little problematic.

South East Asia: In South East Asia, Laos, Cambodia and Myanmar are problematic.

South Asia: Child undernutrition is worst in South Asia where, except for Bhutan and Maldives, all the countries have more than 20 per cent of their under-five children underweight. The Asian Development Bank Report (2012) shows that 60 per cent of Asia's hungry and 81 per cent of its underweight children live in South Asia. According to the MDG Report of 2011, in South Asia, one finds not only a shortage of quality food and poor feeding practices, but a lack of flush toilets and other forms of improved sanitation. Nearly half the population practises open defecation, resulting in repeated bouts of diarrhoeal disease in children, which contribute to the high prevalence of undernutrition. Moreover, more than a quarter of infants in that region weigh less than 2,500 grams at birth. Many of these children are never able to catch up in terms of their nutritional status. All these factors conspire to make underweight prevalence in the sub-region the highest in the world.

High economic growth in India is accompanied by failure on the food security front, with reference to production, availability, distribution, affordability, absorption and nutrition. This has made India one of the most undernourished countries in the world. Bangladesh also has serious food security concerns on all fronts, largely due to natural calamities. In Pakistan, unprecedented inflation has taken food out of the reach of people (The Mahbub ul Haq Development Centre, 2011).

Reduction of Undernourishment

Proportion of the population below the minimum level of dietary energy consumption is the percentage of the population whose food intake falls below the minimum level of dietary energy requirements. This is also referred to as the prevalence of undernourishment, which is the percentage of the population that is undernourished. Table 8.2 shows that there are no or less than five per cent of the population undernourished in countries with very high human development, namely, Hong Kong, Singapore, South Korea and Brunei. Malaysia and Bhutan are also doing well with less than five per cent of their population undernourished. The sub-regions show the following variations.

East Asia: The percentage of undernourished population seems to be minimum in East, Asia, the sub-region that is most developed in Asia.

North and Central Asia: In North and Central Asia, Tajikistan and Mongolia are of concern.

South East Asia: Timor-Leste has the highest proportion, that is, almost a third of their population undernourished in whole of Asia. Laos and Cambodia are also of concern.

South Asia: In South Asia, Bangladesh, Pakistan and India are of concern.

Global Hunger Index

The International Food Policy Research Institute has developed the Global Hunger Index (GHI) that combines the following indicators into one:

- Undernourishment: Percentage of undernourished people in the population
- Child underweight: Percentage of under-weight children under-five
- Under-five child mortality rate

The GHI ranks countries on a 100-point scale in which zero is the best score (no hunger) and 100 he worst, although neither of these extremes is reached in practice.

Table 8.2 shows that in Asia, highest level of GHI is in Timor-Leste (27.3), followed by Vietnam (24.3), Bangladesh (24), India (22.9) and Nepal (20.3).

Implications for Policy for Food Security

Initiatives for Food Security

The major initiatives for food security in the Asia-Pacific region are the green revolution, food self-reliance, social protection programmes of food transfers and cash transfers and resilient community initiatives for mutual support such as everything together, building banks, sharing water, common property resources and food storage and protection.

Green Revolution

Since the mid-1960s, the Asia and the Pacific region has benefitted from a remarkable boost in agricultural output as a result of the Green Revolution, using new varieties of rice and wheat, along with the application of fertilizer and irrigation. The result was a striking increase in cereal yields. To some extent, especially in its initial stages, the Green Revolution benefitted the rural poor. This was partly because the new technology could also be used on small farms, and because the new farming systems, which often involved double or triple cropping, proved to be quite labour intensive, thus generating more work for the landless. Nevertheless, the Green Revolution displaced many smaller farmers, particularly women, as production was consolidated into larger and more integrated farming systems (UNESCAP, 2009).

Food Self-Reliance

While some countries in the Asia and Pacific region grow most of the food that they need, most rely to some extent on international trade. In this region, 25 countries are net food importers. Some of these have, at times, aimed for national food self-sufficiency. However, a more realistic objective is 'food self-reliance', which means being able to earn sufficient foreign exchange from other exports, such as manufactured goods, so as to be able to import food. Countries following this strategy will, however, need to be concerned about the terms of trade. As food prices rise, food self-reliant countries will need to export more manufactured and other goods to be able to import sufficient food (UNESCAP, 2009).

Social Protection Programmes for Food Security

The UNESCAP Report (2009) on food security in Asia and Pacific note the following government social protection programmes for food security in the region.

Food Transfers: Food from reserves and elsewhere can be released into national food markets. Typically, this has been through 'food-for-work' programmes, such as building roads, which are 'self-targetting' on the assumption that only the poorest would be prepared to do this work for the type of food on offer. Other types of conditional programmes include 'food-for-education', whereby food may be distributed through schools to encourage attendance. Food aid has helped achieve many humanitarian and development goals, but it has also been criticized for damaging local markets, fostering dependency, and for being susceptible to corruption.

Cash Transfers: An alternative form of support to food-insecure communities is to offer lump sum payments to vulnerable groups. These too are usually conditional, such as the Primary Education Scholarship Programme in Bangladesh and the Rural Employment Guarantee Scheme in India. Many programmes target women on the grounds that, compared with men, they are more likely to allocate incremental food or cash to their families, especially their children. But the conditions applied also represent extra demands on overworked mothers.

Resilient Communities

The UNESCAP Report (2009) on food security in Asia and Pacific note that communities that are food insecure face different kinds of shocks. To protect themselves, they have established the following systems of mutual support in the region.

Everything Together: Farmers who rely on one or two crops can be at considerable risk if these fail, or market prices fall. In response, many farmers have evolved complex integrated farming systems. In Kazakhstan, for example, some farmers have developed a form of two-track agriculture combining livestock and food production that tides them over during the severe winter months. In China, farmers have developed integrated agriculture centred on fish ponds, combined with cultivating silkworms, along with raising chickens, ducks and other animals – a system that uses almost all waste as nutrient resources.

Building Banks: Farmers can provide a degree of security for themselves by using common resources, such as grain or seed banks. This type of mutual support is promoted, for example, by the Self-employed Women's Association, a trade union based in Gujarat in India, which has used banks for grain, seeds, fodder and tools to help build food security. In some cases, grain banks have been combined with other activities to build the equivalent of public distribution systems.

Sharing Water: Asia has many community-based water delivery systems which serve one-third or more of the total irrigated area. Generally, these have been developed in mountainous or hilly territory, based on the diversion of small and medium streams, especially in the Himalayan regions, China, Laos, Japan, the Philippines and Thailand. In Indonesia, rice farmers in Bali have irrigation systems coordinated through temples that use common planting cycles based on a ritual calendar.

Common Property Resources: The poorest households often rely for food security on common resources – lands, forests, wildlife, fisheries and waterways – which they use as primary or secondary sources of food and fodder. Besides offering extra quantities of food, these can also add to the nutritional quality of their diets.

Food Storage and Protection: Poor communities in rural areas, however, lacking in modern methods of storage, have had to devise some of their own. In the Himalayan regions of India, for example, foodgrains like maize, wheat and rice are stored in special bamboo containers that inhibit the entry of insects and larvae. For protecting crops, people also use indigenous materials, such as leaves from the *neem* tree.

Recommendations for Food Security Measures

According to the UNESCAP Report (2009), food security depends on interlinked short-, medium- and long-term measures as given below:

Short-Term Measures Improving Access to Food

For large numbers of people in Asia-Pacific, food security depends as much on income as on food availability. People who have sufficient money will always have enough economic access to food. Government action to promote the long-term availability of food on a sustainable basis must be complemented by measures to ensure economic and social, and physical access to food, especially with regard to the poor and vulnerable communities of the Asia-Pacific region.

- Economic and social access
- Social protection against shocks
- Physical access: transport and logistics
- Improving choice and utilization of food

Medium-Term Measure

Sustainable Agriculture: The governments of the region stand at a crossroads: business as usual, continuing with short-term profits for the few through chemically cultivated, irrigation- and energy-intensive monoculture, with the burden of long-term costs shouldered by the many; or, a new, long-term commitment to ecologically balanced, socially just and economically equitable agriculture to ensure food security for all.

Long-Term Measure

Adaptation to Climate Change: Climate change holds the potential to radically alter agro-eco systems in the coming decades. Adaptation to climate change should include strengthening regional and national mechanisms for scientific assessment, forecasting and information sharing, while building national and local capacities for greater ecological literacy, monitoring agro-eco systems and for assessing and managing risks. The concept of building the resilience of communities to tackle the impact of climate change in the context of changes in socioeconomic and environmental conditions has to be rapidly developed and widely promoted. Measures include rehabilitating degraded grasslands, as well as improving crop and grazing land use and management.

Amartya Sen (1997) notes that food production remains the central focus of concern for FAO but much else needs to be done. He notes that the trend of food output per head has been persistently upwards in most regions of the world and the growth of world population has started to slow down significantly. According to him, for elimination of hunger in the world, it is critical to understand the problem in an adequately broad framework, involving not only food production and agricultural expansion but also the functioning of the entire economy, and the operation of the political and social arrangements that can influence people's ability to acquire food and to achieve health and nourishment.

References

Asian Development Bank. (2007). *Inequality in Asia, Highlights.* Manila.

——. (2011). *Key Indicators for Asia and the Pacific.* Manila. Retrieved 31 March 2013 from http://www.adb.org/key-indicators/2011/main

——. (2012). *Food Security and Poverty in Asia and the Pacific: Key Challenges and Policy Issues.* Manila.

Girvan, N. (2005). *The Search for Policy Autonomy in the South.* Geneva: United Nations Research Institute for Social Development.

The Institute for Food and Development Policy. (2006). 12 myths about hunger. *Backgrounder,* 12(2), 1–4.

International Food Policy Research Institute. (2012). *Global Hunger Index: The Challenge of Hunger.* Washington, DC.

Kabeer, N. (2005). Social exclusion: Concepts, findings and implications for the MDGs. Paper commissioned as background for the Social Exclusion Policy Paper, Department for International Development (DFID), London. Retrieved 1 July 2012 from http://www.gsdrc.org/docs/ open/SE2.pdf

Lister, R. (2004). *Poverty.* Malden, MA: Polity Press.

The Mahbub ul Haq Human Development Centre. (2011). *Human Development in South Asia: 2010/2011.* Lahore: Oxford University Press.

Mitlin, D. and Hickey, S. (2009). Introduction. In D. Mitlin and S. Hickey (eds), *Rights-based Approach to Development: Exploring the Potential and Pitfalls* (pp. 3–20). Sterling, VA: Kumarian Press.

Muchhala, B. (2007). Introduction. In B. Muchhala (ed.), *Ten Years After: Revisiting the Asian Financial Crisis.* Washington, DC: Woodrow Wilson International Center for Scholars, Asia Program.

Omvedt, G. (1994). *Dalits and the Democratic Revolution: Dr. Ambedkar and the Dalit Movement in Colonial India.* New Delhi: Sage Publications.

Rahnema, M. (2010). Poverty. In W. Sachs (ed.), *The Development Dictionary: A Guide to Knowledge as Power* (2nd ed.). (pp. 174–194). New York: Zed Books.

Rist, G. (2008). *The History of Development: From Western Origins to Global Faith* (3rd ed.). New York: Zed Books.

Sen, A. (1997). Hunger in the contemporary world. Discussion Paper No. 8. London: London School of Economics and Political Science. Retrieved 13 May 2010 from http://sticerd.lse.ac.uk/dps/de/dedps8.pdf

Sen, A. (1999). *Development as Freedom.* New York: Random House.

United Nations. (2010). *Report on the World Social Situation 2010 'Rethinking Poverty'.* Retrieved 15 July 2010 from http://www.un.org/esa/ socdev/rwss/2010_media.html

——. (2011). *Millennium Development Goals Report 2011.* New York. Retrieved 11 August 2011 from http://www.un.org/millenniumgoals/pdf/(2011_E)%20MDG%20Report%202011_Book%20LR.pdf

——. (2012). *The Millennium Development Goals Report 2012.* New York.

United Nations Development Programme. (1994). *Human Development Report: New Dimensions of Human Security.* New York: Oxford University Press.

——. (1997). *Human Development Report: Human Development to Eradicate Poverty.* New York: Oxford University Press.

——. (2010). *Human Development Report: The Real Wealth of Nations: Pathways to Human Development.* New York: Oxford University Press.

——. (2013). *Human Development Report: The Rise of the South: Human Progress in a Diverse World.* New York.

United Nations Economic and Social Commission for Asia and the Pacific. (2007). UNESCAP Fact Sheets on MDGs in North and Central Asia. Retrieved 19 May 2010 from http://www.mdgasiapacific.org/files/shared_folder/documents/fs_nca_mdg_all_en.pdf

——. (2009). *Sustainable Agriculture and Food Security in Asia and the Pacific.* Bangkok. Retrieved 13 May 2010 from http://www.unescap.org/65/theme_study2009.asp

United Nations Economic and Social Commission for Asia and the Pacific, Asian Development Bank and United Nations Development Program. (2012–13). *Perspectives for a Post-2015 Development Agenda: Asia-Pacific Regional MDGs Report 2012/13.*

United Nations Research Institute for Social Development. (2010). *Combating Poverty and Inequality: Structural Change, Social Policy and Politics.* Geneva.

United Nations World Summit for Social Development Programme of Action. (1995). Retrieved 19 November 2010 from http://social.un.org/index/Home/WorldSummitforSocialDevelopment1995/Agreements WSSD1995.aspx

CHAPTER 9

Diversity in Progress in Investment in Health in Asia

Introduction

Concepts of Investment in Health and Education

According to the constitutional preamble of the WHO (1946), 'health is a state of complete physical, mental and social well-being and not merely the absence of disease or infirmity' (cited by WHO, 1998). In 1999, Amartya Sen (1999: 20–21) saw the importance of health and education as leading to basic capabilities, deprivation of which leads to poverty. Investment in people's basic needs is paramount for enhancing their capabilities and enlarging their choices. According to Ranis, Stewart and Ramirez (2000, cited in Spence, 2009), health, primary and secondary education and nutrition raise the productivity of workers, which in turn contribute to economic growth. The capability approach has given rise to a distinct framework for evaluating development policies and processes. Policies are judged to be successful if they have enhanced people's capabilities – whether or not they have also affected income, growth, and other important means to this end (United Nations Educational, Scientific and Cultural Organization, 2002).

Chapter Objectives

This chapter on diversity in progress in investment in health in Asia reviews the following:

1. Concepts of investment in and importance of health, barriers to health and right to health.
2. Progress in investment in health in Asia with reference to public spending on health, life expectancy, reduction of child mortality and maternal mortality and combating HIV/AIDS, Malaria and other diseases.
3. Diversity in progress in investment in health in Asian sub-regions.
4. Implications for health policy in Asia.

Conceptual Framework of Investment in Health

Importance of Health

The Commission on Macroeconomics and Health (CMH) provided evidence that improvements in health are important for economic growth. It confirmed that in countries where people have poor health and the level of education is low, it is more difficult to achieve sustainable economic growth. Health is a cornerstone of economic growth and social development. The Commission showed that increased life expectancy and low infant mortality are linked to economic growth. Healthy people are more productive; healthy infants and children can develop better and become productive adults; and a healthy population can contribute to a country's economic growth. The Commission says that increased investment in health would translate into hundreds of billions of dollars per year of additional income which could be used to improve living conditions and social infrastructure in poorer countries (World Health Organization, no date). Besides being important for economic growth, health is important for educational achievements and cognitive development, employment opportunities, income earning potential, as well as dignity, safety, security and empowerment (Ariana and Naveed, 2009). OECD Policy Brief (2003) noted that substantially improved health outcomes are a prerequisite for developing countries to break out of the cycle of poverty. Good health contributes to development via higher labour productivity, higher rates of domestic and foreign investment, improved human capital, higher rates of national savings and demographic changes such as lower rates of fertility and mortality.

According to UNDP-UNEP Poverty Environment Initiative (2009), environmental conditions account for a significant portion of health risks to poor people. Environmental risk factors, such as occupational exposures to chemicals and indoor air pollution from household solid fuel use, play a role in more than 80 per cent of the diseases regularly reported on by the World Health Organization. Globally, nearly a quarter of all deaths and of the world's total disease burden can be attributed to the environment. As many as 13 million deaths could be prevented every year by making the environment healthier. Improved health from better environmental conditions would also contribute to improvements in livelihoods, economic development and resilience to environmental risks.

Barriers to Health

The poor health of the poor, the social gradient in health within countries, and the marked health inequities between countries are caused by the unequal distribution of power, income, goods, and services, globally and nationally, the consequent unfairness in the immediate, visible circumstances of people's lives – their access to health care, schools, and education, their conditions of work and leisure, their homes, communities, towns, or cities – and their chances of leading a flourishing life. This unequal distribution of health-damaging experiences is not in any sense a 'natural' phenomenon but is the result of a toxic combination of poor social policies and programmes, unfair economic arrangements, and bad politics. Together, the structural determinants and conditions of daily life constitute the social determinants of health and are responsible for a major part of health inequities between and within countries (World Health Organization, 2008).

A Report of the UNESCAP, ADB and UNDP (2007) identified the following obstacles within the health systems in the Asia Pacific region:

Deficiencies in Physical Infrastructure: The unavailability and the inaccessibility of emergency obstetric care and antenatal care facilities in many rural areas are major contributing factors to the slow progress in achieving Goals 4 and 5 in many countries of the region. In at least eight Asian countries, comprising approximately half the population in the Asian and Pacific region, more than 60 per cent of births occur at home. Clinics and hospitals can be overcrowded with patients having to wait for long periods before getting diagnosed or treated.

Deficiencies in Human Resources: Despite having 50 per cent of the world's population, Asia has only 30 per cent of the global stock of health workers, an average of 20 per 10,000 people. Asia also has one of the world's lowest rates of births attended by skilled health personnel. Even where health providers are available, negligence, incompetence or inadequate training may result in misdiagnosis or wrong prescription of treatment. The problem can be compounded by corrupt and illegal practices among health professionals.

Insufficient Spending on Health: In most ESCAP countries health-care services are financed through a mix of government and private arrangements and, in some countries, with external assistance. Government systems include social health insurance systems and tax revenue-based systems. Private spending is largely through out-of-pocket expenditures, community-based and private insurance schemes. When compared with other regions of the world, the Asian and Pacific region has the world's lowest level of government expenditure, on health and the highest contribution of private out-of-pocket expenditures.

Undeveloped Health-Protection Systems: Comprehensive universal health-care coverage is still a distant promise for most countries in Asia. Japan has a well-developed model of universal health-care coverage in place. The establishment of the National Health Insurance programme in the Republic of Korea and the Universal Health Care Scheme in Thailand have been heralded as some of the most successful anywhere in the developing world. These approaches have contributed to significant improvements in health indicators in both countries.

Inequitable Allocations of Health Budgets: A highly inequitable distribution of public investments in health exists in many developing countries in the ESCAP region. Resources are heavily concentrated in urban areas and on secondary and tertiary care, often at the expense of even the most essential health care in rural areas.

Poor Working Conditions and Prospects for Health Professionals: In most developing countries it is common practice for many health personnel to migrate from rural to urban areas and from the public to the private sector. Urban and more accessible areas not only have higher numbers of health professionals per capita but are also able to retain the most qualified staff. These factors further contribute to the rural/urban divide that is created by the imbalance in the pattern of health spending. The drain on human resources also takes place across international borders as health professionals in developing countries look for better economic opportunities abroad.

Poor Governance and Low Efficiency in Health Systems: Deficiencies in the allocation of financial and human resources are often compounded by poor management, lack of performance standards and weak accountability systems. All of these factors contribute ultimately to lower overall levels of efficiency. Such shortfalls can increase the possibility of corrupt and illegal practices occurring within health systems.

Weak Health Information Systems: Many developing countries in the region lack the capacity to put in place systematic health-surveillance systems. Such systems should collect information on births and deaths, data on censuses and household surveys, epidemiological information, data on the services provided, and track resources. Health-surveillance systems are an important component of well-functioning health-information systems. In many developing countries a large proportion of all deaths are not reported to national registration systems. The information that is reported is often not standardized or is not included in national databases even where data about diagnosis and treatments are collected locally. Inefficiency or wastefulness within health systems are often not recognized, thus preventing a more optimum allocation of scarce resources because of the lack of data.

Low Capacity Levels at Local Level in Decentralized Health Systems: Several countries in the region have embarked on a process of decentralizing public health services as part of broader processes of public-sector reform. However, the transfer of managerial responsibilities to lower administrative levels has not always been accompanied by a parallel level of devolution in financial resources and political authority. Many local governments lack the necessary capacity to plan and manage local health services.

Vertical Disease-Specific Campaigns: Many programmes addressing the health-related MDGs have been carried out through vertical disease-specific campaigns. Vertical approaches simplify management, implementation, monitoring and evaluation. Their intensive and focused nature often renders quick outcomes while also offering donor-favoured clear and traceable links to resources. However, the vertical approaches have frequently been found responsible for insufficient allocation of resources for the development and strengthening of health systems.

Right to Health

Article 25 of the Universal Declaration of Human Rights of 1948 states that:

1. Everyone has the right to a standard of living adequate for the health and well-being of himself and of his family, including food, clothing, housing and medical care and necessary social services, and the right to security in the event of unemployment, sickness, disability, widowhood, old age or other lack of livelihood in circumstances beyond his control.
2. Motherhood and childhood are entitled to special care and assistance. All children, whether born in or out of wedlock, shall enjoy the same social protection.

The Alma-Ata Declaration (International Conference on Primary Health Care, 1978) reaffirmed 'that health, which is a state of complete physical, mental and social well-being, and not merely the absence of disease or infirmity, is a fundamental human right and that the attainment of the highest possible level of health is a most important world-wide social goal whose realization requires the action of many other social and economic sectors in addition to the health sector.' It further stated that 'Economic and social development, based on a New International Economic Order, is of basic importance to the fullest attainment of health for all and to the reduction of the gap between the health status of the developing and developed countries. The promotion and protection of the health of the people is essential to sustained economic and social development and contributes to a better quality of life and to world peace.'

Progress in Investment in Health in Asian Sub-Regions

The progress of investment in health is compared in this chapter across Asian sub-regions with reference to public spending on health, life expectancy and the MDG–4 on reduction of child mortality, MDG–5 on improvement of maternal mortality and MDG–6 on combating HIV/AIDS, malaria and other diseases. The following table shows the comparative public spending on health as percentage of the GDP, progress of life expectancy and loss in inequality-adjusted life expectancy index in Asian sub-regions as reported by the latest HDR (United Nations Development Programme, 2013).

Table 9.1
Diversity in Public Spending on Health and Life Expectancy in Asian Sub-Regions

Level of Human Development 2012	Countries in Asia	Public Spending on Health % of GDP 2010	Life Expectancy at Birth (years) 2012	% Loss in Inequality-adjusted Life Expectancy 2012
East Asia				
V High	Japan	7.8	83.6	3.5
V High	South Korea	4.1	80.7	4.3
V High	Hong Kong	—	83.0	2.9
Medium	China	2.7	73.7	13.5
Low	North Korea	NA	69.0	NA
South East Asia				
V High	Singapore	1.4	81.2	2.9
V High	Brunei	2.4	78.1	5.8
High	Malaysia	2.4	74.5	6.7
Medium	Thailand	2.9	74.3	10.1
Medium	Philippines	1.3	69.0	15.2
Medium	Indonesia	1.3	69.4	16.8
Medium	Vietnam	2.6	75.4	13.4
Medium	Timor-Leste	5.1	62.9	30.2
Medium	Laos	1.5	67.8	21.7
Medium	Cambodia	2.1	63.6	28.8
Low	Myanmar	0.2	65.7	25.3
North and Central Asia				
High	Russia	3.2	69.1	10.8
High	Kazakhstan	2.5	67.4	16.2
Medium	Turkmenistan	1.5	65.2	26.7
Medium	Mongolia	3.0	68.8	18.8
Medium	Uzbekistan	2.8	68.6	24.3
Medium	Kyrgyzstan	3.5	68.0	19.8
Medium	Tajikistan	1.6	67.8	27.2
South Asia				
High	Sri Lanka	1.3	75.1	9.4
Medium	Maldives	3.8	77.1	7.3
Medium	India	1.2	65.8	27.1
Medium	Bhutan	4.5	67.6	24.1
Low	Pakistan	0.8	65.7	32.3
Low	Bangladesh	1.2	69.2	23.2
Low	Nepal	1.8	69.1	19.5

Public Spending on Health

According to Table 9.1, in about two-thirds of the countries in Asia, public spending is not more than 3 per cent of their GDP on health. Public spending on health is highest at 7.8 per cent, in the country with the highest level of development that is Japan. At the other extreme, Myanmar and Pakistan that are at low level of human development have the lowest percentage of public spending on health, 0.2 per cent and 0.8 per cent, respectively. However, in general, public spending on health does not always seem to be correlated with the level of human development. Singapore and Brunei, which are at very high level of human development, do not do much public spending on health which is 1.4 per cent and 2.4 per cent, respectively. On the other hand, the next highest percentage of percentage of public spending on health is in Timor-Leste at 5.1 per cent and Bhutan at 4.5 per cent, although both are at the medium level of human development.

Life Expectancy

Table 9.1 shows that life expectancy and equality in life expectancy in Asia is highest in countries at the very high level of human development. It shows the following sub-regional diversity:

East Asia: East Asia is leading in Asia with the highest life expectancy in Japan (83.4 years) and highest equality in life expectancy in Hong Kong. China has the lowest life expectancy in East Asia, at 73.7 years.

South East Asia: Singapore is leading in South East Asia at life expectancy of 81.2 years and loss in inequality at 2.9 per cent. Timor-Leste has the lowest life expectancy of 62.9 years in Asia and highest inequality in life expectancy in South East Asia at 30.2 per cent.

North and Central Asia: North and Central Asian countries are homogenous with reference to life expectancy ranging from 65.2 years in Turkmenistan to 69.1 years in Russia. The loss due to inequality in life expectancy in this sub-region ranges from 10.8 per cent in Russia to 27.2 per cent in Tajikistan.

South Asia: In South Asia, Maldives and Sri Lanka are better in life expectancy at 77.1 years and 75.1 years, respectively, and equality in life expectancy than most of the South East Asian countries and all the North and Central Asian countries. India and

Pakistan are lagging behind on these indicators. Pakistan's loss in inequality in life expectancy is the highest in Asia at 32.3 per cent.

Reduction of Child Mortality

Indicators for Child Mortality

The Target 5 for the MDG–4 is to reduce by two-thirds, between 1990 and 2015, the child mortality rate. The indicators for this target are:

- *Infant Mortality Rate:* The infant mortality rate is typically defined as the number of infants dying before reaching the age of one year per 1,000 live births in a given year.
- *Under-Five Mortality Rate:* The under-five mortality rate is the probability (expressed as a rate per 1,000 live births) of a child born in a specified year dying before reaching the age of five if subject to current age-specific mortality rates.
- *Proportion of One Year-Old Children Immunized against Measles:* The proportion of one year-old children immunized against measles is the percentage of children under one year of age who have received at least one dose of measles vaccine.

Measles is the leading cause of death among vaccine-preventable diseases.

Asia is lagging behind in reducing child mortality (UNESCAP, ADB and UNDP, 2010–11). The 2013 HDR provides the following data on infant and under-five mortality rates in Asian sub-regions.

Table 9.2
Diversity in Reduction of Child Mortality in Asian Sub-Regions

Level of Human Develop-ment 2012	Countries in Asia	Infant Mortality Deaths per 1000 Live Births 2010	Under-Five Mortality Deaths per 1000 Live Births 2010	Immunization against Measles % of Children under-five 2010	Immunization against DTP % of Children under-five 2010
East Asia					
V High	Japan	02	03	94	99
V High	South Korea	04	05	98	96
V High	Hong Kong	—	—	—	—
Medium	China	16	18	99	99
Low	North Korea	26	33	99	94

Cont'd...

...Cont'd

South East Asia					
V High	Singapore	02	03	95	98
V High	Brunei	06	07	94	98
High	Malaysia	05	06	96	98
Medium	Thailand	11	13	98	99
Medium	Philippines	23	29	88	89
Medium	Indonesia	27	35	89	94
Medium	Vietnam	19	23	98	93
Medium	Timor-Leste	46	55	66	75
Medium	Laos	42	54	64	81
Medium	Cambodia	43	51	93	93
Low	Myanmar	50	66	88	93
North and Central Asia					
High	Russia	09	12	98	99
High	Kazakhstan	29	33	99	99
Medium	Turkmenistan	47	56	99	99
Medium	Mongolia	26	32	97	98
Medium	Uzbekistan	44	52	98	99
Medium	Kyrgyzstan	33	38	99	99
Medium	Tajikistan	52	63	94	95
South Asia					
High	Sri Lanka	14	17	99	99
Medium	Maldives	14	15	97	97
Medium	India	48	63	74	83
Medium	Bhutan	44	56	95	94
Low	Pakistan	70	87	86	90
Low	Bangladesh	38	48	94	98
Low	Nepal	41	50	86	85

Infant Mortality

Table 9.2 shows that the infant mortality rate in Asia seems to be the lowest in countries with very high and high level of human development and high in countries at low level of human development. It shows the following sub-regional diversity:

East Asia: In East Asia, infant mortality is lowest in Japan and highest in North Korea. However, North Korea's infant mortality rate is still better than many countries in other sub-regions of Asia.

South East Asia: In South East Asia, infant mortality is lowest in Singapore and highest in Myanmar, Timor-Leste, Cambodia and Laos.

North and Central Asia: In North and Central Asia infant mortality is lowest in Russia and highest in Tajikistan, Turkmenistan and Uzbekistan.

South Asia: In South Asia infant mortality is lowest in Sri Lanka and Maldives and highest in Pakistan, India, Bhutan and Nepal. Pakistan has the highest infant mortality rate in Asia.

Under-Five Child Mortality

Table 9.2 shows that the under-five child mortality rate in Asia is also the lowest in countries with very high and high level of human development and high in countries at low level of human development. It shows the following sub-regional diversity:

East Asia: In East Asia, under-five child mortality rate is lowest in Japan and highest in North Korea.

South East Asia: In South East Asia, it is lowest in Singapore and highest in Myanmar, Timor-Leste, Laos and Cambodia.

North and Central Asia: In North and Central Asia, it is lowest in Russia and highest in Tajikistan, Turkmenistan and Uzbekistan.

South Asia: In South Asia, it is lowest in Maldives and Sri Lanka and highest in Pakistan, India and Bhutan. Again, Pakistan has the highest under-five child mortality in Asia.

Immunization against Measles

Table 9.2 shows that:

East Asia: China and North Korea have 99 per cent of their children immunized against measles.

North and Central Asia: The North and Central Asian countries are doing very well. Russia, Kazakhstan, Turkmenistan, Uzbekistan and Kyrgyzstan have 99 per cent of their children immunized against measles.

South East Asia: In South East Asia, Timor-Leste and Laos are lagging far behind in whole of Asia and Indonesia, Philippines and Myanmar are of concern.

South Asia: In South Asia, Sri Lanka has 99 per cent of their children immunized against measles. India, Pakistan and Nepal are of concern.

Immunization against DTP

DTP stands for diphtheria, pertussis and tetanus. Table 9.2 shows that:

East Asia: Japan and China in East Asia have 99 per cent of their children immunized against DTP.

North and Central Asia: The North and Central Asian countries are doing very well. Kazakhstan, Turkmenistan and Kyrgyzstan have 99 per cent of their children immunized against DTP.

South East Asia: In South East Asia, Timor-Leste and Laos are of concern.

South Asia: In South Asia, Sri Lanka has 99 per cent of their children immunized against DTP. India and Nepal are of concern.

Reduction of Maternal Mortality

Target 6 for MDG–5 is to reduce by three-quarters, between 1990 and 2015, the maternal mortality ratio. The Indicators for this target are the following:

- Maternal mortality ratio
- Proportion of births attended by skilled health personnel

Maternal Mortality Ratio

The maternal mortality ratio is the number of women who die from any cause related to or aggravated by pregnancy or its management (excluding accidental or incidental causes) during pregnancy and childbirth or within 42 days of termination of pregnancy, irrespective of the duration and site of the pregnancy, per 100,000 live births. The 10th revision of the International Classification of Diseases makes provision for including late maternal deaths occurring between six weeks and one year after childbirth.

Proportion of Births attended by Skilled Health Personnel

The proportion of births attended by skilled health personnel is the percentage of deliveries attended by personnel trained to give the necessary supervision, care and advice to women during pregnancy, labour and the post-partum period; to conduct deliveries on their own; and to care for newborn. Skilled health personnel include only those who are properly trained and who have appropriate equipment and drugs. Traditional birth attendants, even if they have received a short training course, are not to be included. Maternal health needs special attention as an unacceptable number of women perish from preventable and treatable complications related to pregnancy (UNESCAP, ADB and UNDP, 2010–11). The Asian Development Bank (2011) provides the following comparative data on maternal mortality ratio and proportion of births attended by skilled personnel in Asian sub-regions.

Table 9.3
Diversity in Reduction of Maternal Mortality in Asian Sub-Regions

Level of Human Development 2012	Country	Maternal Mortality Ratio (per 100,000 Live Births) 2008	% of Births attended by Skilled Health Personnel 2006–09
East Asia			
V High	Japan	008	100
V High	South Korea	018	100
V High	Hong Kong	002	—
Medium	China	038	099
Low	North Korea	—	
South East Asia			
V High	Singapore	009	100
V High	Brunei	021	100
High	Malaysia	031	064
Medium	Thailand	048	099
Medium	Philippines	094	062
Medium	Indonesia	240	075
Medium	Vietnam	056	088
Medium	Timor-Leste	370	029
Medium	Laos	580	020

Cont'd...

...*Cont'd*

Medium	Cambodia	290	044
Low	Myanmar	240	064
North and Central Asia			
High	Russia	—	—
High	Kazakhstan	45	100
Medium	Turkmenistan	77	100
Medium	Mongolia	65	099
Medium	Uzbekistan	30	100
Medium	Kyrgyzstan	81	098
Medium	Tajikistan	64	088
South Asia			
High	Sri Lanka	039	099
Medium	Maldives	037	095
Medium	India	230	053
Medium	Bhutan	200	071
Low	Pakistan	260	039
Low	Bangladesh	340	024
Low	Nepal	380	019

Asia is lagging behind in improving maternal health provision (UNESCAP, ADB and UNDP, 2010–11). Table 9.3 shows that the maternal mortality rate also seems to be the lowest in countries with very high and high level of human development and high in countries at low level of human development. The proportion of births attended by skilled health personnel, defined as a medically trained health-care provider (doctor, nurse or midwife), and the maternal mortality ratio are correlated to some extent. The table shows the following sub-regional diversity:

East Asia: In East Asia, maternal mortality ratio is low in Hong Kong and Japan. The proportion of births attended by skilled health personnel is almost 100 per cent in all the countries in this sub-region.

North and Central Asia: In North and Central Asia, maternal mortality ratio is lowest in Uzbekistan and highest in Kyrgyzstan, but the difference between the two is not much. The proportion of births attended by skilled health personnel in this sub-region is also almost 100 per cent in all the countries except in Tajikistan.

South East Asia: In South East Asia, maternal mortality ratio is low in Singapore and Brunei where the proportion of births attended by skilled health personnel is 100 per cent. Maternal mortality ratio is the highest, rather extremely high in Laos. It is also high in Timor-Leste, Cambodia, and Myanmar. These are countries which also have less than 50 per cent of their births attended by skilled personnel.

South Asia: In South Asia, maternal mortality ratio is low in Sri Lanka and Maldives where the proportion of births attended by skilled health personnel is high. Maternal mortality ratio is high in Nepal, Bangladesh and Pakistan, which have less than 50 per cent of their births attended by skilled personnel.

Combatting HIV/AIDS, Malaria and Tuberculosis

Combatting HIV/AIDS, Malaria and Tuberculosis

Target 7 for the MDG–6 to combat HIV/AIDS, Malaria and other diseases is having halted by 2015 and begun to reverse the spread of HIV/AIDS and incidence of Malaria and other diseases. The Asian Development Bank (2011) provides the following comparative data on prevalence/incidence of HIV, Malaria and Tuberculosis in Asian sub-regions.

Table 9.4
Diversity in Combatting of HIV, Malaria and Tuberculosis in Asian Sub-Regions

Level of Human Develop-ment 2012	Country	HIV Prevalence % Population 15–49 years 2009	Incidence of Malaria per 100,000 population 2008	Mortality Rate due to Malaria per 100,000 people 2008	Incidence of Tuberculosis per 100,000 population 2009
East Asia					
V High	Japan	<0.1	—	0.0	021
V High	South Korea	<0.1	8	0.0	090
V High	Hong Kong	—	—	0.0	082
Medium	China	0.1	3	0.0	096
Low	North Korea	—	—	0.0	
North and Central Asia					
High	Russia	—	—	0.0	—
High	Kazakhstan	0.1	—	0.0	163

Cont'd...

...*Cont'd*

Medium	Turkmenistan	—	—	0.0	067
Medium	Mongolia	<0.1	—	—	224
Medium	Uzbekistan	0.1	0	0.0	128
Medium	Kyrgyzstan	0.3	0	0.0	159
Medium	Tajikistan	0.2	9	0.0	202
South Asia					
High	Sri Lanka	<0.1	0021	0.0	066
Medium	Maldives	<0.1	—	0.9	039
Medium	India	0.3	1124	1.9	168
Medium	Bhutan	0.2	0100	0.2	158
Low	Pakistan	0.1	0881	0.8	231
Low	Bangladesh	<0.1	1510	1.8	225
Low	Nepal	0.4	0103	0.0	163
South East Asia					
V High	Singapore	0.1	—	0.0	036
V High	Brunei	—	—	0.0	060
High	Malaysia	0.5	00075	0.1	083
Medium	Thailand	1.3	00322	0.4	137
Medium	Philippines	<0.1	00096	0.2	280
Medium	Indonesia	0.2	01645	3.2	189
Medium	Vietnam	0.4	00055	0.1	200
Medium	Timor-Leste	—	46380	83.0	498
Medium	Laos	0.2	00327	2.9	089
Medium	Cambodia	0.5	01798	3.7	442
Low	Myanmar	0.6	07943	34.0	404

Sources: Columns 1, 2 and 4: Asian Development Bank, 2011
Column 3: United Nations Development Programme, 2013

Combatting HIV/AIDS

The indicators for combatting HIV/AIDS are:

HIV prevalence among pregnant women aged 15–24 years: HIV prevalence among 15–24 year-old pregnant women is the percentage of pregnant women ages 15–24 whose blood samples test positive for HIV.

Condom use rate of the contraceptive prevalence rate: Condom use rate of the contraceptive prevalence rate is the number of women aged 15–49 years in marital or consensual unions who are practising contraception by using condoms as a proportion of all women of the same age group in consensual unions who are practising, or whose sexual partners are practising, any form of contraception.

Condom use at last high-risk sex: Condom use at last high-risk sex is the percentage of young people ages 15–24 reporting the use of a condom during sexual intercourse with a non-regular sexual partner in the last 12 months.

Percentage of population aged 15–24 years with comprehensive correct knowledge of HIV/AIDS: Percentage of population aged 15–24 years with comprehensive correct knowledge of HIV/AIDS is the share of women and men aged 15–24 years who correctly identify the two major ways of preventing the sexual transmission of HIV (using condoms and limiting sex to one faithful, uninfected partner), who reject the two most common local misconceptions about HIV transmission and who know that a healthy-looking person can transmit HIV.

Contraceptive prevalence rate: The contraceptive prevalence rate is the percentage of women who are practising, or whose sexual partners are practising, any form of contraception. It is usually reported for women ages 15–49 in marital or consensual unions.

Ratio of school attendance of orphans to school attendance of non-orphans aged 10–14 years: Strictly defined, the number of children orphaned by HIV/AIDS is the estimated number of children who have lost their mother, father or both parents to AIDS before age 15. In practice, the impact of the AIDS epidemic on orphans is measured through the ratio of orphans to non-orphans who are in school.

Asia as a whole has already achieved the targets for preventing a rise in HIV prevalence (UNESCAP, ADB and UNDP, 2010–11). The MDG Fact Sheets (UNESCAP, 2006 and 2007a, b) show that Asia has relatively minor contribution (21%) to the world's number of people living with HIV/AIDS due mostly to the huge size of the problem in sub-Saharan Africa. Asia has so far avoided the African numbers for three reasons:

- The onset of the epidemic in parts of Asia occurred in the late 1980s, almost a decade later than in sub-Saharan Africa;

- With few exceptions, HIV infections in Asia stayed confined to specific population groups, such as sex workers, intravenous drug users and men having sex with men; and
- A more stable political environment in many Asian countries has made the implementation of policies and access to resources to combat the epidemic more effective.

However, many Asian countries are witnessing increasing adult HIV prevalence since 1990. Additionally, relatively low national prevalence rates mask localized epidemics that have the potential to escalate dramatically. The large populous countries of China, India and Indonesia are of particular concern. General prevalence in these countries is low, but this masks serious epidemics already under way in certain provinces, territories and states. The highest numbers of infected people are to be found in Russia, India, and China and the prevalence in the first two of these is rising (UNESCAP, 2006 and 2007a, b). Although Asia as a whole has already achieved the targets for preventing a rise in HIV prevalence, access to prevention and treatment services for HIV/AIDS still falls well below universal targets in Asia (UNESCAP, ADB and UNDP, 2010–11).

Table 9.4 shows that:

East Asia: East Asia, which has countries with very high level of human development, has low prevalence of HIV. Japan and South Korea have a very low prevalence of HIV (<0.1 per 100,000 population).

North and Central Asia: Countries in North and Central Asia that are at medium level of development also have low prevalence of HIV. Mongolia has a very low prevalence of HIV (<0.1 per 100,000 population).

South East Asia: The Philippines has a very low prevalence of HIV (<0.1 per 100,000 population). The highest prevalence of HIV is in Thailand (1.3), known for sex tourism. Besides Thailand, in South East Asia, Myanmar, Cambodia, Malaysia and Vietnam are countries of concern with reference to HIV prevalence.

South Asia: In South Asia, Sri Lanka and Maldives have a very low prevalence of HIV (<0.1 per 100,000 population). Nepal is of concern.

Combating Malaria

The indicators for combatting malaria include the following:

Prevalence and Death Rates associated with Malaria: Prevalence of malaria is the number of cases of malaria per 100,000 people. Death rates associated with malaria refers to the number of deaths caused by malaria per 100,000 people.

Proportion of Population in Malaria-Risk Areas using Effective Malaria Prevention and Treatment Measures: Malaria prevention is measured as the percentage of children ages 0–59 months sleeping under insecticide-treated bed-nets. Malaria treatment among children is measured as the proportion of children ages 0–59 months who were ill with fever in the two weeks before the survey and who received appropriate anti-malarial drugs.

Malaria is endemic to the world's poorest countries, mainly those in tropical and subtropical regions of Africa, Asia and the Americas (UNESCAP, 2006 and 2007a, b). Table 9.4 shows that malaria is non-existent in East and North and Central Asia as they are located in the temperate zone. In South Asia, Bangladesh and India are affected but not as much as in many countries of South East Asia. South East Asia is the worst affected by malaria. The South East Asian countries in the region of the Mekong River have been of concern with reference to malaria. It has been the leading cause of morbidity in Myanmar for many decades and remains the leading cause of morbidity in Laos (UNESCAP, 2007a). According to Table 9.4, the highest incidence of malaria is found in Timor-Leste followed by Myanmar, in the whole of Asia. Cambodia, Indonesia and Laos also have high incidence of malaria, higher than any other Asian sub-regions.

Combating Tuberculosis

The indicators for combatting tuberculosis include the following.

Prevalence and Death Rates associated with Tuberculosis: Tuberculosis (TB) prevalence is the number of cases of tuberculosis per 100,000 people. Death rates associated with tuberculosis refers to the number of deaths caused by TB per 100,000 people. A TB case is defined as a patient in whom TB has been bacteriologically confirmed or diagnosed by a clinician.

Proportion of Tuberculosis Cases Detected and Cured under Directly Observed Treatment Short Course DOTS: The TB detection rate is the percentage of estimated new infectious TB cases detected under the internationally recommended TB control strategy, DOTS. DOTS combines five elements – political commitment, microscopy services, drug supplies, surveillance and monitoring systems and use of highly efficacious regimes – with direct observation of treatment. The cure rate is the percentage of new, registered smear-positive (infectious) cases that were cured or in which a full course of DOTS was completed.

Asia, as a whole, has already achieved the targets for stopping the spread of TB (UNESCAP, ADB and UNDP, 2010–11). Table 9.4 shows that the incidence of TB is lowest in Japan and other countries at very high or high level of human development.

North and Central Asia: In North and Central Asia, the incidence of TB is highest in Mongolia and Tajikistan.

South Asia: In South Asia, the incidence of TB is highest in Pakistan and Bangladesh.

South East Asia: In Asia, the incidence of TB is highest in countries of South East Asia namely, Timor-Leste, Cambodia and Myanmar. It is also high in the Philippines.

Discussion

Overall Progress in Investment in Health in Asia

In about two-thirds of the countries in Asia, public spending is not more than three per cent of their GDP on health. In general, public spending on health does not always seem to be correlated with the level of human development. Life expectancy and equality in life expectancy, the child mortality rates and the maternal mortality rate in Asia are best in countries at the very high level of human development and vice versa. Asia is lagging behind in reducing child mortality and maternal mortality though doing well on coverage of children by immunization. The proportion of births attended by skilled health personnel and the maternal mortality ratio are correlated to some extent. Although Asia as a whole has already achieved the targets for preventing a rise in HIV prevalence, access to prevention and treatment services for HIV/AIDS still falls well below universal targets in Asia. Asia as a whole has also already achieved the targets for stopping the spread of TB.

Diversity in Progress in Investment in Health in Asian Sub-Regions

Diversity in progress of investment in health in Asian sub-regions is summarized below.

East Asia: East Asia mainly has countries with very high level of human development. It is leading in most of the health indicators, probably due to social policies concentrated on investment in education and health. The proportion of births attended by skilled health personnel is almost 100 per cent in all the countries in this sub-region. The sub-region has low prevalence of HIV and TB and malaria is non-existent as it is located in the temperate zone. Japan leads in investment in health with reference to highest level of public spending on health, highest life expectancy and child mortality rate. Hong Kong follows Japan in life expectancy but has the highest equality in life expectancy and lowest maternal mortality ratio in Asia. China which is at the medium level of human development has covered 99 per cent of children for immunization against measles and DTP. The only country of concern in East Asia is North Korea which has the highest child mortality rates t; however, it is still better than many countries in other sub-regions of Asia.

North and Central Asia: Russia, which is at the high level of human development, has the highest life expectancy and lowest loss due to inequality in life expectancy and lowest child mortality rate in North and Central Asia. North and Central Asian countries are homogenous with reference to life expectancy. Tajikistan, Turkmenistan and Uzbekistan are problematic with reference to child mortality rates. However, these and other North and Central Asian countries are doing very well on immunization against measles and DTP. Maternal mortality ratio is lowest in Uzbekistan and highest in Kyrgyzstan, but the difference between the two is not much. The proportion of births attended by skilled health personnel in this sub-region is also almost 100 per cent in all the countries except in Tajikistan. Countries in this sub-region have low prevalence of HIV and Malaria is non-existent as they are located in the temperate zone. The incidence of TB is highest in Mongolia and Tajikistan. The North and Central Asian countries are dismantling their socialist universal access to social services and so show moderate progress on health indicators.

South Asia: In South Asia, the Southern countries of Sri Lanka and Maldives are leading in investment in health with better in life expectancy and equality in life expectancy than most of the South East Asian countries and all the North and Central Asian countries. In these two countries, child mortality rates are lowest and maternal mortality ratio is also low as the proportion of births attended by skilled health personnel is high. They also have a very low prevalence of HIV and TB. India which is at the medium level of human development is of concern with reference to life expectancy, child mortality, immunization and incidence of malaria. Public spending on health is highest in Bhutan, which is at the medium level of human development. However, child mortality is of concern in Bhutan. Pakistan is most problematic among the countries at the low level of human development in South Asia. It has the lowest percentage of public spending on health, highest loss in inequality in life expectancy, highest child mortality rates and highest incidence of TB. It is also lagging behind with reference to life expectancy, immunization and maternal mortality ratio with less than 50 per cent of their births attended by skilled personnel. Bangladesh has high maternal mortality ratio, which has less than 50 per cent of their births attended by skilled personnel. Bangladesh is also affected by incidence of malaria and TB. Nepal is of concern with reference to immunization, maternal mortality ratio, with less than 50 per cent of their births attended by skilled personnel, and incidence of TB. South Asia has the weakest form of social policy and lag behind on many health indicators.

South East Asia: In Asia, South East Asia is worse affected by most of the health indicators and urgently need a health policy for universal coverage. Singapore and Brunei, which are at very high level of human development, do not do much public spending on health. However, Singapore is leading in South East Asia in life expectancy and loss in inequality in life expectancy. The child mortality rates are lowest in Singapore and maternal mortality ratio is lowest in Singapore and Brunei where the proportion of births attended by skilled health personnel is 100 per cent.

South East Asia is of concern as none of the countries in this sub-region have 99 per cent of their children immunized against measles or DTP. The sub-region is the worst affected by malaria compared to any other Asian sub-region. Moreover, in Asia, the incidence of TB is highest in countries of South East Asia. Myanmar has the lowest percentage of public spending on health in whole of Asia. In South East Asia, the child mortality rates are highest in Myanmar. Maternal mortality ratio is high in Myanmar with less than 64 per cent of their births attended by skilled personnel. Myanmar is of concern with reference to prevalence of HIV and TB. Public spending on health in Timor-Leste is high although it is at medium level of human development. However, Timor-Leste has the lowest life expectancy and highest inequality in life expectancy in South East Asia. Timor-Leste also has high child mortality rates, low level of immunization and maternal mortality ratio with only 29 per cent of their births attended by skilled personnel. The highest incidence of malaria and TB in Asia are found in Timor-Leste. Laos has high child mortality rates. With reference to immunization, Laos is lagging far behind in whole of Asia. Maternal mortality ratio is the highest in Laos with only 20 per cent of their births attended by skilled personnel. Malaria and TB are also of concern in Laos. Cambodia has high child mortality rates and maternal mortality rate and is of concern with reference to HIV prevalence. The highest prevalence of HIV is in Thailand, known for sex tourism. Besides Thailand, in South East Asia, Myanmar, Cambodia, Malaysia and Vietnam are countries of concern with reference to HIV prevalence.

Implications for Health Policy in Asia

According to the latest MDG Report on Asia Pacific (UNESCAP, ADB and UNDP, 2010–11), most governments have determined to improve the provision of health services but still fall short in terms of coverage and quality, particularly in rural areas. Since expenditure on health has stagnated, the region will require increasing public health expenditure, while seeking new health insurance models and increasing the number of primary health care workers.

The Report of the UNESCAP, ADB and UNDP (2007) makes the following recommendations (among others) for countries in the region to achieve the health-related MDGs:

1. Governments need to ensure the equitable access of all to basic health-care services, with particular attention to covering the poor.
2. Health should be at the forefront of social and economic development policies, including poverty reduction strategy papers.

3. A comprehensive approach by governments should extend beyond the ministry of health to involve all relevant line ministries from the local to the national levels.
4. Government expenditures on health and health-related sectors should be increased in order to encourage synergies.
5. Regulatory frameworks are required to protect the rights to good health of the poor, minorities and other vulnerable groups.
6. Improved management, good performance standards and accountability within health systems are essential.
7. Affordable access to essential drugs should be promoted by encouraging the production and use of generic drugs and taking steps to implement policies that affect the supply of and demand for them.
8. Adequate levels of health literacy should be ensured; as such knowledge is crucial for making informed decisions regarding health risks.
9. Communities should be empowered to assert their right to health because it contributes to making governments accountable for the availability and quality of the services provided.
10. A healthy setting encourages the participation of individuals and communities and emphasizes the responsibilities that local governments should assume.
11. Primary care should be strengthened and integrated with higher-level referral systems to ensure that comprehensive health care is available.
12. Health-information systems should be improved so that they can detect the trends in health and diseases, allow for better responses and improve the efficiency of health systems.
13. Decentralization can result in better alignment of health-care services with specific local needs, provided the necessary financial resources are available and the capacity at the provincial and local levels has been developed.
14. Multisectoral interventions should be promoted so that they contribute to health from the community to the national levels.

15. Coordination and integration of disease-specific approaches within comprehensive frameworks that address the multiple determinants of the health MDGs should be promoted.
16. Multisectoral approaches at the societal level should include the participation of civil society organizations.
17. Vertical and exclusively curative approaches need to be changed to also emphasize preventive and health-promotion strategies.
18. Providing increased access to safe drinking water and improved sanitation will contribute strongly to improving the health status of populations in the region.

References

Ariana, P. and Naveed, A. (2009). Health. In S. Deneulin and L. Shahani (eds), *An Introduction to the Human Development and Capability Approach: Freedom and Agency*. London: Earthscan.

Asian Development Bank. (2011). *Key Indicators for Asia and the Pacific*. Manila. Retrieved 31 March 2013 from http://www.adb.org/key-indicators/ 2011/main

International Conference on Primary Health Care. (1978). Declaration of Alma-Ata. Alma-Ata, USSR. Retrieved 5 May 2013 from http://www.who.int/publications/almaata_declaration_en.pdf

OECD Policy Brief (2003). Poverty and health in developing countries: Key actions. Retrieved 14 March 2012 from https://docs.google.com/viewer?url=http%3A%2F%2Fwww.oecd.org%2Fdataoecd%2F39%2F62%2F18514159.pdf

Sen, A. (1999). *Development as Freedom*. New York: Random House.

Spence, R. (2009). Economic growth. In S. Deneulin and L. Shahani (eds), *Human Development and Capability Approach: Freedom and Agency* (pp. 73–100). London: Earthscan.

United Nations Development Programme. (2013). *Human Development Report: The Rise of the South: Human Progress in a Diverse World*. New York.

UNDP-UNEP Poverty Environment Initiative. (2009). *Mainstreaming Poverty-Environment Linkages into Development Planning: A Handbook for Practitioners*. Retrieved 2 November 2011 from http://www.unpei. org/PDF/PEI-full-handbook.pdf

United Nations Economic and Social Commission for Asia and the Pacific. (2006). UNESCAP Fact Sheets on MDGs in South Asia. Retrieved 19 May 2010 from http://www.mdgasiapacific.org/files/shared_folder/documents/ fs_sa_mdg_all.pdf

——. (2007a). UNESCAP Fact Sheets on MDGs in East and South East Asia. Retrieved 19 May 2010 from http://www.mdgasiapacific.org/files/shared_folder/ documents/fs_sea_mdg_all.pdf

——. (2007b). UNESCAP Fact Sheets on MDGs in North and Central Asia. Retrieved 19 May 2010 from http://www.mdgasiapacific.org/files/shared_folder/ documents/fs_nca_mdg_all_en.pdf

United Nations Economic and Social Commission for Asia and the Pacific, Asian Development Bank and United Nations Development Program. (2010–11). *Paths to 2015: MDG Priorities in Asia and the Pacific.* Retrieved 2 December 2010 from http://www.adb.org/Documents/Reports/Asia-Pacific-MDG-2010/default.asp

——. (2007). *Achieving the Health Millennium Development Goals in Asia and the Pacific: Policies and Actions within Health Systems and Beyond.* New York.

——. (2012–13). *Perspectives for a Post-2015 Development Agenda: Asia-Pacific Regional MDGs Report 2012/13.*

United Nations Educational, Scientific and Cultural Organization. (2002). *EFA Global Monitoring Report: Education for All: Is the World on Track?* Retrieved 15 March 2012 from http://www.unesco.org/new/en/education/themes/leading-the-international-agenda/efareport/reports/2002-efa-on-track/

World Health Organisation. (1998). *Health Promotion Glossary.* Geneva: Author. Retrieved from http://www.who.int/healthpromotion/about/HPR%20Glossary%201998.pdf?ua=1

——. (2008). *Closing the Gap in a Generation: Health Equity through Action on the Social Determinants of Health.* Geneva. Retrieved 14 March 2012 from http://whqlibdoc.who.int/hq/2008/WHO_IER_CSDH_08.1_eng.pdf

——. (no date). *Investing in Health: A Summary of the Findings of the Commission on Macroeconomics and Health.* Retrieved 14 March 2012 from https://docs.google.com/viewer?url=http%3A% 2F%2Fwww.who.int%2Fentity%2Fmacrohealth%2Finfocentre%2Fadvocacy%2Fen%2Finvestinginhealth02052003.pdf

CHAPTER 10

Diversity in Progress in Investment in Education in Asia

Introduction

Education is a key dimension of human development. This chapter on diversity in progress in investment in education in Asia reviews the following:

1. Concepts of investment in and importance of education, barriers to education and right to education.
2. Progress in investment in education in Asia with reference to public spending on education, EFA Development Index, progress in school education and progress in youth and adult literacy.
3. Diversity in progress in investment in education in Asian sub-regions.
4. Implications for education policy in Asia.

Conceptual Framework of Investment in Education

Importance of Education

From the capability perspective, education is important for a number of reasons:

1. First, the skills provided by basic education, such as being able to read and write, are valuable in their own right, as a fundamental outcome of development.

2. Second, education can help to displace other more negative features of life. For example, free and compulsory primary education will reduce child labour.
3. Third, education has a powerful role in empowering those who suffer from multiple disadvantages. Thus, women who have benefitted from education may simply survive better and longer than they would otherwise.

Defined in this way, education that is universal, attained by all, regardless of class or caste or gender, has a powerful impact in addressing social and economic barriers within a society and is central to realizing human freedoms (United Nations Educational, Scientific and Cultural Organization, 2002).

Ranis, Stewart and Ramirez (2000, cited by Spence, 2009) highlight the following ways in which improvements in education contribute to greater economic growth:

1. Health, primary and secondary education and nutrition raise the productivity of workers.
2. Secondary education facilitates the acquisition of skills and managerial capacity.
3. Tertiary education supports the development of basic science, the appropriate selection of technology imports, and the domestic adaptation and development of technologies.
4. Secondary and tertiary education represents critical elements in the development of key institutions, such as government, the law and the financial system.
5. A better educated workforce is more creative, leading to greater technological innovation.
6. A better educated female workforce leads to reduced fertility rates and, hence, higher economic growth per capita.

There is substantial evidence that education can reduce poverty. This connection between education and poverty works through three mechanisms: first, more educated people earn more; secondly, more (and especially better quality) education improves economic growth and, thereby, economic opportunities and incomes; and thirdly, education brings wider social benefits that improve economic development and especially the situation of the poor, such as lower fertility, improved health care of children, and greater participation of women in the labour force (van der Berg, 2008). There is now robust evidence that human capital is a key determinant of economic growth and emerging evidence indicates that it is also associated with a wide range of non-economic benefits such as better health and well-being. Investment in human capital, and by implication in education, has thus moved to centre stage in strategies to promote economic prosperity, fuller employment and social cohesion. As a result, education is increasingly considered an investment in the collective future of societies and nations, rather than simply in the future success of individuals (Organization for Economic Co-operation and Development, 2002).

Barriers to Education

Disparities in access, quality of education and learning outcomes among populations exist in large part due to social, economic and cultural factors. Marginalized individuals and groups do not just accumulate fewer years of education, but often received a poorer quality education that results in low levels of learning achievement. Underlying causes are diverse and interconnected, with household poverty being one of the strongest and most persistent factors for educational marginalization, gender is another important barrier, especially when these are combined with other factors such as culture, language, ethnicity, race, geographical location, disability, health and other socio-political contexts (United Nations Development Group, 2010).

Right to Education

Article 26 of the Universal Declaration of Human Rights of 1948 states that:

1. Everyone has the right to education. Education shall be free, at least in the elementary and fundamental stages. Elementary education shall be compulsory. Technical and professional education shall be made generally available and higher education shall be equally accessible to all on the basis of merit.
2. Education shall be directed to the full development of the human personality and to the strengthening of respect for human rights and fundamental freedoms. It shall promote understanding, tolerance and friendship among all nations, racial or religious groups, and shall further the activities of the United Nations for the maintenance of peace.

3. Parents have a prior right to choose the kind of education that shall be given to their children.

In 1990, United Nations Educational, Scientific and Cultural Organization (UNESCO) organized the World Conference on Education for All (EFA) in Jomtien, Thailand, to make primary education accessible to all children and to massively reduce illiteracy before the end of the decade. The delegates adopted a *World Declaration on Education for All*, which reaffirmed the notion of education as a fundamental human right and urged countries to intensify efforts to address the basic learning needs of all. The *Framework for Action to Meet the Basic Learning Needs* defined targets and strategies to meet the basic learning needs of all by the year 2000. The goals included universal access to learning; a focus on equity; emphasis on learning outcomes; broadening the means and the scope of basic education; enhancing the environment for learning; and strengthening partnerships. Ten years later, with many countries far from having reached this goal, the international community met again in Dakar, Senegal, and affirmed their commitment to achieving EFA by the year 2015. They identified six key education goals which aim to meet the learning needs of all children, youth and adults by 2015:

- Goal 1: Expand early childhood care and education
- Goal 2: Provide free and compulsory primary education for all
- Goal 3: Promote learning and life skills for young people and adults
- Goal 4: Increase adult literacy
- Goal 5: Achieve gender parity
- Goal 6: Improve the quality of education

(http://www.unesco.org/new/en/education/themes/leading-the-international-agenda/education-for-all/efa-goals/).

Progress in Investment in Education in Asian Sub-Regions

The following table shows the comparative public spending on education as percentage of GDP, progress in mean years of schooling and loss in inequality-adjusted education in Asian sub-regions as reported by the latest HDR (United Nations Development Programme, 2013). The data on EDI is taken from UNESCO report (2012).

Table 10.1
Diversity in Public Spending on Education and Education Indicators in Asian Sub-Regions

Level of Human Development 2012	Countries in Asia	Public spending on Education % of GDP 2005–2010	EDI 2010	% Loss in Inequality-adjusted Education 2012
East Asia				
V High	Japan	3.8	0.997	NA
V High	South Korea	5.0	0.972	25.5
V High	Hong Kong	3.6	—	NA
Medium	China	NA	—	23.2
South East Asia				
V High	Singapore	3.3	—	NA
V High	Brunei	2.0	—	NA
High	Malaysia	5.8	—	NA
Medium	Thailand	3.8	—	18.0
Medium	Philippines	2.7	0.898	13.5
Medium	Indonesia	3.0	0.938	20.4
Medium	Vietnam	5.3	—	17.1
Medium	Timor-Leste	14.0	0.769	47.6
Medium	Laos	3.3	0.802	31.2
Medium	Cambodia	2.6	0.801	28.3
Low	Myanmar	—	—	NA
North and Central Asia				
High	Russia	4.1	0.976	NA
High	Kazakhstan	3.1	—	6.5
Medium	Turkmenistan	NA	—	NA
Medium	Mongolia	5.4	0.968	8.9
Medium	Uzbekistan	NA	0.970	1.4
Medium	Kyrgyzstan	6.2	0.978	6.5
Medium	Tajikistan	4.0	0.976	12.2
South Asia				
High	Sri Lanka	2.1	—	14.6
Medium	Maldives	8.7	—	41.2
Medium	India	3.1	0.790	42.4
Medium	Bhutan	4.0	0.803	12.2
Low	Pakistan	2.4	0.656	45.2
Low	Bangladesh	2.2	—	39.4
Low	Nepal	4.7	—	43.6

Public Spending on Education

Table 10.1 shows that:

East Asia: In East Asia, public spending on education as percentage of GDP ranges from 5 per cent in South Korea to 3.6 per cent in Hong Kong.

South East Asia: South East Asia is most diverse where public spending is highest in Timor-Leste (14.0%), which is also the highest in whole of Asia. It is lowest (2.0%) in Brunei which is also the lowest in whole of Asia. Brunei's spending on education is less although it is classified at very high level of development.

North and Central Asia: In North and Central Asia, public spending on education ranges from 6.2 per cent in Kyrgyzstan to 3.1 per cent in Kazakhstan.

South Asia: In South Asia, public spending on education is highest in Maldives (8.7%) and lowest in Sri Lanka (2.1%).

EFA Development Index

The EFA Development Index (EDI) is a composite index that provides a snapshot of overall progress of national education systems towards Education for All. Due to data constraints, the index has until now captured only four of the six goals. The development of an ECCE index this year allows the EDI to be broadened to five goals. The first part of this Annex assesses countries across four dimensions of the EDI. The next part extends the EDI to include the ECCE index and shows how this affects the ranking of countries for which data are available. The value of the standard EDI for a given country is the arithmetic mean of the four components:

- Universal primary education (goal 2), measured by the primary adjusted net enrollment ratio;
- Adult literacy (goal 4), measured by the literacy rate for those aged 15 and above.
- Gender parity and equality (goal 5), measured by the gender-specific EFA index (GEI), an average of the gender parity indices (GPIs) of the primary and secondary gross enrollment ratios and the adult literacy rate.
- Quality of education (goal 6), measured by the survival rate to grade 5; in the absence of comparable indicators on quality,

notably on learning outcomes, the survival rate is used as a proxy because of its positive correlation with average international learning assessment scores.

The EDI value falls between 0 and 1, with 1 representing full achievement of EFA across the four goals (UNESCO, 2012).

Table 10.1 shows the EDI of select countries in Asia. Countries that have high level of EDI (= 0.95) are Japan and South Korea in East Asia, and Kyrgyzstan, Uzbekistan, Russia, and Mongolia in North and Central Asia. Countries with medium level of EDI (0.80 to 0.94) are Indonesia, Philippines, Laos and Cambodia in South East Asia and Bhutan in South Asia. The countries with low level of EDI (<0.80) are India and Pakistan in South Asia and Timor-Leste in South East Asia.

Progress in Pre-Primary Education

The UNESCO (2012) provides the following data for progress in pre-primary education in Asian sub-regions.

Table 10.2

Diversity in Progress in Pre-Primary Education in Asian Sub-Regions

Level of Human Development 2012	Country	Gross Enrolment Ratio in Pre-Primary Education (%)
East Asia		
V High	Japan	43
V High	South Korea	119
V High	Hong Kong	—
Medium	China	54
Low	North Korea	—
South East Asia		
V High	Singapore	—
V High	Brunei	88
High	Malaysia	67
Medium	Thailand	100
Medium	Philippines	51
Medium	Indonesia	18
Medium	Vietnam	82

Cont'd...

...Cont'd

Medium	Timor-Leste	—
Medium	Laos	22
Medium	Cambodia	13
Low	Myanmar	10
North and Central Asia		
High	Russia	90
High	Kazakhstan	48
Medium	Turkmenistan	—
Medium	Mongolia	77
Medium	Uzbekistan	26
Medium	Kyrgyzstan	19
Medium	Tajikistan	09
South Asia		
High	Sri Lanka	—
Medium	Maldives	114
Medium	India	55
Medium	Bhutan	05
Low	Pakistan	—
Low	Bangladesh	13
Low	Nepal	—

The table above shows that:

- Only South Korea, Thailand and Maldives have reached the EFA Goal one and expanded early childhood care and education to all their children in early childhood.
- A majority of children in early childhood in Russia, Brunei, Vietnam, Malaysia, Mongolia, China and India have access to early childhood care and education.
- A majority of children in early childhood in other countries, irrespective of the sub-region and irrespective of the level of human development, do not have access to early childhood care and education.

Progress in School Education

The following table shows the diversity in mean years of schooling and school enrollment ratio at primary, secondary and tertiary levels in Asian sub-regions provided by the 2013 HDR (United Nations Development Programme, 2013).

Table 10.3

Diversity in Progress of School Enrollment Ratio in Asian Sub-Regions

Level of Human Develop-ment 2012	Country	Mean Years of Schooling 2010	Primary Enrolment Ratio % 2002–11	Secondary Enrolment Ratio % 2002–11	Tertiary Enrolment Ratio % 2002–11	% of Primary School Teachers Trained to Teach 2005–11
East Asia						
V High	Japan	11.6	103.0	102.0	059.0	—
V High	South Korea	11.6	104.0	097.0	103.9	—
V High	Hong Kong	10.0	102.0	083.0	059.7	095.6
Medium	China	7.5	111.0	081.0	025.9	—
Low	North Korea	—	—	—	—	—
South East Asia						
V High	Singapore	10.1	101.8	106.9	071.0	094.3
V High	Brunei	8.6	108.0	110.0	017.2	087.1
High	Malaysia	9.5	096.0	068.0	040.2	—
Medium	Thailand	6.6	091.0	079.0	047.7	—
Medium	Philippines	8.9	106.0	085.0	028.9	—
Medium	Indonesia	5.8	118.0	077.0	023.1	—
Medium	Vietnam	5.5	106.0	077.0	022.3	098.3
Medium	Timor-Leste	4.4	117.0	056.0	016.7	—
Medium	Laos	4.6	121.0	045.0	013.4	096.9
Medium	Cambodia	5.8	127.0	046.0	007.8	099.1
Low	Myanmar	3.9	126.0	054.0	011.0	099.9
North and Central Asia						
High	Russia	11.7	099.0	089.0	075.9	—

Cont'd...

...Cont'd

High	Kazakhstan	10.4	111.0	100.0	040.8	—
Medium	Turkmenistan	9.9	—	—	—	—
Medium	Mongolia	8.3	100.0	093.0	053.3	097.8
Medium	Uzbekistan	10.0	095.0	106.0	008.9	100.0
Medium	Kyrgyzstan	9.3	100.0	084.0	048.8	068.4
Medium	Tajikistan	9.8	102.0	087.0	019.7	092.9
South Asia						
High	Sri Lanka	9.3	099.0	087.0	015.5	—
Medium	Maldives	5.8	109.9	071.0	—	077.0
Medium	India	4.4	118.0	060.0	016.2	—
Medium	Bhutan	2.3	111.0	070.0	008.8	091.5
Low	Pakistan	4.9	095.0	034.0	005.4	084.2
Low	Bangladesh	4.8	—	—	010.6	058.4
Low	Nepal	3.2	115.0	044.0	005.6	080.7

Mean Years of Schooling

Table 10.3 shows that with reference to mean years of schooling:

East Asia: Japan and South Korea are leading at 11.6 years of mean years of schooling, giving East Asia a lead. In East Asia, the loss in inequality-adjusted education ranges from 23.2 per cent in China to 25.5 per cent in South Korea, although the latter has a very high level of human development.

North and Central Asia: Russia and the Central Asian countries have between 9 and 10 years of schooling. In North and Central Asia, the loss in inequality-adjusted education ranges from 1.4 per cent in Uzbekistan which is minimum in whole of Asia, to 12.2 per cent in Tajikistan; this sub-region has the minimum percentage loss by inequality in education.

South East Asia: The mean year of schooling is less than 10 years in both Singapore and Brunei although their level of human development is very high. In South East Asia the loss in inequality-adjusted education ranges from 13.5 per cent in the Philippines to 47.6 per cent in Timor-Leste, which is the highest in whole of Asia.

South Asia: In South Asia, Sri Lanka is leading with 9.3 years of schooling and Bhutan has the lowest mean years of schooling (2.3) in whole of Asia. In South Asia, percentage loss by inequality in education ranges from 12.2 per cent in Bhutan to 45.2 per cent in Pakistan.

Goal 2 of EFA is to provide free and compulsory primary education for all. The Target 2 for the MDG–2 is to ensure that, by 2015, children everywhere, boys and girls alike, will be able to complete a full course of primary schooling. The indicators for this target are the following:

Net Enrolment Ratio in Primary Education: Net primary enrollment ratio is the ratio of the number of children of official school age (as defined by the national education system) who are enrolled in primary school to the total population of children of official school age. Primary education provides children with basic reading, writing, and mathematics skills along with an elementary understanding of such subjects as history, geography, natural science, social science, art and music.

Proportion of Pupils Starting Grade One Who Reach Grade Five: The proportion of pupils starting grade one who reach grade five, known as the survival rate to grade five, is the percentage of a cohort of pupils enrolled in grade one of the primary level of education in a given school year who are expected to reach grade five.

School Enrolment and Trained Primary School Teachers

Table 9.3 shows that Asia has achieved primary school enrollment ratio of above 90 per cent. The percentage of primary school teachers trained to teach is not available for many countries. For which it is available, it is highest in Uzbekistan and lowest in Bangladesh. The secondary school enrollment ratio is generally not as good as the primary school enrollment ratio except in Singapore, Brunei and Uzbekistan where it is higher than the primary ratio. At the tertiary level, only South Korea has reached the 100%+ ratio. The table shows the following sub-regional diversity:

East Asia: In East Asia, all the countries have reached the primary school enrollment ratio of 100 per cent or more. The secondary school enrollment ratio in this sub-region ranges from 81 per cent in China to 102 per cent in Japan. With reference to tertiary enrollment ratio, South Korea scores the best in East Asia as well as whole of Asia.

South East Asia: In South East Asia, the primary school enrollment ratio ranges from 91 per cent in Thailand to 127 per cent in Cambodia. The secondary school enrollment ratio in this sub-region ranges from as low as 45 per cent in Laos to 110 per cent in Brunei. With reference to tertiary enrollment ratio, Singapore leads, followed by Thailand and Malaysia. Cambodia is of concern at secondary level and major concern at tertiary level.

North and Central Asia: In North and Central Asia, the primary school enrollment ratio ranges from 95 per cent in Uzbekistan to 111 per cent in Kazakhstan. The secondary school enrollment ratio in this sub-region ranges from 84 per cent in Kyrgyzstan to 106 per cent in Uzbekistan. With reference to tertiary enrollment ratio, Russia leads and Uzbekistan is of major concern.

South Asia: In South Asia, the primary school enrollment ratio ranges from 95 per cent in Pakistan to 118 per cent in India. The secondary school enrollment ratio in this sub-region ranges from as low as 34 per cent in Pakistan to 87 per cent in Sri Lanka. With reference to tertiary enrollment ratio, India leads and Pakistan and Bhutan are of major concern.

Gender Disparities in School Education

Asia as a whole has already achieved the MDG target for reducing gender disparities in primary, secondary and tertiary education enrollment (UNESCAP, ADB and UNDP, 2010–11). Targets for basic education must go beyond universal primary education (UPE) as the broader EFA goals illustrate with their emphasis on early childhood care and education, quality of learning, gender equality, and learning skills for young people, and adult literacy (United Nations Development Group, 2010).

Progress in Youth and Adult Literacy

Goal 4 of EFA is to increase adult literacy. Overall, one-sixth of the world's population, approximately 760 million persons, cannot read or write (United Nations Development Group, 2010). The following table provides comparative data for Asian sub-regions on youth literacy rate by Asian Development Bank (2011) and adult literacy rate by UNESCO (2012).

Table 10.4
Diversity in Progress in Youth Literacy Rate in Asian Sub-Regions

Level of Human Development 2012	Country	% Youth Literacy Rate (15–24 years) 2005–2009	% Adult Literacy Rate (15 years and above) 2005–10
East Asia			
V High	Japan	—	—
V High	South Korea	—	—
V High	Hong Kong	—	—
Medium	China	99.4	94
Low	North Korea	—	—
North and Central Asia			
High	Russia	—	100
High	Kazakhstan	99.8	100
Medium	Turkmenistan	99.8	100
Medium	Mongolia	96.0	97
Medium	Uzbekistan	99.9	99
Medium	Kyrgyzstan	99.8	99
Medium	Tajikistan	99.9	100
South East Asia			
V High	Singapore	99.8	96
V High	Brunei	99.7	95
High	Malaysia	98.5	93
Medium	Thailand	98.1	94
Medium	Philippines	97.8	95
Medium	Indonesia	99.5	93
Medium	Vietnam	96.9	93
Low	Timor-Leste	—	58
Medium	Laos	83.9	73
Medium	Cambodia	87.5	74
Low	Myanmar	95.7	92
South Asia			
High	Sri Lanka	98.0	91
Medium	Maldives	99.3	98
Medium	India	81.1	63
Medium	Bhutan	74.4	53
Low	Pakistan	71.1	55
Low	Bangladesh	75.5	57
Low	Nepal	82.0	60

Table 10.4 shows that Central Asia is leading in youth literacy. Singapore, Brunei, China and Maldives also have more than 99 per cent of literacy among youth. South Asia, especially, Pakistan, Bhutan and Bangladesh lag behind. The table further shows that as far as adult literacy is concerned, Russia, Kazakhstan, Turkmenistan and Tajikistan in North and Central Asia have 100 per cent adult literacy. Although Singapore and Brunei are at very high level of human development, they have not reached this level. Countries of concern are those that have below 80 per cent of adult literacy. These are Cambodia, Laos and Timor-Leste in South East Asia and India, Nepal, Bangladesh, Pakistan and Bhutan in South Asia.

Discussion

Overall Progress in Investment in Education in Asia

A majority of children in early childhood in Asia, irrespective of the sub-region and irrespective of the level of human development, do not have access to early childhood care and education. Asia has achieved primary school enrollment ratio of above 90 per cent. The secondary school enrollment ratio is generally not as good as the primary school enrollment ratio except in Singapore, Brunei and Uzbekistan where it is higher than the primary ratio. At the tertiary level, only South Korea has reached the 100%+ ratio. In primary enrollment and primary completion, Asia without India and China is not on track but slow (UNESCAP, ADB and UNDP, 2012–13).

Diversity in Progress in Investment in Education in Asian Sub-Regions

The diversity in progress of investment in education in Asian sub-regions is summarized below.

East Asia: East Asia is leading in mean years of schooling, achievement of primary education and youth literacy rate, probably due to social policies concentrated on investment in education and health. Public spending on education as percentage of GDP ranges from 5 per cent in South Korea to 3.6 per cent in Hong Kong. Japan and South Korea are leading at 11.6 years of mean years of schooling, giving East Asia a lead. In East Asia, the loss in inequality-adjusted education ranges from 23.2 per cent in China to 25.5 per cent in South Korea, although the latter has a very high level of human development. All the countries have reached the primary school enrollment ratio of 100 per cent or more. The secondary school enrollment ratio in this sub-region ranges from 81 per cent in China to 102 per cent in Japan. With reference to tertiary enrollment ratio, South Korea scores the best in East Asia as well as whole of Asia.

North and Central Asia: Public spending on education ranges from 6.2 per cent in Kyrgyzstan to 3.1 per cent in Kazakhstan. Russia and the Central Asian countries have between 9 and 10 years of schooling. With the background of communist rule, this sub-region has the minimum percentage loss by inequality in education. Although not at the very high level of human development, this sub-region is leading in Asia with reference to primary education completion rate. With the background of communist rule, North and Central Asia are leading in Asia with reference to primary education completion rate and has a near total youth literacy rate and have the minimum percentage loss by inequality in mean years of schooling. However, these countries are in the process of dismantling their socialist universal access to social services.

South East Asia: South East Asia is most diverse where public spending is highest in Timor-Leste (14.0%), which is also the highest in whole of Asia. It is lowest (2.0%) in Brunei which is also the lowest in whole of Asia. Brunei's spending on education is less although it is classified at very high level of development. The mean year of schooling is less than 10 years in both Singapore and Brunei although their level of human development is very high. In South East Asia the loss in inequality-adjusted education ranges from 13.5 per cent in the Philippines to 47.6 per cent in Timor-Leste, which is the highest in whole of Asia. The primary school enrollment ratio ranges from 91 per cent in Thailand to 127 per cent in Cambodia. The secondary school enrollment ratio in this sub-region ranges from as low as 45 per cent in Laos to very high of 110 per cent in Brunei. With reference to tertiary enrollment ratio, Singapore leads, followed by Thailand and Malaysia. Cambodia is of concern at secondary level and major concern at tertiary level.

South Asia: South Asia has the weakest form of social policy and lags behind on most education indicators as well as has high gender gap. Public spending on education is highest in Maldives (8.7%) and lowest in Sri Lanka (2.1%). Sri Lanka is leading with 9.3 years of schooling and Bhutan has the lowest mean years of schooling (2.3) in whole of Asia. In this sub-region, percentage loss by inequality in education ranges from 12.2 per cent in Bhutan to as high as 45.2 per cent in Pakistan. The primary school enrollment ratio ranges from 95 per cent in Pakistan to 118 per cent in India. The secondary school enrollment ratio in this sub-region ranges from as low as 34 per cent in Pakistan to 87 per cent in Sri Lanka. With reference to tertiary enrollment ratio, India leads and Pakistan and Bhutan are of major concern.

Implications for Education Policy in Asia

According to the latest Report the MDGs (UNESCAP, ADB and UNDP, 2010–11), most governments have determined to improve provision of education services but still fall short in terms of coverage and quality, particularly in rural areas. Governments have been allocating more resources to education though as a proportion of GDP but this is still lower than the global average.

EFA will not be achieved unless equal attention is paid to all goals. This requires particular attention to those considered the most neglected, including ECCE and adult literacy. Breaking the intergenerational cycle of education deprivation by providing quality education to all children, including in their early life years, and to their parents, is key (UNESCO, 2012). Since limited progress has been made in narrowing inequality gaps in education, despite this being a key feature of the EFA agenda, in 2013 the following guiding principles have been proposed by the EFA Global Monitoring Report team for setting the post-2015 education goals:

- The right to an education, as guaranteed under international and national laws and conventions, must be at the core of the goals. As a right, education should be free and compulsory. It should help people fulfil their potential and should foster the well-being and prosperity of individuals and society.
- Ensuring that all people have an equal chance of education, regardless of their circumstances, must be at the heart of every goal. No person should be denied access to quality education because of factors such as poverty, gender, location, ethnicity or disability.

- The goals should recognize the learning needs at each stage of a person's life, and that learning takes place in non-formal as well as formal settings.
- One main goal should set the overall ambition for education as part of a broader post-2015 global framework. This overarching goal should be universally applicable, and divided into individual goals that make up a post-2015 education framework. Each of these individual goals should also be linked with other goals to be identified in the broader global framework.
- The goals should enable governments and the international community to be held to account for their education commitments. Each goal must have a specific deadline, be worded clearly and simply, be measurable, and have the ambition of getting to zero. The framework should include a commitment to monitoring the goals regularly and rigorously at the global, national and local levels (http://unesdoc.unesco.org/images/0022/002200/220033E.pdf).

References

Asian Development Bank. (2011). *Key Indicators for Asia and the Pacific.* Manila. Retrieved 31 March 2013 from http://www.adb.org/key-indicators/ 2011/main

Organization for Economic Co-operation and Development. (2002). *Financing Education – Investments and Returns: Analysis of the World Education Indicators.* Retrieved 15 March 2012 from http://www.oecd.org/ dataoecd/27/8/2494749.pdf

Spence, R. (2009). Economic growth. In S. Deneulin and L. Shahani (eds), *Human Development and Capability Approach: Freedom and Agency* (pp. 73–100). London: Earthscan.

United Nations Development Group. (2010). *Thematic Paper on MDG2: Achieve Universal Primary Education.* Retrieved 2 September 2013 from http://www.undg.org/docs/11421/MDG2_1954-UNDG-MDG2-LR.pdf

United Nations Development Program. (2013). *Human Development Report: The Rise of the South: Human Progress in a Diverse World.* New York.

United Nations Economic and Social Commission for Asia and the Pacific, Asian Development Bank and United Nations Development Program. (2010–11). *Paths to 2015: MDG Priorities in Asia and the Pacific.* Retrieved 2 December 2010 from http://www.adb.org/Documents/Reports/Asia-Pacific-MDG-2010/default.asp

——. (2012–13). *Perspectives for a Post-2015 Development Agenda: Asia-Pacific Regional MDGs Report 2012/13.*

United Nations Educational, Scientific and Cultural Organization. (2002). *EFA Global Monitoring Report: Education for All: Is the World on Track?* Retrieved 15 March 2012 from http://www.unesco.org/new/en/education/themes/leading-the-international-agenda/efareport/reports/2002-efa-on-track/

——. (2012). *EFA Global Monitoring Report: 2012. Education for All – Youth and Skills: Putting Education to Work.* Paris. Retrieved 2 September 2013 from http://unesdoc.unesco.org/images/0021/002180/218003e.pdf

van der Berg, S. (2008). *Poverty and Education.* UNESCO, Paris: International Institute for Educational Planning. Retrieved 15 March 2012 from https://docs.google.com/viewer?url=http%3A%2F%2Fwww.iiep.unesco.org%2Ffilea dmin%2 Fuser_upload%2FInfo_Services_Publications%2Fpdf%2F2009%2FEdPol10.pdf

CHAPTER 11

Diversity in Progress in Gender Equality in Asia

Introduction

Concepts of Gender and Gender Equality

For ages, it was believed that the different characteristics, roles and status accorded to women and men in society are determined by biology (that is, sex), that they are natural and, therefore, not changeable. The distinction between sex and gender was introduced to deal with this tendency to attribute women's subordination to their anatomy. Ann Oakley (1972), who was among the first to use the concept of gender, said that 'sex' is a word that refers to the biological differences between male and female: the visible difference in genitalia, the related difference in procreative function. 'Gender', however, is a matter of culture: it refers to the social classification into 'masculine' and 'feminine'. Gender relations are seen as the key determinant of women's position in society, which can be changed if this is desired (Connelly et al., 2000). Gender equality means that the different behaviour, aspirations and needs of women and men are considered, valued and favoured equally. It does not mean that women and men have to become the same, but that their rights, responsibilities and opportunities will not depend on whether they are born male or female (International Labour Organization, 2007: 48).

Chapter Objectives

This chapter on diversity in progress in gender equality in Asia reviews the following:

1. Concepts of gender and gender equality, causes of gender inequality, feminism and women's movement.
2. Progress in Gender Measures in Asian sub-regions with reference to Gender-related Development Index, Gender Empowerment Measure, Gender Inequality Index and sex ratio and diversity in Asian sub-regions.
3. Diversity in progress in MDG targets of gender equality in Asian sub-regions with reference to education, youth literacy, wage employment and political participation and diversity in Asian sub-regions.

Understanding Gender Inequality

Causes of Gender Inequality

Gender Inequality before Industrialization

Origin

Frederic Engels attempted to explain the position of women more fully in *The Origin of the Family, Private Property and the State* in 1884. He claimed that before the family had existed, there had been a situation of entirely free sexual relationships. At this time, it was the women who exercised economic power because reproduction was necessary for the survival of the tribe and because she produced the primary material goods. All this changed as the domestication and breeding of animals, controlled by men, became increasingly important economically. As men became dominant in the production process and created a system of private property, the power relationship between the sexes shifted. Men now wanted to pass on their property to their own children and subjugated women, both through sex and through the division of labour within the household. According to Engels, therefore, emancipation of women could only come about with the abolition of private property (Newman, 2005). Marxist feminists view women's oppression as the outgrowth of the capitalist mode of production, which resulted in the spatial divide between domestic work and wage work and labelled them as non-productive and productive, respectively (Poonacha, 1995).

Patriarchy

Radical feminists conceptualized patriarchy as a system of gender oppression which was primary; it existed in virtually every known society, even those without classes (Connelly et al., 2000). According to them, the origin of patriarchy lies in the structure of family, domestic and personal life. They sought to uncover the influence of patriarchy not only in politics, public life and the economy, but in all aspects of social, personal and sexual existence (Heywood, 2007). Socialist feminists have redefined the radical-feminist conception of patriarchy so that it means a set of hierarchical relations with a material base in men's control over women's sexuality, procreation and labour power. They have added a historical dimension to the concept of patriarchy, arguing that it takes different forms in different historical periods and in different racial, cultural, political, economic and religious contexts (Connelly et al., 2000).

Gender Inequality after Industrialization

Industrialization and Housewifization of Women

Before the Industrial Revolution, most production was subsistence-based and took place within the household and all members participated in it. Industrialization separated work place and home as production, which was no longer a matter of subsistence alone, moved out of the household and into factories (Bhasin, 2000). Mainly in the western countries, men joined industrial employment, women lost their productive roles and stayed at home to look after the family and do household work. Women, thus, became 'dependents' of men in the context of industrialization (Zimmerman, 2001). In her book *Patriarchy and Accumulation on a World Scale,* Maria Mies links the creation of the housewife ideology with the development of European capitalism. She illustrates how the ideal of the domesticated, privatized woman, concerned with love and consumption and dependent on the male breadwinner, first spread among the bourgeoisie, then among the small property owners and finally among the working class (cited by Custers, 2012).

Focus of Development Policy on Men

Gender concerns were missing from early growth-oriented strategies since these strategies generally did not consider the 'human factor' in development. The initial development programmes assumed the 'household' to follow the model of an idealized 'western nuclear family' with a male breadwinner and dependent women and children. This led planners to focus mainstream development interventions on men (Kabeer, 2003). Ester Boserup (1970) discovered that most of the development projects ignored women and many technologically sophisticated projects undermined women's economic opportunities and autonomy. She maintained that national governments and international development agencies had not understood that women had productive, as well as reproductive, roles. Conventional measures of economic activity, based on western market-based economies, significantly underestimated the level of women's economic contributions. They both failed to acknowledge the magnitude and value of women's unpaid work; and undercounted women's paid work outside the 'modern' sector. Training in new technologies was usually offered to men, which meant that most 'modern' projects improved male opportunities and technological knowledge but reduced women's access to both technology and employment. She seriously challenged the argument that benefits from development projects would automatically 'trickle down' to women and other disadvantaged groups in Third World nations. Focus on men also meant that single women (unmarried, divorced, abandoned or separated women) are particularly vulnerable to poverty.

Undervaluation of Women's Work

The HDR on Gender and Human Development (United Nations Development Programme, 1995) observed the undervaluation of women as reflected in the undervaluation of their work and in the absence of recognition of the contribution that they make. It reports data on time usage by women and men for a sample of 31 countries. Women work longer hours than men in nearly every country. Of the total burden of work, women carry on average 53 per cent in developing countries and 51 per cent in industrial countries. Of men's total work time in industrial countries, roughly two-thirds is spent in paid activities and one-third in unpaid activities. For women, the situation is the reverse. In developing countries, more than three-quarters of men's work is in market activities. So, men receive the lion's share of income and recognition for their economic contribution, while most of women's work remains unpaid, unrecognized and undervalued. With no economic value given to these activities, the contribution of women is seriously underestimated, and there is no adequate reward or recognition for the burden of work that women carry. In fact, the failure to value most of their work reduces women to virtual non-entities in most economic transactions such as property ownership or offering collateral for bank loans.

Women's Vulnerability to Poverty

Development led to increased migration together with increased unemployment among men due to replacement by automatic machines. It resulted in a major expansion of the unprotected, unorganized labour force. This force was joined by an increasing number of women, who were left out of development projects, and children. On the other hand, when countries shifted from import-substituting industrialization to the export of labour-intensive goods, their competitive advantage shifted from a protected and better-paid male workforce to an unprotected and less well-paid female one (Kabeer, 2003). The unorganized sector does not provide social security and scope for unionization or application of anti-discrimination laws and so on. This has led to increased poverty among the female-headed families or feminization of poverty. Focus on men also meant that single women (unmarried, divorced, abandoned or separated women) are particularly vulnerable to poverty. As Illich (1983) puts it, higher labour force participation by women implies that more women have been incorporated into the population that is economically discriminated against on the ground of sex. Lister (2004) notes that hidden female poverty exists in other families as well due to women's economic dependence and male power which inhibit women's access to an adequate independent income. It also results in unequal distribution of income and resources within the family. Even where resources are shared fairly, a woman who has insufficient income in her own right, is vulnerable to poverty because she is reliant on the discretion of her partner and is ill-prepared should the partnership break down (Lister, 2004).

Progress of the World's Women 2005 by UNIFEM provides data to show that:

- The proportion of women workers engaged in informal employment is generally greater than the proportion of men workers.
- Women are concentrated in the more precarious types of informal employment.
- The average earnings from these types of informal employment are too low, in the absence of other sources of income, to raise households out of poverty.

While women's work is undervalued, various welfare programmes, such as maternal and child health, family planning and nutrition, are directed to women. These programmes make women dependent instead of supporting women's productive role. The result is the emergence and widening of a gender-based productivity gap and negative impacts on women's status in the economy (Kabeer, 2003).

Feminism and Women's Movement

It is feminism and women's movement that brought about the understanding of gender, gender equality and causes of gender inequality in society. Since the rise of radical feminism in the 1960s, feminism developed into a distinctive and established ideology, whose ideas and values challenge the most basic assumptions of conventional political thought (Heywood, 2007). Born out of women's experience of powerlessness, feminist ideologies seek to understand the nature of power as it operates in women's lives. They attempt to explain not just the origins of gender subordination, but also the tenacity of such normative values in a changing socioeconomic scenario. These explanations go beyond sexism, to provide different perspectives on all kinds of social exclusion including racism and casteism. The underlying contention is that the perceived disparities between the sexes is the earliest known form of social differentiation, it provides the script for the development of other known forms of oppressive practices (Poonacha, 1995). According to Bhasin and Khan (1986), anyone who recognizes the existence of sexism, male domination or patriarchy, in society, and who takes some action to change the situation, is a feminist. They emphasized that feminists not only ask and fight for equality, dignity and freedom of choice to control their lives and bodies, but for a just society for women and men, both.

Brandwein (1990) listed the following interrelated components of feminism: Feminists see the world in a holistic way, encompassing macro and micro levels. Emerging from a holistic approach is a process orientation, rejecting the ends/means split, emphasizing the connection between the individual and her/his community. This leads to the importance of unity in diversity. By rejecting an either/or approach, feminists prefer a win-win rather than a win-lose approach to conflict, as power is seen as an empowerment of self, rather than control over others. A consensual, inclusionary decision-making process and authority structure is, therefore, compatible with feminism. Finally, feminism implies a respect for nature, which does not exist just for human beings. Thus, feminism means replacing an outmoded value system with an alternative way of viewing the world.

The different schools of feminist ideology that have historically emerged to analyse and address gender inequality are liberal feminism, Marxist feminism, radical feminism, socialist feminism, postcolonial third-world feminism, postmodernist feminism and eco-feminism, linked to women's movement and policy approaches for women. The term women's movement describes a sum of campaigns around issues of importance to women, campaigns that feed into a network of women's groups and increase awareness of women's problems and rights (Kumar, 1995, cited by Burn, 2000).

Progress in Gender Measures in Asian Sub-Regions

The measures for gender equality used in this chapter are the gender measures and progress in the MDG 3. Gender Measures comprise Gender-related Development Index (GDI) and Gender Empowerment Measure (GEM) were introduced in the Human Development Report (HDR) on *Gender and Human Development* (United Nations Development Programme, 1995) for ranking countries on a global scale by their performance in gender equality. Since 2010 HDR, Gender Inequality Index (GII) is used as an experimental composite measure of inequality in achievement between women and men. The following table reports on GDI, GEM and GII in Asia.

Table 11.1
Diversity in Gender Measures in Asian Sub-Regions

Level of HD 2012	Countries in Asia	HDI Rank 2012	HDI Value 2007	GDI Value 2007	GDI % of HDI 2007	GEM Value 2007	GII Rank 2012	Sex Ratio 2013 Males/ Females
North and Central Asia								
High	Russia	055	0.817	0.816	99.9	0.556	051	0.86
High	Kazakhstan	069	0.804	0.803	99.8	0.532	051	0.92
Medium	Turkmenistan	102	0.739	—	—	—	—	0.98
Medium	Mongolia	106	0.727	0.727	100.0	0.410	056	1.00
Medium	Uzbekistan	114	0.710	0.708	99.7	—	—	0.99
Medium	Kyrgyzstan	125	0.710	0.705	99.4	0.575	064	0.96
Medium	Tajikistan	125	0.688	0.686	99.6	—	057	0.99
East Asia								
V High	Japan	010	0.960	0.945	98.4	0.567	021	0.95
V High	South Korea	012	0.937	0.926	98.8	0.554	027	1.00
V High	Hong Kong	013	0.944	0.934	98.9	—	—	0.94
Medium	China	101	0.772	0.770	99.8	0.533	035	1.06
South East Asia								
V High	Singapore	018	0.944	—	—	0.786	013	0.96
V High	Brunei	030	0.920	0.906	98.5	—	—	1.00
High	Malaysia	064	0.829	0.823	99.2	0.542	042	1.03
Medium	Thailand	103	0.783	0.782	99.8	0.514	066	0.98
Medium	Philippines	114	0.751	0.748	99.6	0.560	077	1.00
Medium	Indonesia	121	0.734	0.726	99.0	0.408	106	1.00
Medium	Vietnam	127	0.725	0.723	99.7	0.554	048	1.00
Medium	Timor-Leste	134	0.489	—	—	—	—	1.01
Medium	Laos	138	0.619	0.614	99.3	—	100	0.99
Medium	Cambodia	138	0.593	0.588	99.2	0.427	096	0.94
Low	Myanmar	149	0.586	—	—	—	080	0.99

Cont'd...

...Cont'd

South Asia								
High	Sri Lanka	092	0.759	0.756	99.6	0.389	075	0.96
Medium	Maldives	104	0.771	0.767	99.5	0.429	064	1.34
Medium	India	136	0.612	0.594	97.1	—	132	1.08
Medium	Bhutan	140	0.619	0.605	97.7	—	092	1.10
Low	Pakistan	146	0.572	0.532	93.0	0.386	123	1.06
Low	Bangladesh	146	0.543	0.536	98.7	0.264	111	0.95
Low	Nepal	157	0.553	0.545	98.4	0.486	102	0.96

Sources: Columns 1 and 6: United Nations Development Programme, 2013
Columns 2 to 5: United Nations Development Programme, 2009
Column 7: Central Intelligence Agency, 2013

Gender-related Development Index

The GDI is HDI adjusted for gender inequality, measuring achievement in the same basic capabilities as the HDI does, but takes note of inequality in achievement between women and men. The methodology used imposes a penalty for inequality, such that the GDI falls when the achievement levels of both women and men go down or when the disparity between their achievements increases. The greater the gender disparity in basic capabilities, the lower a country's GDI compared with its HDI (The Human Development website http://hdr.undp.org/en/humandev/hdi/). Table 11.1 shows that GDI data is not available for Turkmenistan, Singapore, Timor-Leste and Myanmar. As far as the GDI percentage of HDI is concerned, the distribution of the remaining Asian countries is as follows:

- Countries with GDI Value almost same as HDI Value (99+ to 100%): All the North and Central Asian countries (with Mongolia noted for 100% congruence between the two), China, all the South East Asian countries, except Brunei, Sri Lanka, and Maldives.
- Countries with GDI Value moderately lower than HDI Value (98+ to 99%): The East Asian countries except China, Brunei, Bangladesh and Nepal.

- Countries with GDI Value much lower than HDI Value (93+ to 98%): Bhutan, India and Pakistan.

Gender Empowerment Measure

The GEM is a measure of agency with reference to gender equality in economic and political participation and decision-making. It examines the extent to which women and men are able to actively participate in economic and political life and take part in decision-making. While the GDI focuses on expansion of capabilities, the GEM is concerned with the use of those capabilities to take advantage of the opportunities of life (The Human Development website http://hdr.undp.org/en/humandev/hdi/).

Table 11.1 shows that the GEM Value is not available for many countries: Hong Kong, Brunei, Turkmenistan, Uzbekistan, Tajikistan, Bhutan, Laos, India, Myanmar and Timor-Leste. The remaining Asian countries can be ranked as follows with reference to their GEM Value, where Singapore ranks the highest and Bangladesh the lowest. East Asia is doing better than South East Asia and North and Central Asia. South Asia is lagging behind all:

- High: Singapore (0.786)
- Medium: East Asia: Japan (0.567), South Korea (0.554) and China (0.533); South East Asia: Philippines (0.560), Vietnam (0.554), Malaysia (0.542) and Thailand (0.514); North and Central Asia: Russia (0.556), Kyrgyzstan (0.575) and Kazakhstan (0.532)
- Low: South Asia: Nepal (0.486), Maldives (0.429), Sri Lanka (0.389) and Pakistan (0.386); South East Asia: Cambodia (0.427) and Indonesia (0.408); and Mongolia (0.410)
- Lowest: Bangladesh (0.264)

Gender Inequality Index

Since 2010 HDR, Gender Inequality Index (GIi) is used as an experimental composite measure of inequality in achievement between women and men in three dimensions: reproductive health, empowerment and the labour market. Table 11.1 shows that in 2011, gender inequality is lower in countries of Singapore, Japan and South Korea where the human development is very high. Citywise, the GII is minimum in Singapore (13) and maximum in India (132). Sub-regionwise, it is minimum in East Asia and maximum in South Asia. It is more or less homogenous in North and Central Asia, ranging from 51 in Russia and Kazakhstan to 64 in Kyrgyzstan. South East Asia and South Asia are most diverse. In the former it ranges from 13 in Singapore to 106 in Indonesia and in the latter it ranges from 75 in Sri Lanka to 132 in India.

Sex Ratio

Sex ratio of populations is an indicator of gender discrimination at the level of basic survival chances. Women's biologically longer life expectancies should logically lead to more females in a population. Masculine sex ratios, that is, more men than women in the population, are associated with high levels of excess female mortality in the younger age groups. This is often induced through sex-selective female abortions with the motive of preference for sons (Kabeer, 2003). Table 11.1 shows that China and most of the South Asian countries of Maldives, India, Bhutan and Pakistan have masculine sex ratios, that is, ratio of more than 105 males per 100 females. According to the Mahbub ul Haq Human Development Centre's HDR on South Asia (2012), South Asia is the only sub-region in the world where men outnumber women.

Conclusion

Gender inequality is lower in countries of Singapore, Japan and South Korea where the human development is very high. Gender inequality is more or less homogenous in North and Central Asia and diverse in Southeast Asia and South Asia. While in 2007, North and Central Asia and most of the Southeast Asian countries had a high level of GDI; in 2011 East Asia is leading in GII, which was already leading in GEM in 2007. South Asia which is most backward in the overall human development in Asia lags behind on all the three Gender Measures as well as in sex ratio.

Progress in Gender Equality as a Millennium Development Goal in Asia

The Millennium Summit placed gender equality at the heart of achieving the MDGs. The MDG–3 specifically aims to promote gender equality and empower women, targetting at gender equality in education, work and political participation. The Asian Development Bank (2011) provides the following data on the MDG–3 in Asian sub-regions

Gender Equality in Education

Target 4 for MDG–3 is to eliminate gender disparity in primary and secondary education, preferably by 2005, and in all levels of education no later than 2015. Table 11.2 provides data on progress in gender equality in education in Asian sub-regions.

Table 11.2
Diversity in Gender Equality in Education in Asian Sub-Regions

Level of HD 2012	Countries in Asia	Gender Equality in Primary School 2009	Gender Equality in Secondary School 2009	Gender Equality in Tertiary Education 2009	Female Population with at least Secondary Education % ages 25 and older 2006–10
North and Central Asia					
High	Russia	—	—	—	93.5
High	Kazakhstan	1.01	0.98	1.45	99.3
Medium	Turkmenistan	—	—	—	—
Medium	Mongolia	0.99	1.07	1.55	83.0
Medium	Uzbekistan	0.98	0.99	0.70	—
Medium	Kyrgyzstan	1.00	1.01	1.32	81.0
Medium	Tajikistan	0.96	0.87	0.41	93.2
East Asia					
V High	Japan	1.00	1.00	0.89	80.0
V High	South Korea	0.98	0.96	0.70	79.4
V High	Hong Kong	1.02	1.03	1.03	68.7
Medium	China	1.04	1.07	1.07	54.8
South East Asia					
V High	Singapore	—	—	—	71.3
V High	Brunei	1.01	1.02	1.76	66.6
High	Malaysia	0.99	1.07	1.30	66.0
Medium	Thailand	0.98	1.09	1.24	29.0

Cont'd...

...*Cont'd*

Medium	Philippines	0.98	1.09	1.24	65.9
Medium	Indonesia	0.97	0.99	0.96	36.2
Medium	Vietnam	0.95	0.92	0.73	24.7
Medium	Timor-Leste	0.97	1.00	0.71	—
Medium	Laos	0.91	0.81	0.78	22.9
Medium	Cambodia	0.94	0.82	0.54	11.6
Low	Myanmar	0.98	1.02	1.37	18.0
South Asia					
High	Sri Lanka	1.00	1.02	—	72.6
Medium	Maldives	0.95	1.05	2.40	20.7
Medium	India	0.97	0.88	0.70	26.6
Medium	Bhutan	1.01	0.99	0.59	34.0
Low	Pakistan	0.84	0.79	0.85	18.3
Low	Bangladesh	1.04	1.12	0.56	30.8
Low	Nepal	0.86	0.89	0.40	17.9

Sources: Columns 1 to 3: Asian Development Bank, 2011, pp. 81–82
Column 4: United Nations Development Programme, 2013

Table 11.2 shows that gender equality of 0.95 was achieved at the primary level by 2009 in most countries. There is less gender equality at the secondary level. At the tertiary level, some countries are behind their primary and secondary levels, whereas, some countries have ratios in favour of females.

North and Central Asia: At the primary level, all the countries of North and Central Asia have achieved gender equality up to 0.95. At the secondary level, Tajikistan has not yet achieved this ratio by 2009. At the tertiary level, Uzbekistan and Tajikistan are lagging behind. On the other hand, high ratios in favour of women are observed at this level in Kazakhstan (1.45), Kyrgyzstan (1.32) and Mongolia (1.55). As far as female population with at least secondary education (% ages 25 and older) is concerned, North and Central Asia leads, ranging from 81 per cent in Kyrgyzstan to 99.3 per cent in Kazakhstan.

East Asia: In East Asia China is doing the best with reference to gender equality in education, although it is at medium level of human development. However, although Japan and South Korea are at very high level of human development, their progress in gender equality at the tertiary level is slow. The level of education in their female population is also not so high among the countries at very high level of human development in East Asia, ranging from 68.7 per cent in Hong Kong to 80 per cent in Japan.

South East Asia: Cambodia and Laos lag behind in gender equality at all the three levels of education. At the secondary level, Vietnam also lags behind. At the tertiary level, Vietnam and Timor-Leste also lag behind. On the other hand, high ratios in favour of women are observed at the tertiary level in Brunei (1.76) and Thailand (1.24). Female population with at least secondary education (% ages 25 and older) in Asia is lowest in Cambodia at 11.6 per cent. Among the countries at very high level of human development, the level of education in their female population is not so high; it is 66.6 per cent in Brunei and 71.3 per cent in Singapore.

South Asia: Nepal and Pakistan are lagging behind in gender equality at all the three levels of education. At the secondary level, India is also lagging behind. At the tertiary level, India, Bhutan and Bangladesh are also lagging behind. On the other hand, at this level, Maldives has a very high gender ratio of 2.40, highest in Asia.

Gender Equality in Youth Literacy

Gender equality in youth literacy is the ratio of the female literacy rate to the male literacy rate for the age group 15–24. The Asian Development Bank (2011) provides the following comparative data on youth literacy rate in Asian sub-regions.

Table 11.3
Diversity in Progress of Gender Equality in Youth Literacy Rate in Asian Sub-Regions

Level of Human Development 2012	Country	% Literacy Rate among Youth (15–24 years) 2005–2009		
		Total	Girls	Boys
East Asia				
V High	Japan	—	—	—
V High	South Korea	—	—	—
V High	Hong Kong	—	—	—

Cont'd...

...Cont'd

Medium	China	99.4%	99.3%	99.5%
Low	North Korea	—	—	—
North and Central Asia				
High	Russia	—	—	—
High	Kazakhstan	99.8%	99.9%	99.8%
Medium	Turkmenistan	99.8%	99.9%	99.8%
Medium	Mongolia	96.0%	97.4%	94.6%
Medium	Uzbekistan	99.9%	100.0%	99.9%
Medium	Kyrgyzstan	99.8%	99.8%	99.7%
Medium	Tajikistan	99.9%	99.9%	99.9%
South East Asia				
V High	Singapore	99.8%	99.8%	99.7%
V High	Brunei	99.7%	99.6%	99.7%
High	Malaysia	98.5%	98.7%	98.4%
Medium	Thailand	98.1%	97.9%	98.2%
Medium	Philippines	97.8%	98.5%	97.0%
Medium	Indonesia	99.5%	99.4%	99.5%
Medium	Vietnam	96.9%	96.4%	97.3%
Low	Timor-Leste	—	—	—
Medium	Laos	83.9%	78.7%	89.2%
Medium	Cambodia	87.5%	85.5%	89.4%
Low	Myanmar	95.7%	95.3%	96.1%
South Asia				
High	Sri Lanka	98.0%	98.6%	97.3%
Medium	Maldives	99.3%	99.4%	99.2%
Medium	India	81.1%	74.4%	88.4%
Medium	Bhutan	74.4%	68.0%	80.0%
Low	Pakistan	71.1%	61.2%	79.4%
Low	Bangladesh	75.5%	76.8%	74.1%
Low	Nepal	82.0%	76.7%	86.9%

Table 11.3 showed that:

East Asia and North and Central Asia: All the countries in East Asia and North and Central Asia have above 99 per cent youth literacy rate with gender equality.

South East Asia: In South East Asia, Singapore, Brunei and Indonesia have a near total youth literacy rate with gender equality.

Laos and Cambodia are problematic with reference to youth literacy and gender equality.

South Asia: In South Asia, except for Maldives and Sri Lanka, all the northern South Asian countries have a higher rate of youth literacy among boys compared to girls.

Gender Equality in Wage Employment

MDG–3 measures the share of women in wage employment in the non-agricultural sector which measures the degree to which labour markets are open to women in the industry and service sectors. Table 11.4 provides the data on share of women in wage employment as well as overall female labour force participation in Asia.

Table 11.4
Diversity in Gender Equality in Wage Employment in Asian Sub-Regions

Level of HD 2012	Countries in Asia	Share of Women in Wage Employment (%) 2009	Female Labour Force Participation (% ages 15 and older) 2011
North and Central Asia			
High	Russia	—	56.3
High	Kazakhstan	50.0	66.6
Medium	Turkmenistan	—	46.4
Medium	Mongolia	51.1	54.3
Medium	Uzbekistan	39.4	47.7
Medium	Kyrgyzstan	50.6	55.5
Medium	Tajikistan	37.1	57.4
East Asia			
Very High	Japan	42.3	49.4
Very High	South Korea	42.1	49.2
Very High	Hong Kong	49.9	51.0
Medium	China	—	67.7
South East Asia			
Very High	Singapore	45.4	56.5
Very High	Brunei	30.3	55.5

Cont'd...

...Cont'd

High	Malaysia	39.2	43.8
Medium	Thailand	45.5	63.8
Medium	Philippines	41.9	49.7
Medium	Indonesia	32.4	51.2
Medium	Vietnam	40.4	73.2
Medium	Timor-Leste	—	38.4
Medium	Laos	32.1	76.5
Medium	Cambodia	43.5	79.2
Low	Myanmar	—	75.0
South Asia			
High	Sri Lanka	31.0	34.7
Medium	Maldives	30.0	55.7
Medium	India	18.1	29.0
Medium	Bhutan	26.8	65.8
Low	Pakistan	12.6	22.7
Low	Bangladesh	20.1	57.2
Low	Nepal	—	80.4

Sources: Column 1: Asian Development Bank, 2011, pp. 81–82.
Column 2: United Nations Development Programme, 2013

Table 11.4 shows that the labour force participation of women is much higher than share of women in wage employment. This shows more women in the non-wage agricultural labour which is unorganized, leading to increased poverty among women. The following are sub-regionwise trends about gender equality in wage employment in Asia:

North and Central Asia: The sub-region leads in Asia with share of women in wage employment being 50 per cent and above in Mongolia, Kyrgyzstan and Kazakhstan. Its labour force participation of women in general is also above 46 per cent in all the countries and as high as 66.6 per cent in Kazakhstan.

East Asia: In this sub-region, share of women in non-agricultural wage employment is the second-highest in Asia. It ranges from 42.1 per cent in South Korea to 49.9 per cent in Hong Kong. Its labour force participation of women in general is above 49 per cent and as high as 67.7 per cent in China.

South East Asia: Female share in wage employment is above 45 per cent only in Singapore and Thailand and only 30.3 per cent in Brunei. Although Cambodia has low level of female education, the labour force participation among women in this country is the highest in this sub-region (79.2%). Laos, Myanmar and Vietnam also have above 70 per cent of women's share in labour force in general.

South Asia: The sub-region lags behind with female share in wage employment ranging from 12.6 per cent in Pakistan to 31 per cent in Sri Lanka. The lowest labour force participation among women in Asia is in Pakistan at 22.7 per cent and India at 29 per cent. Although Nepal has low level of female education, the labour force participation among women in this country is the highest in Asia (80.4%).

Gender Equality in Political Participation

Gender equality in political participation is measured by the proportion of seats held by women in national parliament, linked to women's empowerment.

Table 11.5
Diversity in Gender Equality in Political Participation in Asian Sub-Regions

Level of HD 2012	Countries in Asia	Seats in National Parliament (% female) 2011
North and Central Asia		
High	Russia	11.1
High	Kazakhstan	18.2
Medium	Turkmenistan	16.8
Medium	Mongolia	12.7
Medium	Uzbekistan	19.2
Medium	Kyrgyzstan	23.3
Medium	Tajikistan	17.5
East Asia		
V High	Japan	13.4
V High	South Korea	15.7

Cont'd...

...Cont'd

V High	Hong Kong	—
Medium	China	21.3
South East Asia		
V High	Singapore	23.5
V High	Brunei	—
High	Malaysia	13.2
Medium	Thailand	15.7
Medium	Philippines	22.1
Medium	Indonesia	18.2
Medium	Vietnam	24.4
Medium	Timor-Leste	38.5
Medium	Laos	25.0
Medium	Cambodia	18.1
Low	Myanmar	4.6
South Asia		
High	Sri Lanka	5.8
Medium	Maldives	6.5
Medium	India	10.9
Medium	Bhutan	13.9
Low	Pakistan	21.1
Low	Bangladesh	19.7
Low	Nepal	33.2

Source: United Nations Develbpment Programme, 2013

Table 11.5 shows that political participation by women is low in every sub-region, including the highly developed East Asia and the otherwise gender-equal North and Central Asia:

North and Central Asia: Political participation of women in North and Central Asia ranges from 11.1 in Russia to 23.3 per cent in Kyrgyzstan.

East Asia: Political participation of women is least diverse in East Asia, ranging from 13.4 per cent in Japan to 21.3 per cent in China.

South East Asia: Political participation of women in South East Asia is most diverse, ranging from very low of 4.6 per cent in Myanmar to 38.5 per cent in Timor-Leste, highest in Asia.

South Asia: Political participation of women in South Asia ranges from very low (5.3%) in Sri Lanka to 33.2% in Nepal.

True, Niner, Parashar and George (2012) note that women's economic participation, gender quotas and reservations have significantly improved women's political participation in countries such as Timor-Leste and Nepal. However, according to them, women's political participation in Asia is below the global average as there is strong resistance to it evidenced in the formal statements of its leaders and politicians and in the mentalities of the broader societies.

Conclusion

The overall observations with reference to the MDG on gender equality in Asia are as follows:

- Gender equality at the primary level of education is achieved in most countries. There is less gender equality at the secondary level. At the tertiary level, some countries are behind their primary and secondary levels, whereas, some countries have ratios in favour of females.
- The labour force participation of women is much higher than share of women in wage employment, indicating higher level of poverty among women.
- Political participation by women is low in every sub-region, including the highly developed East Asia and the otherwise gender-equal North and Central Asia.

Discussion

Diversity in Gender Equality in Asia

Gender Equality in North and Central Asia

North and Central Asia is homogenously leading in Asia with reference to gender equality in education, youth literacy, wage employment and sex ratio, although most of its countries are at a medium level of human development. In fact, high ratios in favour of women are observed at tertiary level of education in three countries. The explanation for high level of gender equality in these countries seems to lie in the history of communist rule when they were part of the former Soviet Union. According to Lapidus (1982), an extensive reliance on female labour had been a central feature of the Soviet pattern of industrialization over several decades, with important consequences for virtually every aspect of economic and social life. The highest female labour force participation rates of any industrial society were to be found in the Soviet Union. However, as he further noted, beginning in the mid-1960s, a growing array of scholarly studies, to which female economists, sociologists, and demographers were important contributors, began to document in some detail the low level of skill, mobility, and income of women workers, the heavy and conflicting demands of their dual roles, and the harmful effects of poor working conditions and inadequate social services on the health and well-being of working mothers and their families.

Newman (2005) noted that in many respects, the Soviet Union remained more advanced in relation to gender than capitalist societies, in terms of higher educational attainment and professional and political status. However, patriarchy is still prevalent in Russia today; the HDR of UNDP Russia (2010: 49) notes that Russian government policy towards women is increasingly driven by the assumption that the traditional labour division between men and women (where the man is the main breadwinner, while the woman combines the tasks of earning money for the family with household duties and raising children) is the only feasible and socially acceptable paradigm! The HDR of the UNDP Regional Bureau for Europe and CIS (2011: 6) notes that in Central Asia also, the wholesale rejection of the previous system's values is resulting in a return to traditional gender and cultural norms, which can create new sources of exclusion for women.

Gender Equality in East Asia

All the countries in East Asia have above 99 per cent youth literacy rate with gender equality. Although East Asia is very high on the HDI, on the GDI it falls behind. China at the medium level of human development is doing better than countries at very high level of human development with reference to gender equality in education, wage employment and political participation. This fact shows that overall human development does not necessarily lead to gender equality. In East Asia, share of women in non-agricultural wage employment is the second-highest in Asia.

Probably influenced by patriarchal Confucianism, in East Asia, kinship structures are predominantly patrilineal: descent is traced and property transmitted through the male members. Marriage tends to be exogamous and patrilocal: women marry outside their kin and often outside their village community, leaving their own homes at marriage to join their husband's family. Households are organized along highly corporate lines, with strong conjugal bonds and cultural rules that emphasize male responsibility for protecting and provisioning women and children. Household resources and income are pooled under the management and control of the male patriarch. Female chastity is emphasized and considered essential to ensure that property is transmitted based on biological fatherhood. Female sexuality is controlled through a strong public-private divide, with women secluded in the private domain. 'Son preference' is also marked (Kabeer, 2003).

When East and South East Asian countries shifted from import-substituting industrialization to the export of labour-intensive goods, their competitive advantage shifted from a protected and better-paid male workforce to an unprotected and less well-paid female one. Women's high rate of labour force participation started in the East Asian 'miracle' economies. The development states of South Korea and Taiwan (and Singapore) suspended free trade union activity and repressed workers' rights and drew on cultural norms about female docility and secondary worker status to reinforce patriarchal controls over female labour and ensure a compliant workforce for fast economic growth (Kabeer, 2003).

Gender Equality in South East Asia

South East Asia is diverse with reference to gender equality in education, youth literacy, wage employment and political participation. However, it has high level of female labour force participation. South East Asia is known for female farming systems where women played the major role in food production with some help from men (Boserup, 1970). Boserup's classical study on women's role in economic development made a distinction between two patterns of subsistence agriculture: female system of farming in which food production is mainly taken care of by women with little help from men and the male system of farming in which food production is mainly taken care of by men with little help from women. She noted that gender roles in farming had a distinct geographical pattern. Female farming systems are found in areas of shifting cultivation of South East Asia (and North-East and Southern India). Female labour force participation tended to be extremely high in these regions. Women also played an active role in trading activities in some of them. Traditionally, female family labour made up around 50 per cent of the total agricultural force in Thailand and 75 per cent in Cambodia, both areas of female farming. Women also made up around half of the labour force engaged in trade and commerce in Burma (now Myanmar), Cambodia, Laos, the Philippines, Thailand and Vietnam.

In the modern times, like the fast economic growth, women's high rate of labour force participation also spread from East Asia to the South East Asian countries of Indonesia, Malaysia, the Philippines and Thailand which not only have high levels of female labour force participation, they also have a more even distribution of female labour force across agriculture, industry and services. Women made up over a third of the labour in each sector during 1970–1990, with their representation increasing in services over this period. However, following the Asian Financial Crisis, unemployment was more among women than among men (Kabeer, 2003).

Dube (1997) noted that as far as kinship systems are concerned, South East Asia is predominantly bilateral, where both parents are relevant for reckoning kinship and for claiming rights to resources. This sub-region also has some patrilineal and some matrilineal communities. Women in this sub-region exercise an unusual degree of autonomy in economic and social life due to relative egalitarianism between sexes. Certain elements of these societies are inclination towards matrilineality and matrilocality, flexibility in the composition of households, no insistence of family continuity, equal rights of inheritance of sons and daughters, access to resources by both men and women, optation of choice in marital residence, respect for age and hierarchy of status as a cultural element, but a general ethos of non-authoritarian interpersonal relationships among kin, no great compulsion to remain married in the face of intense conflict and suffering, strong cultural approval of children remaining with their mothers in the event of divorce and so on.

According to Kabeer (2003), compared to East Asia, somewhat less rigid gender relations are found in South East Asia in the way kinship and family are organized. However, she noted that the absence of any marked restrictions on women's mobility, and some degree of symmetry in the division of labour in the household should not be taken to imply an absence of gender inequality in these societies. Studies from Indonesia, the Philippines and Vietnam reveal mild gender bias/discrimination in well-being in the household. Even though Philippine women may have high status relative to women in some other countries, this needs to be assessed in relation to Philippine men to be meaningful. She also noted that it is in the relatively more egalitarian regimes of South East Asia – Thailand and the Philippines – that sex tourism has emerged as a key source of income for women (Kabeer, 2003).

Gender Equality in South Asia

South Asia lags behind other Asian sub-regions with reference to gender equality in human development, sex ratio and gender equality in education, youth literacy and wage employment. According to Kabeer (2003), like in East Asia, in South Asia also kinship structures are predominantly patrilineal and patriarchal. Burn (2000) notes that in classical Hinduism that influences the culture of this sub-region, it is believed that no woman can gain salvation except in a future when she has been reborn as a man. In India, the landless poor mainly belong to the 'untouchable' caste. Women from this group are mainly found in agricultural waged employment, among the least well-paid forms of work available in the economy (Kabeer, 2003). Dube (1997) noted that though women in South Asia have a high profile presence in the tertiary sector, most of the women in this sub-region have limited rights over resources, including inheritance, are dependent, secluded and segregated, with no or limited choices.

According to Boserup (1970), the northern region of South Asia is known for male farming systems, where agriculture was largely the responsibility of men, with women confined to a limited number of tasks that could be carried out in the domestic domain. These were mainly found in regions of settled farming with plough-based cultivation and private ownership of land in India and Pakistan (and Middle East). Instead of their own women, the cultivating families relied on hired labour from landless families. These were also regions with very low female participation in trading activities. Boserup further noted that within South Asia, women's participation in trade traditionally varied from two to six per cent in Bangladesh, the northern plains of India and Pakistan, to around 17 per cent in the southern states of India which is known for female farming. Kabeer

(2003) noted that only in South Asia, has female labour remained largely concentrated in the agricultural sector. In South Asia, female labour force participation took off only in Bangladesh due to the emergence of an export-oriented garment industry.

However, South Asia is not a homogenous sub-region. For most of the targets, it is the northern countries of this sub-region that lag behind and the southern countries of Maldives and Sri Lanka are doing better on gender equality, more like the countries of East and South East Asia. Razavi and Miller (1995) noted that these northern countries of South Asia lag behind as part of the so-called belt of classic patriarchy that stretches from North Africa across the Middle East and the northern plains of the Indian subcontinent to Bangladesh. In this sub-region, kinship structures are predominantly patrilineal, marriage tends to be patrilocal and cultural rules emphasize patriarchal family management.

Implications for Gender Policy in Asia

Social policy in Asia and, therefore, the policy for women in Asia use the residual welfare, or welfare pluralism, or informal or insecure welfare approach. Gender policy in Asia needs to be mainstreamed into all the economic and social policies. It needs to use the gender and development (GAD) approach that is concerned with the interconnection of gender, class, and race. It stresses the need for women to organize themselves for more effective political voice. It questions the underlying assumptions of current social, economic and political structures. It leads not only to the design of intervention and affirmative action strategies which will ensure that women are better integrated into ongoing development efforts. It leads, inevitably, to a fundamental re-examination of social structures and institutions and, ultimately, to the loss of power of entrenched elites, which inevitably will affect women as well as men (Rathgeber, 1988).

According to Kabeer (1995), policies that recognize no gender difference, incorporate biases in favour of existing gender relations and tend to exclude women are called gender-blind policies. Gender aware policies recognize gender differences and may be of three types:

- *Gender-Neutral Policies,* in light of gender differences, target delivery to men and women's practical gender needs and work within existing gender division of resources and responsibilities.

- *Gender-Specific Policies*, in light of gender differences, respond to the practical needs of either men or women specifically and work within existing gender division of resources and responsibilities.
- *Gender Redistributive Policies* intend to transform existing gender relations to create a more balanced relationship, may target both men and women, or one specifically, work on practical gender needs in a transformatory way and work on strategic gender needs.

In spite of high level of gender inequality in South Asia, the sub-region has many success stories of civil society organizations working for empowerment of women. The Self-Employed Women's Association (SEWA) in India has moved from organizing women in the informal economy through a combination of trade union and cooperative principles to seeking to put pressure on the state government for greater responsiveness to the needs of poor women. It has been lobbying to make the ILO less a voice for the organized, predominantly male workers and more representative of the world's informal workers. Studies of micro-credit in rural Bangladesh, where women have traditionally been excluded from the cash economy, found that women's access to credit led to a number of changes in women's own perception of themselves and their role in household decision-making. It also led to long-term reduction in domestic violence as well as increase in women's assets. Women workers in the garment industry in this country expressed their satisfaction at having a proper job and regular wages compared to the casualized and poorly paid forms of employment that had previously been their only options. Many had used their new-found earning power to renegotiate their relations within marriage, others to leave abusive marriages. Yet others used their earnings to postpone early marriage and to challenge the practice of dowry (Kabeer, 2003).

Note

This chapter is an updated version of my article published as 'Diversity and Contradictions in Gender Equality in Asia', in C. Noble and M. Henrickson (eds) *Social Work Education: Voices from the Asia-Pacific* (2nd ed). Sydney: the University of Sydney Press, in 2013.

References

Asian Development Bank. (2011). *Key Indicators for Asia and the Pacific.* Manila. Retrieved 31 March 2013 from http://www.adb.org/key-indicators/ 2011/main

Bhasin, K. (2000). *Understanding Gender.* New Delhi: Kali for Women.

Bhasin, K. and Khan, N.S. (1986). *Some Questions on Feminism and its Relevance in South Asia.* New Delhi: Kali for Women.

Boserup, E. (1970). *Woman's Role in Economic Development.* New York: St. Martin's Press.

Brandwein, R. (1990). Women's issues, women's studies and feminism. In F.M. Yasas and V. Mehta (eds), *Exploring Feminist Visions: Case Studies on Social Justice Issues* (pp. 4–8). Pune: Streevani and International Association of Schools of Social Work.

Burn, S.M. (2000). *Women across Cultures: A Global Perspective.* London: Mayfield Publishing Co.

Central Intelligence Agency. (2013). *The World Factbook.* Washington, DC. Retrieved 6 May 2013 from https://www.cia.gov/library/publications/the-world-factbook/fields/print_2018.html

Connelly, P., Li, T.M., MacDonald, M. and Parpart, J.L. (2000). Feminism and development: Theoretical perspectives. In J.L. Parpart, M.P. Connelly and V.E. Barriteau (eds), *Theoretical Perspectives on Gender and Development.* Ottawa: International Development Research Center. Retrieved 8 December 2009 from http://www.idrc.ca/es/ev-27444-201-1- DO_TOPIC.html

Custers, P. (2012). *Capital Accumulation and Women's Labour in Asian Economies.* New York: Monthly Review Press.

Dube, L. (1997). *Women and Kinship: Comparative Perspectives on Gender in South and South-East Asia.* New Delhi: Vistaar Publications.

Heywood, A. (2007). *Political Ideologies: An Introduction* (4th ed.) New York: Palgrave Macmillan.

Ilich, I. (1983). *Gender.* London: Marion Boyars.

International Labour Organization. (2007). *ABC of Women Workers' Rights and Gender Equality* (2nd ed.). Geneva. Retrieved 4 April 2013 from http://www.ilo.org/wcmsp5/groups/public/...dgreports/...gender/documents/publication/wcms_087314.pdf

Kabeer, N. (1995). *Reversed Realities: Gender Hierarchies in Development Thought.* New Delhi: Kali for Women.

——. (2003). *Gender Mainstreaming in Poverty Eradication and the Millennium Development Goals: A Handbook for Policy-Makers and Other Stakeholders.* Ottawa: Commonwealth Secretariat.

Lapidus, G.W. (1982). *Women, Work, and Family in the Soviet Union.* Armonk, NY: M.E. Sharpe. Retrieved 3 February 2011 from http://www.questia.com/library/book/women-work-and-family-in-the-soviet-union-by-gail-warshofsky-lapidus.jsp

Lister, R. (2004). *Poverty.* Malden, MA: Polity Press.

The Mahbub ul Haq Human Development Centre. (2012). *Human Development in South Asia: 2012: Governance for People's Empowerment.* Lahore: Oxford University Press.

Newman, M. (2005). *Socialism: A Very Short Introduction.* New York: Oxford University Press.

Oakley, A. (1972). *Sex, Gender and Society.* London: Temple Smith. Reprinted in 1985 with new Introduction, London: Gower.

Poonacha, V. (1995). *Gender within the Human Rights Discourse.* Bombay: Research Centre for Women's Studies, SNDT Women's University.

Rathgeber, E.M. (1988). *WID, WAD, GAD: Trends in Research and Practice.* Ottawa: International Development Research Centre.

Razavi, S. and Miller, C. (1995). *From WID to GAD: Conceptual Shifts in the Women and Development Discourse.* Geneva: United Nations Research Institute for Social Development.

True, J., Niner, S., Parashar, S. and George, N. (2012). Women's political participation in Asia and the Pacific. Conflict Prevention and Peace Forum. Retrieved 9 June 2013 from http://artsonline. monash. edu.au/thebordercrossingobservatory/files/2013/02/UNDPA-Women%E2%80%99s-Political-Participation-in-Asia-and-the-Pacific.pdf

United Nations Development Programme. (1995). *Human Development Report: Gender and Human Development.* New York: Oxford University Press.

——. (2009). *Human Development Report: Overcoming Barriers: Human Mobility and Development.* New York: Oxford University Press.

——. (2010). *Human Development Report: The Real Wealth of Nations: Pathways to Human Development.* New York: Oxford University Press.

——. (2013). *Human Development Report: The Rise of the South: Human Progress in a Diverse World.* New York.

United Nations Development Programme Regional Bureau for Europe and CIS. (2011). *Beyond Transition: Towards Inclusive Societies.* Bratislava. Retrieved 4 April 2013 from http://hdr.undp.org/en/reports/regional/europethecis/RBEC_HDR_2011_EN.pdf

United Nations Development Programme Russia. (2010). *Millennium Development Goals in Russia: Looking into the Future.* Moscow. Retrieved 4 April 2013 from http://hdr.undp.org/en/reports/national/europethecis/russia/ Russia_NHDR_2010_EN.pdf

UNIFEM. (2005). *Progress of the World's Women: 2005.* Retrieved 25 September 2011 from https://docs.google.com/viewer?url=http%3A%2F%2Fwww. unifem.org%2Fattachments%2Fproducts%2FPoWW2005_overview_eng.pdf

Zimmerman, S.L. (2001). *Family Policy: Constructed Solutions to Family Problems.* London: Sage Publications.

CHAPTER 12

Diversity in Progress in Environmental Sustainability in Asia

Introduction

Concepts of Environmental Sustainability

The environment comprises a diversity of ecosystems: those that occur in deserts, forests, wetlands, mountains, lakes, rivers, and agricultural landscapes. Ecosystems are self-regulating natural systems, composed of both living and non-living elements (Heywood, 2007). In each ecosystem, living creatures, including humans, form a community, interacting with one another and with the air, water, and soil around them. It is the combination of life forms and their interactions with each other and with the rest of the environment that has made earth a uniquely habitable place for humans (Convention on Biological Diversity, 1993). According to Article 2 of the Convention on Biological Diversity (CBD), 1993, the term biodiversity is defined as '... the variability among living organisms from all sources including, *inter alia*, terrestrial, marine and other aquatic ecosystems and the ecological complexes of which they are part; this includes diversity within species, between species and of ecosystems.' Biodiversity provides a large number of goods and services that sustain living beings and the loss of biodiversity often reduces the productivity of ecosystems, thereby shrinking nature's basket of goods and services, from which we constantly draw. It destabilizes ecosystems, and weakens their ability to deal with natural disasters such as floods, droughts, and hurricanes, and with human-caused stresses, such as pollution and climate change. Environmental degradation is the deterioration of the environment through depletion of resources such as air, water and soil; the destruction of ecosystems; and the extinction of wildlife (UN Millennium Project, 2005).

In 1987, the World Commission on Environment and Development, also known as the Brundtland Commission, produced a report called *Our Common Future* or the Brundtland Report, which is a pioneering report in the field of sustainable development. According to this Report, 'Sustainable development is development that meets the needs of the present without compromising the ability of future generations to meet their own needs ... the goals of economic and social development must be defined in terms of sustainability in all countries – developed or developing, market-oriented or centrally planned' (United Nations, 1987). The Millennium Development Goal–7 to ensure environmental sustainability has the following targets:

Target 9: Integrate the principles of sustainable development into country policies and programmes and reverse the loss of environmental resources.

Target 10: Halve, by 2015, the proportion of people without sustainable access to safe drinking water and basic sanitation.

Target 11: By 2020, to have achieved a significant improvement in the lives of at least 100 million slum dwellers.

Chapter Objectives

This chapter on diversity in progress in environmental sustainability in Asia reviews the following:

1. Concepts, causes and effects of environmental degradation, ecologism and environmental movement.
2. Progress in reversal of the loss of environmental resources in Asia with reference to forest cover, protected area, and CO_2 emissions and ODP CFC consumption and diversity in Asian sub-regions.
3. Progress in access to sustainable water sources and sanitation facilities in urban and rural Asia and diversity in Asian sub-regions.

4. Progress in the lives of slum dwellers in Asia and diversity in Asian sub-regions.

Understanding Environmental Degradation

Causes of Environmental Degradation

Science and Industrialization

Most preindustrial societies considered nature as akin to god due to its importance for survival. The reverential attitude towards plants, animals, rivers and the earth reflects an ecocentric view of traditional societies (Ramakrishnan, 2001). However, the advent of science saw nature as inert, passive and accessible for human research and industrialization sought to use nature for promoting production for consumption. As Capra (1982, cited by Heywood, 2007) emphasized, science has treated nature as a machine, implying that it can be tinkered with, repaired, improved on or even replaced. According to the eminent eco-feminist Vandana Shiva (2010), left to themselves, natural resources maintained their renewability and provided sustenance and livelihood to people. However, since the scientific and industrial revolution, technology and economics have mutually reinforced the assumption that nature's limits must be broken for the creation of abundance. The modern efficient and productive technologies created within the context of growth in market economic terms are associated with heavy ecological costs. The resource- and energy-intensive production processes demand ever-increasing withdrawals from the ecosystems. These withdrawals convert the renewable natural systems into non-renewable 'resources'.

Disempowerment of People

Sachs (2010) notes that poverty was long regarded as unrelated to environmental degradation, which was attributed to the impact of industrialization; the world's poor entered the equation only as future claimants to an industrial lifestyle. However, as Vivian (1991) observed, environmental degradation in rural areas of the Third World is not due to the poverty of rural communities; rather, poverty is a symptom of one of the primary underlying causes of local level environmental decline in the Third World today: the disempowerment of these communities. Furthermore, to the extent that local level degradation forms a major component of global environmental problems, this growing inability of communities to participate in resource management decisions has an important impact on the potential for sustainable development. Disempowerment in the course of development can take many forms. People may be deprived of access to the resources on which they depend, their traditional tenure rights and rights to exclude outsiders may be abrogated, or their ability to make their own decisions regarding resource management may be curtailed. In all of the cases the result is similar: resource management decisions are taken over by those with insufficient stake in the local environment, and resources are extracted at unreplenishable levels in order to benefit other, often richer, societies. Rist (2008) notes that whereas an economy based upon local resources can make people sensitive to any deterioration in their environment, and in most cases eager to preserve it, the market (globalization) makes it possible to take resources from one region, to consume them in another region, and to dispose of the waste in yet another.

Effects of Environmental Degradation

Effects on Health and Productivity

In 1992, the *World Development Report* by World Bank had identified the following effects of the major environmental problems on both health and productivity: water pollution and water scarcity, air pollution, solid and hazardous wastes, soil degradation, deforestation, loss of biodiversity and atmospheric changes.

Water Pollution and Water Scarcity

More than two million deaths and billions of illnesses a year are attributable to water pollution; water scarcity compounds these health problems. Productivity is affected by the costs of providing safe water, by constraints on economic activity caused by water shortages, and by the adverse effects of water pollution and shortages on other environmental resources.

Air Pollution

Urban air pollution is responsible for 300,000 to 700,000 deaths annually and creates chronic health problems for many more people. In addition, 400 million to 700 million people, primarily women and children in poor rural areas, are affected by smoky indoor air. Restrictions on vehicles and industrial activity during critical periods affect productivity, as does the effect of acid rain on forests and water bodies.

Solid and Hazardous Wastes

Diseases are spread by uncollected garbage and blocked drains; the health risks from hazardous wastes are typically more localized, but often acute. Wastes affect productivity through the pollution of groundwater resources.

Soil Degradation

Depleted soils increase the risk of malnutrition for farmers. Productivity losses on tropical soils are estimated to be in the range of 0.5 to 1.5 per cent of GNP, while secondary productivity losses are due to siltation of reservoirs, transportation channels and other hydrologic investments.

Deforestation

Death and disease can result from the localized flooding caused by deforestation. Loss of sustainable logging potential and of erosion prevention, watershed stability and carbon sequestration provided by forests, are among the productivity impacts of deforestation.

Loss of Biodiversity

The extinction of plant and animal species will potentially affect the development of new drugs; it will reduce ecosystem adaptability and lead to the loss of genetic resources.

Atmospheric Changes

Ozone depletion is responsible for, perhaps, 300,000 additional cases of skin cancer a year and 1.7 million cases of cataracts. Global warming may lead to a shift in vector-borne diseases and increase the risk of climatic natural disasters. Productivity impacts may include sea-rise damage to coastal investments, regional changes in agricultural productivity and disruption of the marine food chain.

Effects on Poverty

The world's poor depend disproportionately on ecosystems for their livelihood systems of small-scale agriculture, grazing, harvesting, hunting, and fishing (UN Millennium Project, 2005). The Poverty-Environment Initiative (PEI) of the United Nations Development Programme (UNDP) and the United Nations Environment Programme (UNEP) is a global UN-led programme that supports country-led efforts to mainstream poverty-environment linkages into national development planning. According to the UNDP-UNEP PEI (2009), poverty-environment linkages can be conceptualized in many ways, notably in terms of their relationship to livelihoods, resilience to environmental risks, health and economic development as discussed below.

Livelihoods

Ecosystems provide services (including provisioning services such as food and freshwater, regulating services such as the regulation of climate and water and air quality, cultural services such as recreation and aesthetic enjoyment, and supporting services needed to produce all other ecosystem services such as soil formation) on which poor people rely disproportionately for their well-being and basic needs. Populations also depend on the environment to earn incomes in sectors such as agriculture, fishing, forestry and tourism, through both formal and informal markets. Livelihoods can be sustainable or not, depending on the way the environment is managed.

Resilience to Environmental Risks

Poor people are more vulnerable to natural disasters such as floods and droughts, the effects of climate change and other environmental shocks that threaten their livelihoods and undermine food security. Improving the ways in which environmental resources, such as forests, are managed increases the resilience of poor people and their livelihoods to environmental risks.

Health

Environmental conditions account for a significant portion of health risks to poor people. Environmental risk factors, such as occupational exposures to chemicals and indoor air pollution from household solid fuel use, play a role in more than 80 per cent of the diseases regularly reported on by the World Health Organization. Globally, nearly a quarter of all deaths and of the world's total disease burden can be attributed to the environment. As many as 13 million deaths could be prevented every year by making the environment healthier. Improved health from better environmental conditions would also contribute to improvements in livelihoods, economic development and resilience to environmental risks.

Economic Development

Environmental quality contributes directly and indirectly to economic development and employment. These contributions are particularly important in developing countries in such sectors as agriculture, energy, forestry, fisheries and tourism.

Effects on Common Resource Management Systems

People who rely immediately on natural resources for their livelihood have always developed methods to ensure the conservation of their environment. In general, these methods are more explicit and more formalized in situations where resources are very scarce, such as in arid lands, although implicit rules governing resource use exist as well in situations of relative abundance. On the community level, resource management systems have generally been more evident among the disadvantaged and rural dwellers than among the urban rich, simply because means of livelihood other than direct resource exploitation are less readily available to the former groups. Common property tenure and usufruct systems are central to many traditional management systems. Rural Third World communities often do not have as pervasive a sense of individual private property ownership as has developed in the industrialized world, instead, systems of group ownership prevail. They not only have the highest incentives for managing their resources sustainably, but they have historically often been able to develop a variety of effective and adaptable means of doing so. There are numerous descriptions, for instance, of religious or spiritual significance being attached to certain plants or animals, which are thereby protected (Vivian, 1991). However, as Shiva (2010) noted, the destruction or privatization of the commons was essential for the creation of natural resources as a supply of raw materials for industry.

Effects on Social Structure

UNRISD (1994) notes that the responses to environmental degradation by local people who are negatively affected can be grouped under four general headings, which in the medium to long term, contribute to changing social structures:

1. Individuals and households can adapt customary production and consumption patterns to the new circumstances.
2. They can attempt to find alternative sources of livelihood in the same locality (such as engaging in commerce, services or wage labour, often made available by the same processes that caused the degradation).
3. They can migrate temporarily to supplement family livelihoods with income from elsewhere, or migrate with their families permanently to find alternative livelihoods elsewhere.
4. They can organize collectively to undertake production and investment activities that would not be feasible individually, as well as to protect their livelihoods by resisting environmental degradation caused by outsiders.

Climate Change

Rising fossil fuel burning and land use changes have emitted, and are continuing to emit, increasing quantities of greenhouse gases into the earth's atmosphere. These greenhouse gases include carbon dioxide (CO_2), methane (CH_4) and nitrogen dioxide (N_2O), and a rise in these gases has caused a rise in the amount of heat from the sun withheld in the earth's atmosphere, heat that would normally be radiated back into space. According to the World Meteorological Organization, which issues annual updates on the status of climate change and greenhouse gas emissions, the decade 2001–2010 was the warmest on record since 1880 in terms of average global temperatures. It was warmer than the previous record decade 1991–2000. This increase in heat has led to the greenhouse effect, resulting in climate change. The main characteristics of climate change are:

- Increases in average global temperature (global warming).
- Changes in cloud cover and precipitation particularly over land.
- Melting of ice caps and glaciers and reduced snow cover.
- Increases in ocean temperatures and ocean acidity, due to seawater absorbing heat and carbon dioxide from the atmosphere (United Nations Framework Convention on Climate Change, no date).

Climate change has wide-ranging effects on the environment, and on socioeconomic and related sectors, including water resources, agriculture and food security, human health, terrestrial ecosystems and biodiversity and coastal zones. Changes in rainfall pattern are likely to lead to severe water shortages and/or flooding. Melting of glaciers can cause flooding and soil erosion. Rising temperatures will cause shifts in crop growing seasons which affects food security and changes in the distribution of disease vectors putting more people at risk from diseases such as malaria and dengue fever. Temperature increases will potentially severely increase rates of extinction for many habitats and species (up to 30 per cent with a 2° C rise in temperature) (United Nations Framework Convention on Climate Change, no date).

Climate change is a serious risk to poverty reduction and could undo decades of development efforts. While climate change is global, its negative impacts are more severely felt by poor people and poor countries. They are more vulnerable because of their high dependence on natural resources and limited capacity to cope with climate variability and extremes. Restoring and maintaining key ecosystems can help communities in their adaptation efforts and support livelihoods that depend upon the services of these ecosystems. Moving towards low-carbon societies can help reduce greenhouse gas emissions, improving human health and well-being and creating green jobs (United Nations Environment Programme, no date).

Effects on 'Natural Disasters'

Most environmental problems, which are described as 'natural disasters', are in fact created as a result of scientists and planners overstepping boundaries in order to create limitless growth and limitless consumption (Shiva, 2010).

Ecologism and Environmental Movement

Ecologism is an ideology based on the belief that nature is an interconnected whole, embracing humans and non-humans, as well as the inanimate world. Capra (1975, cited by Heywood, 2007) argued that the ancient pagan religions and the eastern religions such as Hinduism, Buddhism and Taoism have long preached the unity of oneness of all things, a discovery that western science made only in the 20th century. However, ecologism is mainly a reaction against the process of industrialization.

Deep ecology is strong ecologism, based on the more challenging idea that the purpose of human life is to help sustain nature, and not the other way round (Heywood, 2007). According to Capra (1996), a deep ecologist, the world is not a collection of isolated objects, but a network of phenomena that are fundamentally interconnected and interdependent. In nature, there is no 'above' or 'below', and there are no hierarchies. There are only networks nesting within other networks. Ultimately, such deep ecological awareness is spiritual or religious awareness, he said. According to him, the principles of the planet's ecosystems organize themselves through interdependence, recycling, partnership, flexibility, and diversity. One of the most significant assumptions of deep ecology is biocentric equality, which views natural entities as morally independent of their perceived usefulness for human purposes. This underscores the intrinsic worth of all natural things. From this assumption flows deep ecology's ideas of non-anthropocentrism, tolerance of different views, open relational communication with nature, the inclusion of animals and plants in the community and creating the need for heightened preservation and conservation efforts (Naess, 1995, cited by Besthorn, 2003).

According to Gadgil and Guha (1998), an environmental movement is an organized social activity consciously directed towards promoting sustainable use of natural resources, halting environmental degradation or bringing about environmental restoration. Through the process of struggle, the spreading of consciousness, and constructive work, action groups in the environment field have come to develop an incisive critique of the development process itself. More hesitantly, they have tried to outline an alternate framework for development, which, they argue, would be both ecologically sustainable and socially just.

Progress in Reversal of the Loss of Environmental Resources in Asian Sub-Regions

Indicators of Reversal of the Loss of Environmental Resources

Following are the indicators for the second half of Target 9 of MDG–7 on reversal of the loss of environmental resources (described at http://www.mdgasiapacific.org/node/44):

- Proportion of land area covered by forest.
- Ratio of area protected to maintain biological diversity to surface area.
- Energy use (kg oil equivalent) per $1 GDP (PPP).
- Carbon dioxide emissions per capita and consumption of ozone-depleting CFCs (ODP tons) (this indicator is used to monitor the reduction in the usage of Ozone Depleting Substances).
- Proportion of population using solid fuels.

Asian Development Bank (2011) provides comparative data (Table 12.1) on reversal of the loss of environmental resources in Asian sub-regions.

Table 12.1
Diversity in Reversal of the Loss of Environmental Resources in Asian Sub-Regions

Level of HD 2012	Country	Reversal of Loss of Environmental Resources			
		% of Land Area covered by Forest 2010	% of Marine Areas Protected 2010	Per capita metric tons CO_2 Emissions 2008	Consumption of ODP metric tons 2009
East Asia					
V High	Japan	68.5%	10.9%	09.5	699.5
V High	South Korea	63.0%	03.0%	10.6	4272.3
V High	Hong Kong	—	41.8%	05.5	—

Cont'd...

...Cont'd

Medium	China	21.9%	16.0%	05.3	20371.2
Low	North Korea	—	—	—	
South East Asia					
V High	Singapore	02.9%	03.4%	07.0	226.9
V High	Brunei	72.1%	29.6%	27.0	5.0
High	Malaysia	62.3%	13.7%	07.7	604.5
Medium	Thailand	37.1%	17.3%	04.2	1012.0
Medium	Philippines	25.7%	05.0%	00.9	403.4
Medium	Indonesia	52.1%	06.4%	01.8	374.8
Medium	Vietnam	44.5%	04.6%	01.5	289.3
Medium	Timor-Leste	49.9%	06.4%	00.2	0.9
Medium	Laos	68.2%	16.6%	00.2	2.1
Medium	Cambodia	57.2%	23.4%	00.3	17.1
Low	Myanmar	48.3%	05.2%	00.3	4.1
North and Central Asia					
High	Russia	—	—	—	—
High	Kazakhstan	01.2%	02.5%	15.3	130.2
Medium	Turkmenistan	08.8%	03.0%	09.5	13.1
Medium	Mongolia	07.0%	13.4%	04.1	1.9
Medium	Uzbekistan	07.7%	02.3%	04.6	1.8
Medium	Kyrgyzstan	05.0%	06.9%	01.1	7.7
Medium	Tajikistan	02.9%	04.1%	00.5	2.6
South Asia					
High	Sri Lanka	28.8%	15.0%	00.6	13.5
Medium	Maldives	03.3%	—	03.0	5.1
Medium	India	23.0%	04.8%	01.5	977.0
Medium	Bhutan	69.1%	28.4%	01.1	0.3
Low	Pakistan	02.2%	09.8%	00.9	245.3
Low	Bangladesh	11.1%	01.6%	00.3	195.9
Low	Nepal	25.4%	17.0%	00.1	1.2

Forest Cover

The proportion of land area covered by forest is the forest area as a share of total land area, where land area is the total surface area of the country less the area covered by inland waters, such as major rivers and lakes. Forest includes both natural forests and forest plantations. It refers to land with an existing or expected tree canopy of more than 10 per cent and an area of more than 0.5 hectare where the trees should be able to reach a minimum height of five meters. Forests are identified by both the presence of trees and the absence of other land uses. Land from which forest has been cleared but that will be reforested in the foreseeable future is included. Excluded are stands of trees established primarily for agricultural production, such as fruit tree plantations (http://www.mdgasiapacific.org/node/44). According to the MDG Report of 2012 (United Nations, 2012), Asia registered a net gain of some 2.2 million hectares annually in the past 10 years, mostly because of large-scale afforestation programmes in China, India and Vietnam. With reference to forest cover, without China and India, Asia is regressing. This is due to the shrinkage of forest cover in East and Northeast Asia, South East Asia (excluding the Philippines, Singapore and Viet Nam) and in some countries of South Asia (UNESCAP, ADB and UNDP, 2012–13).

Table 12.1 shows that maximum percentage of land area covered by forests is in the mountainous countries of Brunei, Bhutan, Japan, Laos, South Korea and Malaysia where it ranges from 72.1 per cent in Brunei to 62.3 per cent in Malaysia.

East Asia: In East Asia, maximum percentage of land area covered by forests is in the mountainous countries of Japan and South Korea and China has made maximum progress on this indicator.

South East Asia: In South East Asia, percentage of forest land ranges from 2.9 per cent in the island city state of Singapore to 72.1 per cent in Brunei. In this sub-region, maximum percentage of land area covered by forests is in the mountainous countries of Brunei, Laos and Malaysia and Vietnam has made the fastest progress for this indicator.

South Asia: In South Asia, maximum percentage of land area covered by forests is in the mountainous country of Bhutan. In this sub-region, forest land ranges from 2.2 per cent in Pakistan to 69.1

per cent in the mountainous Bhutan. India has made fastest progress on this indicator.

North and Central Asia: North and Central Asia have minimum forest land in Asia as this sub-region is known for vast deserts and treeless grassy steppes. In this sub-region, forest land ranges from 1.2 per cent in Kazakhstan to 8.8 per cent in Turkmenistan. Forest cover is a less relevant indicator in these arid and sparsely populated countries (UNESCAP, 2007).

Protected Marine Area

The ratio of area protected to maintain biological diversity to surface area is defined as nationally protected area as a percentage of total surface area of a country. The generally accepted IUCN-World Conservation Union definition of a protected area is an area of land or sea dedicated to the protection and maintenance of biological diversity and of natural and associated cultural resources and managed through legal or other effective means (http://www.mdgasiapacific.org/node/44). The MDG report of 2012 shows that since 1990, protected areas have increased in number by 58 per cent and in their extent by 48 per cent. By 2010, protected area covered 12.7 per cent of the world's land area and 1.6 per cent of the total ocean area (United Nations, 2012: 49). Table 12.1 shows that in Asia the maximum percentage of marine areas protected is in the island of Hong Kong (41.8%) and minimum in Bangladesh (1.6%).

East Asia: The maximum percentage of marine areas protected in East Asia is in the island of Hong Kong (41.8%) and minimum in South Korea (3%).

South East Asia: The percentage of marine areas protected in South East Asia ranges from 3.4 per cent in Singapore to 29.6 per cent in Brunei.

North and Central Asia: The North and Central Asian countries are landlocked and that explains low percentage of marine area protected by them (from 2.3 per cent in Uzbekistan to 13.4 per cent in Mongolia).

South Asia: The percentage of marine areas protected in South Asia ranges from 1.6 per cent in Bangladesh to 28.4 per cent in Bhutan.

CO_2 Emissions and ODP CFC Consumption

Carbon dioxide emissions per capita is the total amount of carbon dioxide emitted by a country as a consequence of human (production and consumption) activities, divided by the population of the country. Consumption of ozone-depleting chlorofluorocarbons (CFCs) in ODP (ozone-depleting potential) tons is the sum of the consumption of the weighted tons of the individual substances in the group-metric tons of the individual substance (defined in the Montreal Protocol on Substances that Deplete the Ozone Layer) multiplied by its ozone-depleting potential. An ozone-depleting substance is any substance containing chlorine or bromine that destroys the stratospheric ozone layer. The stratospheric ozone layer absorbs most of the biologically damaging ultraviolet radiation (http://www.mdgasiapacific.org/node/44). The MDG report of 2012 shows that defying the long-term trend, CO_2 emissions decreased globally by 0.4 per cent from 2008 to 2009 due to the slowing economic activity during the global crisis. Emissions from the developed regions were especially affected. On the other hand, the emissions in the developing regions continued to increase. Even with the dip, 2009 emissions were still 39 per cent above the 1990 level, the per capita emissions being 10 metric tons of CO_2 in the developed world as compared to three metric tons in the developing world (United Nations, 2012: 47–48).

Asia as a whole has already achieved the targets for reducing consumption of ozone-depleting substances (UNESCAP, ADB and UNDP, 2010–11). Table 12.1 shows that per capita metric tons of CO_2 emissions in Asia is maximum in Brunei (27) and minimum in the less developed countries of Nepal (0.1), Timor-Leste and Laos (0.2), and Cambodia, Myanmar and Bangladesh (0.3). On the other hand, the consumption of ODP metric tons is very high in China (20371.2) and low in Bhutan (0.3) and Timor-Leste (0.9).

East Asia: In East Asia, the per capita metric tons of CO_2 emissions range from 5.3 in China to 10.6 in South Korea. In this sub-region, the consumption of ODP metric tons range from 699.5 in Japan to a very high of 20371.2 in China.

North and Central Asia: In North and Central Asia, the per capita metric tons of CO_2 emissions range from 0.5 in Tajikistan to 15.3 in Kazakhstan. The 2005 MDG Report for Asia and the Pacific (UNESCAP, ADB and UNDP, 2005) noted that many of the Central

Asian countries have reduced industrial output. In this sub-region, the consumption of ODP metric tons range from 1.8 in Uzbekistan to 130.2 in Kazakhstan.

South Asia: In South Asia, the per capita metric tons of CO_2 emissions range from 0.1 in Nepal to 3 in Maldives. In this sub-region, the consumption of ODP metric tons range from 0.3 in Bhutan to 977 in India.

South East Asia: In South East Asia, the per capita metric tons of CO_2 emissions range from 0.2 in Timor-Leste and Laos to 27 in Brunei. In this sub-region, the consumption of ODP metric tons range from 0.9 in Timor-Leste to 1012 in Thailand.

Progress in Sustainable Water Sources and Sanitation Facilities in Asian Sub-Regions

Indicators of Access to Sustainable Water Sources and Sanitation Facilities

According to the WHO, inadequate access to sanitation and safe drinking water is the second most important risk factor (after malnutrition) contributing to the global burden of disease. Earlier WHO 1997 figures indicated that 19 per cent of deaths among children under five in the developing world in 1995 were attributable to diarrhoeal disease, which is closely associated with contaminated water (Labonte, Schrecker, Sanders and Meeus, 2004).

Following are the Indicators for Target 10 of MDG–7 on reducing by half the proportion of people without sustainable access to safe drinking water.

Proportion of population with sustainable access to an improved water source, urban and rural: The proportion of the population with sustainable access to an improved water source, urban and rural, is the percentage of the population who use any of the following types of water supply for drinking: piped water, public tap, borehole or pump, protected well, protected spring or rainwater. Improved water sources do not include vendor-provided water, bottled water, tanker trucks or unprotected wells and springs.

Proportion of population with access to improved sanitation, urban and rural: Proportion of the urban and rural population with access to improved sanitation refers to the percentage of the population with access to facilities that hygienically separate human excreta from human, animal and insect contact.

Asian Development Bank (2011) provides comparative data in Asian sub-regions on improved water source and sanitation facilities, shown in Table 12.2.

Table 12.2
Diversity in Sustainable Water Sources and Sanitation Facilities in Asian Sub-Regions

Level of Human Develop-ment 2012	Country	% Urban Population using Improved Water Sources 2008	% Rural Population using Improved Water Sources 2008	% Urban Population using Improved Sanitation Facilities 2008	% Rural Population using Improved Sanitation Facilities 2008
East Asia					
V High	Japan	100%	100%	100%	100%
V High	South Korea	100%	088%	100%	100%
V High	Hong Kong	—	—	—	—
Medium	China	098%	082%	058%	052%
Low	North Korea	—	—	—	—
South East Asia					
V High	Singapore	100%	NA	100%	NA
V High	Brunei	—	—	—	—
High	Malaysia	100%	99%	96%	95%
Medium	Thailand	099%	98%	95%	96%
Medium	Philippines	093%	87%	80%	69%
Medium	Indonesia	089%	71%	67%	36%
Medium	Vietnam	099%	92%	94%	67%
Medium	Timor-Leste	086%	63%	76%	40%
Medium	Laos	072%	51%	86%	38%
Medium	Cambodia	081%	56%	67%	18%
Low	Myanmar	075%	69%	86%	79%
North and Central Asia					
High	Russia	—	—	—	—
High	Kazakhstan	99%	90%	097%	098%

Cont'd...

...Cont'd

Medium	Turkmenistan	97%	72%	099%	097%
Medium	Mongolia	97%	49%	064%	032%
Medium	Uzbekistan	98%	81%	100%	100%
Medium	Kyrgyzstan	99%	85%	094%	093%
Medium	Tajikistan	94%	61%	095%	094%
South Asia					
High	Sri Lanka	98%	88%	088%	92%
Medium	Maldives	99%	86%	100%	96%
Medium	India	96%	84%	054%	21%
Medium	Bhutan	99%	88%	087%	54%
Low	Pakistan	95%	87%	072%	29%
Low	Bangladesh	85%	78%	055%	52%
Low	Nepal	93%	87%	051%	27%

Improvement in Sustainable Water Sources

The MDG target of halving the proportion of the population without sustainable access to safe drinking water has been met five years ahead of the 2015 target. In 2010, 89 per cent of the world's population was using improved drinking water sources, up from 76 per cent in 1990. China and India alone recorded almost half of global progress. The urban-rural difference is wide. In 2010, 96 per cent of the urban population used an improved drinking water source, compared to 81 per cent of the rural population. However, in absolute terms, because of population growth, the number of people without an improved source in urban areas actually increased and in rural areas this number decreased (United Nations, 2012: 52–53). Asia as a whole has already achieved the targets for halving the proportion of people without access to safe drinking water (UNESCAP, ADB and UNDP, 2010–11). The 2005 MDG Report for Asia and the Pacific (UNESCAP, ADB and UNDP, 2005) shows that the situation of water supplies in the rural areas is typically 10 to 20 percentage points lower than that in the urban areas. Table 12.2 shows that in all the countries except Japan and Singapore, the rural population covered is less than the urban population.

East Asia: Japan is leading in Asia and East Asia with 100 per cent urban and rural population using improved water sources. China has the lowest coverage in East Asia. According to the MDG Report of 2011 (United Nations, 2011), East Asia registered the largest gains in drinking water coverage – from 69 per cent in 1990 to 86 per cent in 2008.

South Asia: Maldives and Bhutan are leading in South Asia with 99 per cent urban population using improved water sources. As far as rural population is concerned, Sri Lanka and Bhutan are leading with 88 per cent coverage. Country with the lowest coverage in urban (85%) and rural areas (78%) is Bangladesh. There is significant progress in South Asia; however, an analysis of trends over the period 1995–2008 for three countries in South Asia shows that improvements in sanitation disproportionately benefitted the better off, while sanitation coverage for the poorest 40 per cent of households hardly increased (United Nations, 2011).

South East Asia: Singapore and Malaysia are leading in South East Asia with 100 per cent urban population using improved water sources and Malaysia is leading with 99 per cent rural population using improved water source (Singapore does not have a rural component). Countries with the lowest coverage in urban areas are Laos (72%), Myanmar (75%), Cambodia (81%) and Timor-Leste (86%). Same countries have still less coverage in rural areas: Laos (51%), Cambodia (56%), Timor-Leste (63%), and Myanmar (69%).

North and Central Asia: Kazakhstan and Kyrgyzstan are leading in North and Central Asia with 99 per cent urban population using improved water sources and other countries follow closely. Kazakhstan is leading with 90 per cent of the rural population using improved water source but other countries are trailing behind. Mongolia has only 49 per cent rural coverage.

Conclusion: Improvement in water supply has made good progress in urban Asia, but not in rural areas. Lately, East Asia registered the largest gains in drinking water coverage. There is significant progress in South Asia, with most of the increase attributable to India. However, an analysis of trends over the period 1995–2008 for three countries in South Asia shows that improvements in sanitation disproportionately benefitted the better off, while sanitation coverage for the poorest 40 per cent of households hardly increased. South East Asia is very diverse with countries doing very well and those that are of concern. North and Central Asian countries are doing well with reference to urban water sources but not with reference to rural water source.

Improvement in Sanitation Facilities

Asia is lagging behind in providing basic sanitation (UNESCAP, ADB and UNDP, 2010–11). Sanitation coverage increased from 36 per cent in 1990 to 56 per cent in 2010 in the developing regions as a whole. The number of people who do not use any facility and resort to open defecation has decreased but there still remain 1.1 billion people or 15 per cent of the global population with no sanitation facilities at all. Nearly 60 per cent of those practicing open defecation live in India. Rural-urban disparities in access to sanitation are even more pronounced than for access to drinking water. Eight out of 10 urban people use an improved sanitation facility, compared to only half of the rural population (United Nations, 2012). The 2005 MDG Report for Asia and the Pacific (UNESCAP, ADB and UNDP, 2005) shows that access to improved sanitation is also far better in urban than rural areas, 73 against 31 per cent. Table 12.2 shows the urban-rural gap except in Japan, South Korea, Uzbekistan and Singapore (which has no rural area).

East Asia: Japan and South Korea both have covered 100 per cent of their urban and rural population with improved sanitation facilities. China has covered only 58 per cent of urban and 52 per cent of rural population with improved sanitation facilities.

North and Central Asia: Uzbekistan is leading in North and Central Asia with 100 per cent coverage of sanitation in urban and rural areas. Only Mongolia is problematic with reference to urban (64%) and rural (32%) sanitation.

South Asia: Maldives is leading in South Asia with 100 per cent coverage of urban sanitation and 96 per cent coverage of rural sanitation. India is of concern with only 54 per cent coverage of urban sanitation and 21 per cent coverage of rural sanitation. In the world, nearly 60 per cent of those practicing open defecation live in India (United Nations, 2012: 55). Bangladesh (55%) and Nepal (51%) are of concern with reference to urban sanitation and Pakistan (29%) and Nepal (27%) are of concern with reference to rural sanitation.

South East Asia: Besides 100 per cent coverage in Singapore, Malaysia (96%, 95%) and Thailand (95%, 96%) are doing well in

South East Asia with reference to urban and rural sanitation. Indonesia and Cambodia (both 67%) are lagging behind with reference to urban sanitation. Cambodia has the lowest rural coverage of sanitation facilities (18%) in South East Asia as well as in Asia as a whole. Indonesia (36%), Laos (38%) and Timor-Leste (40%) are also countries of concern about rural sanitation.

Progress in Lives of Slum Dwellers in Asian Sub-Regions

The share of urban slum residents in the developing world declined from 39 per cent in 2000 to 33 per cent in 2012. More than 200 million of these people gained access to improved water sources, improved sanitation, facilities, or durable or less crowded housing, thereby exceeding the MDG target. However, the absolute number of slum dwellers continues to grow, fed by an accelerating pace of urbanization (United Nations, 2012: 56). Asian Development Bank (2011) provides comparative data in Asian sub-regions on slum population as percentage of urban population, shown in the table below.

Table 12.3
Diversity in Percentage of Slum Population in Asian Sub-Regions

Level of Human Development 2012	Country	Slum Population as % of Urban Population 2007
East Asia		
Medium	China	31.0%
South East Asia		
Medium	Indonesia	23.0%
Medium	Vietnam	38.8%
Low	Myanmar	42.3%
North Asia		
Medium	Mongolia	57.9%
South Asia		
Medium	India	32.1%
Low	Pakistan	47.0%
Low	Bangladesh	70.8%
Low	Nepal	59.4%

Table 12.3 shows that:

East Asia: China is the only country in East Asia to have population living in slums.

North and Central Asia: Mongolia is the only country in North and Central Asia to have population living in slums.

South East Asia: In South East Asia, Myanmar and Vietnam are of concern. Indonesia has minimum (23%) proportion of slum population in Asian countries that have slums.

South Asia: South Asia has the maximum percentage of slum population in urban areas. Bangladesh has more than 70 per cent of its urban population living in slums. India which has the lowest proportion of slum population, in this sub-region, also has almost a third of its urban population living in slums. The rapid expansion of urban areas in South Asia is creating cities of unprecedented size and complexity and new challenges for providing a decent environment for the poor (UNESCAP, 2006).

Discussion

Overall Progress of Environmental Sustainability in Asia

The UN Report (2006) on State of the Environment in Asia and the Pacific observes that while this region has limited access to natural resources in comparison with the levels and nature of economic activity that these resources must support, consumption and production patterns are becoming less environmentally sustainable. As regional economies grow to reduce poverty and to meet the demands of its growing populations for a better quality of life, environmental pressures are mounting. The result is continued declines in natural capital, as evidenced in the loss of natural forests, changes to freshwater systems, air pollution, coastal and marine ecosystem stress, declining biodiversity and climate change. The rapid rate of growth and the tremendous unmet needs for socio-economic progress mean that a focus on improving environmental performance cannot mitigate the environmental pressures exerted by current patterns of development.

Diversity in Progress in Environmental Sustainability in Asian Sub-Regions

East Asia

In the most developed sub-region of East Asia, South Korea has one of the maximum percentages of land area covered by forests and has covered 100 per cent of their urban and rural population with improved sanitation facilities. However, it has minimum percentage of marine areas protected and maximum per capita metric tons of CO_2 emissions. Japan also has one of the maximum percentages of land area covered by forests and the lowest consumption of ODP metric tons. It is also leading in Asia and East Asia with 100 per cent urban and rural population using improved water sources and sanitation facilities.

China has made maximum progress on land area covered by forests and the per capita metric tons of CO_2 emissions are minimum in China. However, the consumption of ODP metric tons is very high (20371.2) in China and this huge country has the lowest coverage of people's access to improved water sources in East Asia. Moreover, China has covered only 58 per cent of urban and 52 per cent of rural population with improved sanitation facilities and it is the only country in East Asia to have population living in slums. The theme of China's HDR of 2009–10 is *China and a Sustainable Future: Towards a Low Carbon Economy and Society* (United Nations Development Programme China, 2009–10). This Report notes that the rapid economic growth and large population are responsible for China's damage to its environment. Its poverty is most serious in mountainous areas where natural conditions are harsh, and socio-economic development lags behind the more prosperous coastal areas. Many areas in China's vast territory have fragile ecosystems prone to unfavourable climate shifts. To support China in its transition to a lower carbon pathway, this report concludes that the shift to a low carbon development pathway is an imperative for sustaining its human development.

South East Asia

In South East Asia, the maximum percentage of land area covered by forests is in the mountainous countries. The percentage of forest land and the percentage of marine areas protected in South East Asia are maximum in Brunei. However, the per capita metric tons of CO_2 emissions are also maximum in Brunei. The percentage of forest land and the percentage of marine areas protected in South East Asia are minimum in Singapore. Singapore leads in South East Asia with 100 per cent urban population using improved water sources and has 100 per cent coverage of urban and rural sanitation. Malaysia leads in South East Asia with 100 per cent urban population using improved water sources and 99 per cent rural population using improved water sources. With reference to urban and rural sanitation, Malaysia and Thailand are doing well. However, the consumption of ODP metric tons is maximum in Thailand. In South East Asia, the per capita metric tons of CO_2 emissions and the consumption of ODP metric are the lowest in Timor-Leste.

Countries with the lowest coverage improved water sources in urban areas are Laos, Myanmar, Cambodia and Timor-Leste. Same countries have still less coverage in rural areas. Indonesia and Cambodia are lagging behind with reference to urban and rural sanitation. Cambodia has the lowest rural coverage of sanitation facilities in South East Asia as well as in Asia as a whole. In South East Asia, Myanmar and Vietnam are of concern with reference to slum dwelling. Indonesia has minimum (23%) proportion of slum population in Asian countries that have slums. The UN Report (2006) observes that South East Asian economies have benefitted from, and supported, consumption in East Asia and economies further afield. As a result, environmental pressures are rising, perhaps, the fastest in this sub-region, as exemplified by the dwindling natural forests, air pollution and problems of industrial and solid waste management.

North and Central Asia

North and Central Asia have minimum forest land in Asia as this sub-region is known for vast deserts and treeless grassy steppes. Forest cover is a less relevant indicator in these arid and sparsely populated countries. The North and Central Asian countries are landlocked and that explains low percentage of marine area protected by them. Kazakhstan and Kyrgyzstan are leading in North and Central Asia with high proportion of urban population using improved water sources and other countries follow closely. As far as rural water sources are concerned, Kazakhstan is leading but other countries are trailing behind. Uzbekistan is leading in North and

Central Asia with 100 per cent coverage of sanitation in urban and rural areas. In this sub-region, Kazakhstan has the maximum per capita metric tons of CO_2 emissions and the consumption of ODP metric tons. The per capita metric tons of CO_2 emissions are minimum in Tajikistan and the consumption of ODP metric tons is minimum in Uzbekistan. Only Mongolia is problematic with reference to improved water sources and urban and rural sanitation and it is the only country in North and Central Asia to have population living in slums.

South Asia

Maldives is leading in South Asia with reference to urban population using improved water sources, and coverage of urban and rural sanitation. On the other hand, Maldives has maximum per capita metric tons of CO_2 emissions in South Asia. As far as access of rural population to sustainable water sources is concerned, Sri Lanka is leading with 88 per cent coverage. Bhutan is leading in South Asia with reference to urban and rural population using improved water sources. Bhutan has the maximum percentage of land area covered by forests and marine areas protected in South Asia. In this sub-region, the consumption of ODP metric tons is also minimum in Bhutan.

India has made fastest progress on reversal of forest cover. However, in this sub-region, the consumption of ODP metric tons is maximum in India. India is also of concern with reference to urban and rural sanitation. In the world, nearly 60 per cent of those practicing open defecation live in India. India which has the lowest proportion of slum population, in this sub-region, also has almost a third of its urban population living in slums. Pakistan is of concern with reference to forest cover and rural sanitation. Bangladesh has minimum percentage of marine areas protected in South Asia. It also has the lowest coverage of sustainable water sources in urban and rural areas. It is also of concern with reference to urban sanitation. Bangladesh has more than 70 per cent of its urban population living in slums. In South Asia, the per capita metric tons of CO_2 emissions are minimum in Nepal. However, Nepal is of concern with reference to urban and rural sanitation. South Asia has the maximum percentage of slum population in urban areas. The rapid expansion of urban areas in South Asia is creating cities of unprecedented size and complexity and new challenges for providing a decent environment for the poor.

Thakur and Wiggen (2004) identify the following factors responsible for environmental degradation in South Asia:

- A very high population growth rate coupled with a lack of appropriate infrastructure.
- Somewhat unfettered industrial growth without due environmental considerations.
- Major demographic shifts, including intense urbanization.

Other factors, in particular poverty and lack of education, further exacerbate the impacts on the environment. In turn, the environmental impacts adversely affect livelihoods and the availability of natural resources, forming a vicious cycle of destruction (Thakur and Wiggen, 2004). However, the underdeveloped infrastructure and still low levels of consumption in South Asia may prove to be an opportunity to meet its needs in an environmentally sustainable manner (United Nations, 2006).

Implications for Environment Policy in Asia

The plan of implementation of the UN World Summit on Sustainable Development held at Johannesburg, in 2002 (United Nations, 2002), was built on the achievements made since the UN Earth Summit in 1992, to expedite the realization of the remaining goals:

- The integration of the three components of sustainable development: economic development, social development and environmental protection as interdependent and mutually reinforcing pillars.
- Poverty eradication, changing unsustainable patterns of production and consumption and protecting and managing the natural resource base of economic and social development.
- The implementation of the outcomes of the Summit should benefit all, particularly women, youth, children and vulnerable groups.
- The implementation should involve all relevant actors through partnerships, especially between governments of the North and South, on the one hand, and between governments and major groups.

- Good governance within each country and at the international level is essential for sustainable development.
- Continued need for a dynamic and enabling international economic environment supportive of international cooperation.
- Peace, security, stability and respect for human rights and fundamental freedoms, including the right to development, as well as respect for cultural diversity.

The findings from 15 years of the UNRISD research (2002) have a variety of policy and analytical implications, which are summed up as follows:

- Environmental degradation can be addressed through reforms in policies and institutions and shifts in the balance of social forces.
- Environmental protection policies and programmes need to consider and address the basic questions about why the environment should be protected, for whose benefit, who will incur the costs and how those costs will be compensated.
- Policies and institutions are required that recognize and defend the property rights, including customary rights, of less powerful stakeholders; that prevent gross inequalities in ownership of and access to land and other natural resources.
- Local knowledge, resources, participation and experimentation have a crucial role in natural resource management and conservation initiatives.
- Participation and empowerment are crucial for the design and implementation of many environmental protection initiatives given their role in ensuring that environmental goals are balanced with human welfare considerations.
- NGOs, trade unions, researchers and grassroot activists have an important role to play in monitoring and watchdog activities to ensure that agency and corporate discourse is applied in practice, and to keep alive the search for alternatives.

References

Asian Development Bank. (2011). *Key Indicators for Asia and the Pacific.* Manila. Retrieved 31 March 2013 from http://www.adb.org/key-indicators /2011/main

Besthorn, F.H. (2003). Radical ecologisms: Insights for educating social workers in ecological activism and social justice. *Critical Social Work*, 4(1). Retrieved 30 July 2011 from http://www.uwindsor.ca/criticalsocialwork/radical-ecologisms-insights-for-educating-social-workers-in-ecological-activism-and-social-justice

Capra, F. (1996). *The Web of Life.* New York: Anchor Books.

Convention on Biological Diversity. (1993). Convention on Biologicl Diversity. Retrieved 14 October 2010 from http://www.cbd.int/doc/legal/cbd-en.pdf

Gadgil, M. and Guha, R. (1998). Towards a perspective on environmental movements in India. In M. Desai, A. Monteiro and L. Narayan (eds), *Towards People-centred Development*, Part 2 (pp. 450–472). Mumbai: Tata Institute of Social Sciences.

Heywood, A. (2007). *Political Ideologies: An Introduction* (4th ed.). New York: Palgrave Macmillan.

Labonte, R., Schrecker, T., Sanders, D. and Meeus, W. (2004). *Fatal Indifference: The G8, Africa, and Global Health.* Cape Town: University of Cape Town Press. Retrieved 14 March 2012 from http://web.idrc.ca/en/ ev-45682-201-1- DO_TOPIC.html

Ramakrishnan, P.S. (2001). Man and nature: Indigenous wisdom. *Humanscape*, 5, 270–275.

Rist, G. (2008). *The History of Development: From Western Origins to Global Faith* (3rd ed.). New York: Zed Books.

Sachs, W. (2010). Environment. In W. Sachs (ed.), *The Development Dictionary: A Guide to Knowledge as Power* (2nd ed.). (pp. 24–37). New York: Zed Books.

Shiva, V. (2010). Resources. In W. Sachs (ed.), *The Development Dictionary: A Guide to Knowledge as Power* (2nd ed.). (pp. 228–242). New York: Zed Books.

Thakur, R. and Wiggen, O. (2004). Introduction: South Asia's manifold challenge to the international community. In R. Thakur and O. Wiggen (eds), *South Asia in the World: Problem Solving Perspectives on Security, Sustainable Development and Good Governance.* Tokyo: United Nations University Press.

United Nations. (1987). *Our Common Future: Report of the World Commission on Environment and Development.* Retrieved 23 January 2010 from http://conspect.nl/pdf/Our_Common_Future-Brundtland_Report_1987.pdf

——. (1992). Conference on environment and development. Rio de Janeiro.

——. (2002). *Report of the World Summit on Sustainable Development.* Johannesburg.

——. (2006). *State of the Environment in Asia and the Pacific 2005: Economic Growth and Sustainability.* Thailand. Retrieved 15 May 2010 from http://www.unescap.org/esd/environment/soe/2005/mainpub/documents/Title.pdf

——. (2011). *Millennium Development Goals Report 2011.* New York. Retrieved 11 August 2011 from http://www.un.org/millenniumgoals/pdf/(2011_E)%20MDG%20Report%202011_Book%20LR.pdf

——. (2012). *Millennium Development Goals Report 2012.* New York.

United Nations Development Programme China. (2009–10). *China Human Development Report 2009–10: China and a Sustainable Future: Towards a Low Carbon Economy and Society.* Beijing: China Translation and Publishing Corporation.

UNDP-UNEP Poverty Environment Initiative. (2009). *Mainstreaming Poverty-Environment Linkages into Development Planning: A Handbook for Practitioners.* Retrieved 2 November 2011 from http://www.unpei.org/PDF/PEI-full-handbook.pdf

United Nations Economic and Social Commission for Asia and the Pacific. (2006). UNESCAP Fact Sheets on MDGs in South Asia. Retrieved 19 May 2010 from http://www.mdgasiapacific.org/files/shared_folder/documents/fs_sa_mdg_all.pdf

——. (2007). UNESCAP Fact Sheets on MDGs in North and Central Asia. Retrieved 19 May 2010 from http://www.mdgasiapacific.org/files/shared_folder/ documents/fs_nca_mdg_all_en.pdf

United Nations Economic and Social Commission for Asia and the Pacific, Asian Development Bank and United Nations Development Program. (2005). *A Future within Reach: Reshaping Institutions in a Region of Disparities to Meet the Millennium Development Goals in Asia and the Pacific.* New York.

——. (2010–11). *Paths to 2015: MDG Priorities in Asia and the Pacific.* Retrieved 2 December 2010 from http://www.adb.org/Documents/Reports/Asia-Pacific-MDG-2010/default.asp

——. (2012–13). *Perspectives for a Post-2015 Development Agenda: Asia-Pacific Regional MDGs Report 2012/13.*

United Nations Environment Programme. (no date). *Climate Change.* Paris. Retrieved 17 September 2011 from https://docs.google.com/viewer?url=http%3A%2F%2Fwww.unep.org%2Fpdf%2FUNEP_Profile%2FClimate_change.pdf

United Nations Framework Convention on Climate Change. (no date). *Climate Change: Impact, Vulnerabilities and Adaptation in Developing Countries.* Retrieved 6 March 2011 from http://unfccc.int/resource/docs/publications/impacts.pdf

United Nations Millennium Project. (2005). *Environment and Human Well-being: A Practical Strategy*. Summary version of the report of the Task Force on Environmental Sustainability. New York: The Earth Institute at Columbia University.

United Nations Research Institute for Social Development. (1994). Environmental degradation and social integration. UNRISD Briefing Paper No. 3, World Summit for Social Development. Retrieved 6 March 2011 from http://www.unrisd.org/80256B3C005BCCF9/httpNetITFrame

PDF?ReadForm&parentunid=52B8B9CA2197847380256B65004C9CC9&parentdoctype=paper&netitpath=80256B3C005BCCF9/%28httpAuxPages%29/52B8B9CA2197847380256B65004C9CC9/$file/bp3.pdf

——. (2002). *People, Power and the Environment: 15 Years of UNRISD Research.* Geneva.

Vivian, J.M. (1991). *Greening at the Grassroots: People's Participation in Sustainable Development.* Geneva: United Nations Research Institute for Social Development.

World Bank. (1992). *World Development Report 1992: Development and the Environment.* Oxford. Retrieved 31 May 2010 from http://www.wds.worldbank.org/external/default/WDSContentServer/IW3P/IB/2000/12/13/000178830_9810191106175/Rendered/PDF/multi_page.pdf

CHAPTER 13

Discussion of Diversity in Social Development Progress in Asia and Implications

Introduction

Book Objectives

The aim of the book is to carry out an analysis of social development progress in Asia in order to explore the following questions:

- What is the status of social development in Asia with reference to progress, gaps and contradictions if any?
- Is social development in Asian sub-regions homogenous or diverse?
- Why is Asia rising? Is it a miracle? What factors explain the diversity in social development progress across Asian sub-regions?
- Are there Asian values or development approaches that cut across Asian sub-regions? What are they and what determine them?
- What does Asia and the Asian sub-regions need to do for better progress in social development?
- What are the implications for international social development if Asia is rising?

Chapter Objectives

This chapter on discussion of diversity and contradictions in social development in Asia aims to discuss the book objectives through a summarization of the following:

1. Overall social development progress, gaps and contradictions in Asia.
2. Diversity in social development progress in Asia.
3. Factors affecting diversity in social development progress in Asia.
4. Policy implications for social development in Asia and for international social development.

Overall Social Development Progress in Asia

Achievements

Asia has made achievements with reference to the following MDGs:

- Reduce by half the proportion of people living on less than one US dollar a day.
- Ensure that all boys and girls complete a full course of primary schooling.
- Halt and begin to reverse the spread of HIV/AIDS.
- Halt and begin to reverse the spread of TB.
- Eliminate gender disparity in primary and secondary education preferably by 2005, and at all levels by 2015.
- Reduce consumption of ozone-depleting substances.
- Reduce by half the proportion of people without sustainable access to safe drinking water.

Gaps

Asia has not achieved the following MDGs:

- Reduce by half the proportion of people who suffer from hunger.
- Ensure that girls and boys reach the last grade of primary education.
- Reduce the mortality rate among children under five by two-thirds.
- Reduce the maternal mortality ratio by three quarters.
- Eliminate gender disparity in youth literacy.
- Eliminate gender disparity in wage employment.

- Eliminate gender disparity in political participation.
- Halt and begin to reverse the incidence of malaria.
- Reverse loss of environmental resources.
- Improve sanitation facilities.
- Achieve significant improvement in lives of at least 100 million slum dwellers, by 2020.

Contradictions

Following are the major contradictions in social development progress in Asia:

- The Income Gini Coefficient, which shows that inequality in income is prevalent throughout Asia, cuts across the levels of economic development.
- In all the countries, the Inequality-adjusted HDI Value is lower than the HDI Value, indicating the major contradiction in the progress of social development in all the countries of Asia.
- Public spending on health and education does not always seem to be correlated with the level of human development.
- Level of human development is not correlated with gender equality.

Diversity in Social Development Progress in Asian Sub-Regions

The temptation to see Asia as one unit reveals a distinctly Eurocentric perspective. The analysis in the book shows that there are very few commonalities across Asian sub-regions. The overall progress of social development shows the diversity in Asian countries that ranges from very high human development to low human development. Most of the countries in Asia are categorized as medium human development level. In all the countries, the Inequality-adjusted HDI Value is lower than the HDI Value, indicating the major contradiction in the progress of social development in all the countries of Asia. Diversity is seen in East Asia leading in social development, North and Central Asia leading in equality, South East Asia being most diverse, and South Asia marked with the lowest level of social development and highest level of inequality.

Social Development Progress in East Asia

Pre-modern Chinese civilization has not only made an impact in the whole of Asia but also contributed significantly to the world. East

Asia is leading today in social development in Asia with three countries at very high level of human development and one country, China, at the medium level of human development. North Korea is the only country of concern in this sub-region.

Economic Development and Poverty Eradication

East Asia has mainly high income economies with fastest growth and sharpest reduction in poverty, particularly in China. The Confucian cultural features such as filial piety, respect for authority, collectivism and diligence are the most prominent in explanations of East and South East Asian economic development. East Asia was the focus of the Cold War, as a result of which, the US allies received enormous aid from the US which promoted their development. East and South East Asia are known for authoritarian states that seem to have led to the developmental state approach that resulted in high level of economic development in these sub-regions. However, the developmental state approach is critiqued for leading to significant human rights and environmental costs. Moreover, it was the absence of democracy in these states that has been one of the key problems behind the Asian Financial Crisis.

Food Security and Investments in Health and Education

East Asia is leading in Asia with reference to food security and in most of the health and education indicators. The proportion of births attended by skilled health personnel is almost 100 per cent in all the countries in this sub-region. The sub-region has low prevalence of HIV and TB and malaria is non-existent as it is located in the temperate zone. The causes for high level of investment in health and education may be due to productivist welfare regimes in these sub-regions where social policies are concentrated on investment in education and health. The productivist welfare regimes are influenced by Confucian familism which involves a strong reliance on the family as the site of social welfare and service delivery. After the Asian Financial Crisis, some East Asian countries strengthened their social protection policy besides that on health and education. In East and South East Asia (except in Philippines), civil society has been weak; NGOs are a very recent phenomenon as in the past they have been discouraged by authoritarian regimes.

Gender Equality

All the countries in East Asia have above near total youth literacy rate with gender equality. Although this sub-region is very high on the HDI, on the GDI it falls behind. China at the medium level of human development is doing better than Japan and South Korea which are at very high level of human development with reference to gender equality in education, wage employment and political participation. Influence of patriarchal Confucianism and fast economic growth are responsible for gender inequality in East Asia.

Environmental Sustainability

Japan and South Korea are leading in Asia with reference to forest cover and urban and rural improved water sources and sanitation facilities. However, due to fast economic growth, China has very high consumption of ODP metric tons and the lowest coverage of people's access to improved water sources improved sanitation facilities in urban and rural areas. It is the only country in East Asia to have population living in slums. North Korea is the only country of concern regarding food insecurity and child mortality rate.

Social Development Progress in South East Asia

South East Asia is most diverse with reference to social development. In this sub-region, compared to Indo-China, countries in the Maritime South East Asia are at a higher level of human development. In the Maritime South East Asia, Singapore and Brunei are at very high level of human development, Malaysia is at high level of human development, and three countries are at medium level of human development. In Indo-China, four countries are at medium level and Myanmar is at low level of human development.

Economic Development and Poverty Eradication

South East Asia is similar to East Asia with reference to influence of Confucius religion, authoritative state, and developmental state approach. However, except for Singapore and Brunei, countries in South East Asia are mainly lower middle income economies. Poverty in South East Asia is problematic as in whole of Asia, Timor-Leste has maximum MPI Vietnam has second-largest percentage of people living below the poverty line and Malaysia has maximum income inequality. All the South East Asian countries (except Thailand) faced colonization by diverse European countries which may explain why there is diversity in social development in this sub-region. In the context of the Cold War, Indo-China was devastated by the Vietnam War, for two decades, and is still lagging behind.

Food Security and Investments in Health and Education

Timor-Leste, Laos, Cambodia and Myanmar are of concern regarding food insecurity. South East Asia is not doing well on most of the health indicators. The mean year of schooling is less than 10 years in both Singapore and Brunei although their level of human development is very high. Timor-Leste, Laos and Cambodia are of concern with reference to different indicators on education. Like in East Asia, social policy in South East Asia is also characterized by productivist welfare regimes and weak civil society, but unlike East Asia, this sub-region continues to focus only on health and education even after the Asian Financial Crisis. On the other hand, the family structure is going through rapid changes, leading to its diminishing role in welfare.

Gender Equality

South East Asia is diverse with reference to gender equality in education, wage employment and political participation. However, it has high level of female labour force participation due to the legacy of female farming systems where women played the major role in food production with some help from men combined with fast economic growth in the modern times.

Environmental Sustainability

In this sub-region, Brunei has the maximum percentage of land area covered by forests and the percentage of marine areas protected. However, the per capita metric tons of CO_2 emissions are also maximum in Brunei. Singapore and Malaysia lead in South East Asia with improved water sources and sanitation facilities. Countries with the lowest coverage improved water sources in urban areas and still lower coverage in rural areas are Laos, Myanmar, Cambodia and Timor-Leste. Indonesia and Cambodia are lagging behind with reference to urban and rural sanitation. Myanmar and Vietnam are of concern with reference to slum dwelling.

Social Development Progress in North and Central Asia

North and Central Asian countries, which were under the former Soviet Union, seem to be quite homogenous with five out of seven countries at medium level of social development. These countries are leading in Asia in equality in social development, a legacy of the former communist rule. However, all the North and Central Asian countries that are in transition from communism to democracy are high on corruption or low on transparency as they have minimized or eliminated the accountability and transparency mechanisms of the state institutions. The Central Asian governments have largely subdued, coopted or in some cases eliminated the civic actors that earlier helped the process of democratization.

Economic Development and Poverty Eradication

Having used the centrally planned economy approach when under the former Soviet Union, these countries have emphasized intentional social and economic planning over the automatic adjustments of capitalist markets. This sub-region has mainly upper middle income economies, the lowest multi-dimensional poverty and the lowest percentage of people below the poverty line. However, the one US dollar a day poverty line may not be appropriate for cold climate countries where spending on food, heat, and winter clothing is higher than in other sub-regions.

Food Security and Investments in Health and Education

Tajikistan in Central Asia and Mongolia in North Asia are of concern regarding food insecurity. The North and Central Asian countries show moderate progress on health indicators. Countries in this sub-region have low prevalence of HIV and Malaria is non-existent as they are located in the temperate zone. It leads in Asia with reference to primary education completion rate and have the minimum percentage loss by inequality in mean years of schooling. Their progress may be attributed to the background of communist rule with universal access to basic social services; however, these countries are in the process of dismantling this socialist system. However, they are in the process of dismantling the socialist system of universal and comprehensive access to health, education and social protection, to a privatized fee-for-service system and most social relief is ad hoc and uncertain.

Gender Equality

North and Central Asia is again leading in Asia with reference to gender equality in education, youth literacy, wage employment and sex ratio, although most of its countries are at a medium level of human development. The explanation for high level of gender equality in these countries again seems to lie in the history of communist rule. However, with democratization, these countries are regressing to patriarchal gender roles.

Environmental Sustainability

North and Central Asia have minimum forest land in Asia as this sub-region is known for vast deserts and treeless grassy steppes. Forest cover is a less relevant indicator in these arid and sparsely populated countries. The North and Central Asian countries are landlocked and that explains low percentage of marine area protected by them. Only Mongolia is problematic with reference to improved water sources and urban and rural sanitation and it is the only country in North and Central Asia to have population living in slums.

Social Development Progress in South Asia

India has had strong foundation of pre-modern civilization that has contributed significantly to the civilizations in South and South East Asia as well as the whole world. At the same time, the other-worldly philosophy of Hinduism gives less importance to improving the conditions in this world. The belief in *karma* makes Hindus fatalistic about the caste system which hinders development in South Asia. South Asia is marked with the lowest level of social development and highest level of inequality in Asia. In this sub-region, compared to the countries in the mainland, the island countries, namely, Sri Lanka and the Maldives are better developed, similar to the Maritime South East Asian countries. The only two countries that have democracy in Asia are Sri Lanka and India in South Asia which are at high and medium level of development, respectively. These democratic countries seem to have moderate level of corruption and weak states which have not allowed very high level of human development. Social democracy has a democratic and parliamentary oriented politics that arose out of socialism, although its socialist content has been diluted over time.

Economic Development and Poverty Eradication

The social democracy-based South Asia used the mixed economy approach. This sub-region has mainly lower middle income economies and the second-highest MPI in the world. The Northern countries of South Asia have high level of MPI and high percentage of people below the poverty line. The Southern countries of Maldives and Sri Lanka have low level of MPI and population below the poverty line but have high level of income inequality.

Food Security and Investments in Health and Education

South Asian countries are problematic with different health and education indicators. This is due to South Asia having the weakest social policy and low level of human development. All the countries in this sub-region have established some components of social protection, but these are piecemeal and ad hoc, and social protection is not yet an entitlement that people claim as citizens. This sub-region is known for a vibrant civil society organizations that help fill the void that is left by a weak public sector in the provision of social services. The Southern countries of Sri Lanka and Maldives are leading in investment in health with better in life expectancy and equality in life expectancy than most of the South East Asian countries and all the North and Central Asian countries. In these two countries, child mortality rates are lowest and maternal mortality ratio is also low as the proportion of births attended by skilled health personnel is high. They also have a very low prevalence of HIV and TB.

Gender Equality

South Asia lags behind other Asian sub-regions with reference to gender equality in human development, sex ratio and gender equality in education, youth literacy and wage employment. However, South Asia is not a homogenous sub-region. For most of the targets of gender equality, the Northern countries of this sub-region that had the male farming system lag behind. For most of the targets of gender equality, the Southern countries that had the female farming system are doing better on, more like the countries of South East Asia.

Environmental Sustainability

India is of concern with reference to the consumption of ODP metric tons and urban and rural sanitation. Pakistan is of concern with reference to forest cover and rural sanitation, Bangladesh is of concern with reference to protection of marine areas, sustainable water sources in urban and rural areas, urban sanitation and slum dwelling. Nepal is of concern with reference to urban and rural sanitation. Maldives, Sri Lanka and Bhutan are leading in South Asia with reference to improved water sources and sanitation facilities in urban and rural areas.

Factors Affecting Diversity in Social Development Progress in Asian Sub-Regions

Independent Constructs

Geographical Background

- Adjacency between sub-regions and countries and geo-politics affect the diversity in social development.
- The temperate/tropical zones, the landlocked developing countries and Small Island Developing States only partly affect the diversity in social development progress.

Religious Background

- Asian religious ideologies, namely, Hindu, Buddhist and Confucius ideologies, affect the diversity in the type of state and social development progress.

Cultural Background

- Collectivistic cultural values cut across Asia.

Pre-Colonial Civilizations:

- Asia rising is not a miracle as China and India have had pre-colonial civilizations that have contributed significantly to the adjacent civilizations as well as to the world.

Political Background

- Colonization/communism and neo-colonialism in the context of the Cold War affect the diversity in the type of state, economic and social policy approaches and social development progress.

Intermediate Constructs

Role of Development Systems

- Type of state and corruption affect diversity in role of civil society and social development progress.
- Role of civil society affect diversity in social development progress.

- Sub-regional institutions strengthen economic development but do not contribute to social development.

Social Development Policy Approaches

- Economic policy approaches affect diversity in social development progress.
- Social policy approaches affect diversity in social development progress.

Conclusion

The following table summarizes the factors responsible for diversity in social development in Asia.

Table 13.1
Factors Affecting Diversity of Social Development

Independent Constructs			
Geographical Background:	Religious Background:	Cultural Background:	Political Background:
Adjacency between Sub-Regions and Countries and Geopolitics	Hindu Ideologies Buddhist Ideologies Confucius Ideologies	Collectivism	Colonization/ Communism Neocolonialism/ The Cold War
Intermediate Constructs			
Role of Development Systems:		Social Development Policy Approaches:	
State Civil Society Sub-Regional Institutions		Economic Policy Approaches Social Policy Approaches	
Dependent Construct: Progress of Social Development			
Economic Development, Poverty Eradication and Food Security	Investments in Basic Needs: Health and Education	Social Justice: Gender Equality	Environmental Sustainability

The following table gives a comparison between factors affecting development in the West and that in Asia.

Table 13.2
Comparison of Factors Affecting Social Development in the West and in Asia

	In the West	In Asia
Background of Development		
Geographical Background	Temperate Zone	Temperate and Tropical Zones
Ideological-Cultural Background	Judeo-Christian Religious Ideologies	Hindu/Confucius/Buddhist Religious Ideologies
	Individualism	Collectivism
	Modernism	Post-Colonialism Multiculturalism
	Social Darwinism	
Political Background	Colonizer	Colonized
	Capitalism	Communism
	Aid Donor	Aid Receiver
Strength of Development Systems		
State	Liberal Democracy	Mostly Authoritarianism
Civil Society	Strong	Mostly Weak
Sub-Regional Institutions	Strong	Weak
Social Development Policy Approaches		
Economic Policy Approach	Liberal Capitalism	State Capitalism
		Mixed Economy
Social Policy Approach	Welfare Capitalism	Welfare Pluralism

Implications for Policy for Social Development

Implications for Policy for Social Development in Asia

For social development progress in Asia, it is imperative that the Asian sub-regions urgently work in the following directions:

1. Development Systems need to work towards:
    - Good governance and local self-governance by the state.

- Focus on natural civil society systems of CBOs and cooperatives.
- Stronger sub-regional institutions for sub-regional cooperation for social development.

2. Social Development Policies need to comprise:
    - Pro-poor economic policies.
    - Poverty eradication targetting at landless and marginal farmers, migrant workers, unemployed, unorganized labour and slum/pavement dwellers.
    - Rights-based social policy for food, health, education, housing, livelihood/employment.
    - Inclusion and empowerment policy for women, children, adolescents, young adults, persons with disability, older persons, labour and racially/ethnically marginalized groups.
3. Sub-Regional Institutions need to be strengthened and contribute to sub-regional social development.

Implications for Policy for International Social Development

From 'Human Development' to 'Social Development'

The current development agenda is centred on the MDGs, which have an overall target date of 2015. Post-2015, the term 'human development' needs rethinking. It has two problems. One, the word 'human' has individualistic connotations. The term 'human development', therefore, gets confused with the discipline of human development that deals with individual development through the life span. 'Human development' may, therefore, be replaced with the term used in the international development systems as well as in education and literature, that is, 'social development' and the goals may be called the social development goals.

Post-2015 Development Goals

The post-2015 goals need to be comprehensive for development to be comprehensive and preventative:

- Economic development with equality.

- Poverty eradication: Targetting at landless and marginal farmers, migrant workers, unemployed, unorganized labour and slum/pavement dwellers
- Investments in basic needs: food, health, education, housing, livelihood/employment.
- Social justice: Inclusion and empowerment of women, children, adolescents, young adults, persons with disability, older persons, labour and racially/ethnically marginalized groups.
- Environmental sustainability: water sources and sanitation facilities.

Since social development goals should be comprehensive, the measures may also truly be made comprehensive by including measuring of all the social development goals listed above. Moreover, gender disaggregation is needed in all the human development measures and MDGs.

Rights-based Development

Simma and Zoeckler (2003) noted that as long as we regard lack of food, health care, housing, and basic education as a deplorable tragedy and do not treat this disrespect for human dignity as a violation of an individual's rights, we are not taking these needs seriously enough. They recommend approaching development policies from a human rights perspective to turn vague humanitarian aspirations and advisable policies into clear-cut obligations. According to Munro (2009), the existence of international human rights conventions means that development policy is no longer simply a matter of charity, or morality, or social preference, or economic or social benefit, as it is legally enforceable. According to Jolly, Emmerji, Ghai and Lapeyre (2004, cited in Munro, 2009), the explicit incorporation of human rights considerations into development work is meant to add value in five ways:

- Human rights have universal international legitimacy as an organizing framework.
- States have legal obligations to respect, protect and help fulfil rights.
- Rights are universal, so their use draws attention to the most marginalized groups whose rights are least respected.

- Human rights, having legal force, bring with them the possibility of legal redress.
- The realization of rights is not just of mere instrumental value for the fulfillment of other objectives, rights are end in themselves.

Universal, Comprehensive and Preventative Social Policy

Among the human rights principles are universality, interdependence and interrelatedness, which require a comprehensive and preventative approach.

Universal Approach: According to the UNRISD report (2007), a universal approach to the provision of social services is essential to realizing their full potential as a component of rights-based social policy. Universalism is grounded in the principles of solidarity and citizenship; it can foster social cohesion and build coalitions across classes, groups, and generations. If the poor are provided with access to the same kinds of services enjoyed by the rich, universalism may also act as an instrument for redistribution and social mobility. A universal approach should, thus, seek to limit conditionality and targetting (Sen, 1999).

Comprehensive Approach: Because the social problems are interlinked, the social policy approach has to be comprehensive to be effective. Developing countries have different ministries, specializing in the vertically organized delivery of particular services, each operating independently from others, and with little regard to the cross-cutting nature of social needs of the bulk of the population. Such bureaucratization of the social sectors established strong vested interests among politicians and civil servants for their continuation along the sectoral lines and set ministries in competition against each other for allocation of scarce public resources (Devereux and Cook, 2000, cited in Kabeer, 2004). According to the UNRISD report (2010), systems that are fragmented, with multiple providers, programmes, and financing mechanisms aimed at different population groups, have limited potential for redistribution, and generally result in high costs, poor quality, and limited access for the poor. The report highlights that integrated systems of social service provision that are grounded in universal principles can be redistributive, act as powerful drivers of solidarity and social inclusion, and improve the capabilities of the poor (UNRISD, 2010).

Preventative Approach: The preventative approach is an imperative in the rights-based approach as it is the only way to prevent social problems, rather than merely deal with them as they arise. It is grounded in the ecological perspective, oriented to the future, empowerment-focused, developmental and cost-effective. Desai (2013) has applied the three-tier public health prevention model to the rights-based, comprehensive, and preventative social policy approach for social transformation as follows:

1. At the primary prevention level, social policy needs to aim at social regulation, to facilitate the fulfillment of rights of basic needs of all persons, and develop their capabilities, thereby preventing the need for the secondary and tertiary level interventions.
2. At the secondary prevention level, social policy needs to aim at social redistribution, to fulfill rights of those who cannot do so themselves due to social exclusion and/or poverty, by ensuring their inclusion, empowerment, and social protection, thereby preventing the need for tertiary level interventions.
3. At the tertiary prevention level, social policy needs to aim at restoration of rights of those who are victims of societal violence through socio-legal protection.

International Development Systems

As the HDR of 2013 notes, with the rise of the South, the current institutions and principles for international governance require rethinking as they were designed in the post-Second World War context that does not match the contemporary reality. The UN Security Council is a significant body that has the ultimate responsibility for meeting threats to international peace and security. However, the five permanent veto-wielding seats are reserved for the victors of the Second World War, namely the US, Soviet Union (now Russia), the UK, France and China (earlier Taiwan). In the two most powerful international financial institutions, the IMF and the World Bank, the current voting system allows the West to dominate. Moreover, no Asian has been the head of either of these organizations. India's Prime Minister Manmohan Singh said in his speech in

2006, '...we need global institutions and new global 'rules of the game' that can facilitate the peaceful rise of new nations in Asia. It also means that existing global institutions and frameworks of cooperation must evolve and change to accommodate this new reality. This is as true for the reform and revitalization of the United Nations and the restructuring of the United Nations Security Council, as it is true for the management of multilateral trading system, or for the protection of global environment or for the security of world energy supplies.' According to Mahubani (2008), with the rise of Asia, rethinking of these structures has become an imperative as only monarchies and dictators enjoy perpetual rule, without seeking re-election and without being held accountable.

References

Desai, M. (2013). *The Paradigm of International Social Development: Ideologies, Development Systems and Policy Approaches.* New York: Routledge.

Kabeer, N. (2004). *Imagining 'The Social': Social Policy Analysis for the Poor in Poor Countries.* Brighton, Sussex: Institute of Development Studies.

Mahubani, K. (2008). *The New Asian Hemisphere: The Irresistible Shift of Global Power to the East.* New York: Public Affairs.

Munro, L.T. (2009). The 'human rights-based approach to programming': A contradiction in terms? In D. Mitlin and S. Hickey (eds), *Rights-based Approach to Development: Exploring the Potential and Pitfalls* (pp. 187–208). Sterling, VA: Kumarian Press.

Sen, A. (1999). *Development as Freedom.* New York: Random House.

Simma, B. and Zoeckler, M. (2003). Global social standards. In K. Marshall and O. Butzbach (eds), *New Social Policy Agendas for Europe and Asia: Challenges, Experience, and Lessons* (pp. 467–480). Washington, DC: World Bank.

United Nations Development Programme. (2013). *Human Development Report: The Rise of the South: Human Progress in a Diverse World.* New York.

United Nations Research Institute for Social Development. (2007). *Conference News: Poverty Reduction and Policy Regimes: Report of the UNRISD Workshop in Geneva.* Geneva.

——. (2010). *Combating Poverty and Inequality: Structural Change, Social Policy and Politics.* Geneva.

Index